SEX
CAN
SAVE YOUR
HEART...
AND
LIFE

SEX CAN SAVE YOUR HEART... AND LIFE

BY EUGENE SCHEIMANN, M.D.

CROWN PUBLISHERS, INC., NEW YORK

T O
my brother George—
may his wish come true

Library of Congress Catalog Card Number: 73–91513

Printed in the United States of America

Published simultaneously in Canada by
General Publishing Company Limited

Designed by Ruth Smerechniak

CONTENTS

ACKNOWLEDGMENTS

Many people have helped me in my search to discover the relationship between sex and coronary heart disease: some were medical colleagues; some were patients; some were simply concerned human beings who heard about my work and voluntarily contacted me. I couldn't begin to thank, or even think of, all of them, yet to each of them I am undeniably indebted.

Leonard A. Carney, an accomplished circulation director of the publishing company that printed a magazine article of mine, "Sex Can Save Your Heart," became a crusader for my thesis. He introduced me to Walter B. J. Mitchell, Jr., who not only encouraged me, but helped me to write this book. He is its godfather, so to speak. Without his professional publishing guidance, this project would never have been completed.

It was Herbert Michelman, vice-president of Crown, my publishers, whose critical analysis of my first draft crystallized my intent in this book. My personal gratitude to him is immense, as it is, too, to Paul Nadan of Crown and Mildred Hird of Bantam Books.

Bettina Smith, a top Chicago professional writer and editor, collaborated with me on the research and the initial writing. She did so with extraordinary enthusiasm and total dedication. Wendy O'Donnell, Emilie Carter Cook, and Carol Carmen worked with me as well.

But, one person, and she alone, inspired me to start my search to discover the relationship between sex and coronary heart disease—June, my beloved wife, whose love cured my own masculinity crisis and coronary insufficiency. Words aren't enough, June.

E. S.

Chicago, February 19, 1974

vii

INTRODUCTION

"SEX . . . SEX CAN SAVE MY HEART, DOCTOR?" HOW MANY
of my patients have asked me this question in astonish-
ment? Then, after reflecting on my explanation, they react:
"Okay—I'll buy it—your theory makes sense, but if it's true,
how come other doctors don't know about it?" (My private
and unprofessed—up till now—opinion is: they do and they
don't *at their own convenience*. Some doctors do, but don't
want to discuss it. Others don't, and don't discuss sex,
period, either with their patients, professionally, or seemingly in their own lives.)

But why indeed do most physicians strenuously avoid
the entire issue of sex? Why has the medical profession as
a whole virtually ignored sex in the study of heart disease?
Why doesn't a heart specialist of necessity *have* to obtain
a sexual history or current profile of his or her patients?
Why do doctors assiduously avoid mentioning sexual intercourse—except, perhaps, after a heart attack to warn
against it? Worse—why do countless doctors overlook sex
both as a precipitating factor in disease or as a positive
influence on health?

Part of the answer lies in the fact that in truth many
doctors are plainly ignorant about sex. Medical schools
hardly teach much more than the structure and function of
the reproductive organs. The scientific, objective study of

sexual behavior is still in its infancy. Authoritative, direly needed information based on case history research is not available—despite the spate of so-called sex books in our day. Even as noted a sexologist as William Masters openly admits: "Physicians know no more and no less than others [about sex]. . . . They share most of the common misconceptions, taboos, and fallacies of their non-medical confreres."

Another reason for overlooking sex in medicine is that doctors are trained to concentrate on the physical, chemical, *measurable* aspects of a patient. The science of medicine, as many have observed, sees man not as a whole human being, but as a bundle of isolated physical symptoms. Naturally, most physicians feel more comfortable dealing with a patient's cardiogram, cholesterol level, and caloric intake than with his private sexual problems, proclivities, permissiveness (or nonpermissiveness), and, God forbid, perversions. Needless to say it's *verboten*—particularly if the physician himself happens to be sexually inhibited or puritanical.

Medical students reportedly are often inexperienced and highly anxious, even troubled, in their own sex lives. I have known some doctors who believe, some consciously and some unconsciously, that sex is dangerous and harmful. They don't trust it. They don't trust their patients' capabilities in knowing how to deal with sex either. One of my colleagues recently warned me, "You can't go around telling middle-aged men and women to have more sex. No telling what they'll do. If you tell them sex is good for them, they might go wild—and you'll be to blame." (For the record I espouse moderation in all things, including sex. But sex differs according to one's demands and needs and is totally harmless as long as it is in harmony with oneself and one's partner. *Chacun à son goût*, or "tastes differ."

As our rapidly expanding society undergoes shifts in political, social, and moral values, this *medi*eval (sic) sex attitude is due for a change. But, in the meantime, doctors are not offering the wisdom, understanding, and tolerance desperately needed—not to mention practical, sound advice. Lacking this advice and guidance, *men and women are dying at an alarmingly increasing rate from heart disease. Sex Can Save Your Heart . . . and Life* is my single-handed attempt to remove a serious contributing factor.

Lennart Levi, director of the Laboratory for Clinical Stress Research, Karolinska Institute, Stockholm, wrote in his preface to *Society, Stress and Disease*, the printed record of the symposium held in April 1970, sponsored by the University of Uppsala and The World Health Organization: ". . . most people agree that modern man's rapidly changing psychosocial environment does, indeed, confront him with serious medical, psychological, social and economic problems, the solution of which is urgent." Urgent mind you. The index of that book (485 pages) carries just six short references to sex.

My own ideas on sex and heart disease have evolved gradually over fifty years of general medical practice. I am especially proud, particularly since I was born a Hungarian Jew and came to America in 1924 with naught save a medical degree from the University of Budapest and a borrowed ten dollars, to have on my office walls personally signed citations from three of our presidents: Roosevelt, Truman, and Eisenhower.

My research has not been formal and systematic. I have not used statistics, computers, and many of the other tools of so-called orthodox medical research, nor have I analyzed tissues or observed animals in laboratories. On the contrary, my everyday lab is the human maze of Chicago's near North Side, not in the ivory tower of abstract science. Many of my patients are average, everyday human beings. But many more are derelicts, prostitutes, drug addicts, sex deviates, and other lost souls who frequent this area. Others are wealthy Gold Coast residents whom I first visited as an emergency doctor on the roster of the Chicago Medical Society. As a syndicated columnist I have also received countless letters from readers telling me their most intimate medical, emotional, and sexual problems.

During fifty years I have observed and recorded the health problems, personal habits, life-styles, and emotional problems of thousands of patients of many races, and all ages and economic and social classes. I saw at first hand during the last two and a half decades *a sharp increase in heart attacks*—especially among middle-aged men (and now more frequently women!). This book expresses my deep concern over this increase. I observed, too, in this same group an increase in sexual dysfunction. At least 75 percent of the patients I attended with current or impending heart attacks suffered from anxiety related to impotence and to aging problems. My conflicting, and seemingly contradictory, observations of older men who did not seem to be susceptible to heart disease confirmed my suspicion. These older men in the main had vigorous, active, uncomplicated sex lives. I am convinced, therefore, that heart disease is related to the sexual anxiety that strikes middle-aged men. Further, I strongly believe that a satisfying, active sex life is *the single most effective protection against heart attacks* that is available today . . . or perhaps ever was.

This book does not report a new medical breakthrough. It does not offer a magic formula to prevent or cure heart disease. It addresses the layman, but also it is an emphatic, heartfelt plea to the medical profession to study the role of sex seriously. Efforts to reduce coronary heart disease by changing dietary and smoking habits are useful, but they are not enough. A new approach is needed to achieve this goal. Sexual stress, I implore, should be the starting point.

Doctors can no longer afford to be concerned only with changes in the coronary arteries—they must tackle the far bigger problems and perplexities of the societal changes that are related to coronary arteries. For example, the medical profession must become aware of the women's liberation movement, the sexual revolution, and the meta-morphosis of marriage and monogamy. These can be factors in what is occurring in diseased coronary arteries. We must face up to the world we live in. Coronary artery disease demands a multifactorial approach for prevention and treatment. This approach can no longer ignore the two most important elements related to our hearts—LOVE and SEX.

Dr. A. R. Herrman of the University of Texas, in agreeing with my thesis that emotional stress is a crucial factor in heart disease, says: "Each patient presents individual problems that must be solved for him by his physician. . . . Most patients need some advice as to how to live more sanely and reasonably. . . . Any sense of fear, inadequacy, and insecurity must be allayed and personal contentment assured. We must recognize the fact that sex and love problems are the most common causes of fear, inadequacy, impotence, and insecurity today. Contrarily, we must openly admit and accept the fact that a patient who experiences regularly the full joys of sex is assured of personal contentment."

This book is also an appeal to the lay reader, especially to coronary-prone men and women, husbands and wives. It is an appeal not to neglect sex and love during the struggle to obtain status and success, for ours is an age of extraordinarily pronounced sexual tensions that play a significant part in the onset of heart attacks. It's time we faced up to it.

The key to relief of sexual anxiety is sexual liberation. Therefore, I propose that marriage should be liberated from the taboos of yesterday, while retaining its intimacy; that women should be liberated from their old roles, while still maintaining their deep and abiding concern for their children and family life; that men should be liberated from the old ideas of masculinity, while learning how to live as modern men; that sexuality must be liberated from the guilt and darkness of the past and stripped of its association with sickness and sin.

How can we in our enlightened twentieth century account for the fact that the earliest peoples knew instinctively about the association between sexuality and health and protected themselves, while we don't? Thousands of years ago making love played an open and important part in community rituals. It was accepted naturally as a concomitant of ensuring health, vigor, fertility, and longevity. Unfortunately for us, centuries later, sex was redefined under a two-faced, double-standard morality as being sinful, self-indulgent, and dangerous. The positive association between sex and health decidedly has been too long under official suppression. This must end.

When Sigmund Freud observed that many physical illnesses have their roots in sexual repression, he shocked the world. Although his wary contemporaries found his ideas unorthodox and unsettling, we can ill afford to deny today the essential underlying truth of his findings. Freud once stated that "in normal sex there is no neurosis." Even though the definition of "normal sex" has undergone many changes in the intervening years, Freud's statement still holds true. The keynote of *Sex Can Save Your Heart . . . and Life* amplifies Freud's further discovery: "In normal sex and love there is *a healthy heart*" (italics added).

PART ONE

THE BROKEN HEART

1

HEART
DISEASE:
THE
MYSTERIOUS
EPIDEMIC

In 1972, 600,000 Americans—men and women—died of heart attacks, and countless more were disabled. About two-thirds of those who died were men, which should come as no surprise. But what is surprising is that women accounted for 212,000 of the total deaths. *Indeed, 60 percent more women died of heart attacks than of cancer!*

When compiled for 1973, fatality figures will be larger—at least 650,000—and an increased number will be women. Heart disease and strokes are on an alarming and unrelenting increase. The chance of a heart attack today in the United States is *four times* greater than it was in 1935. What has happened, and *is* happening, is that in just under four decades the United States has become second only to Finland in coronary heart disease death rate in the entire world. Heart disease is the number-one threat to life today.

How is it possible that life expectancy today for the middle-aged American male is only a few years more than it was at the turn of the century? (The two chief culprits then, pneumonia and tuberculosis, have been drastically curtailed.) The annual rate of heart attacks today is: at age forty, three per 1,000; *at fifty, it is one out of every 100!* Before age sixty, one out of every five will have coronary disease. More often than not, unfortunately, the heart attack itself is the first sign.

These formidable figures for American males should not blind us to the incredible indices for females. True, up to age forty-five men have thirteen times as many heart attacks as do females. And from that age to just over sixty, men continue to have twice as many. But after that age, women are equally susceptible. It is an epidemic for both sexes to take seriously, as *both* are becoming increasingly vulnerable victims. Why? And, what are we going to do about it? The need for immediate answers and action is critical.

And, since the need is so dire, I have chosen to publish my thesis, that sex can save your heart and life, before becoming involved in costly, but more important today, time-consuming, scientific research that might (or might not) medically prove it. I am aware of my grave responsibility to prove it to you and I recollect, not without proper humility, a line from Vauvenargues's *Maxims and Reflections* published in France in 1746: "The mind of man is more intuitive than logical, and comprehends more than it can coordinate."

If you already are, or suspect you are, a coronary-prone man or woman, then it is imperative for you to change your mode of living. In the face of the ever-increasing death rate, immediate action is mandatory for many. I shall endeavor to prove this vitally important point. It is based on the theory that a multifactorial approach for the prevention of heart attacks is clearly indicated and must be emphatically prescribed.

Frank G. Slaughter, the celebrated surgeon-novelist, put it aptly in his book *Medicine for Moderns:* "We strive to be healthy in order to be happy, but how many of us strive to be happy in order to be healthy?" He also predicted in that same book the terrifying statistics that opened this book, i.e.: "Coronary heart disease and angina pectoris represent perhaps the most dangerous of all psychosomatic disorders and are rapidly becoming one of the characteristic diseases of civilization." And his book was published over twenty-five years ago!

As witness to how necessary it is that we do change our attitude forthwith, let us heed this recent ominous warning from the Council of the World Health Organization:

> Ischemic [of a temporary deficiency of blood, often from blood vessel constriction] heart disease, or coronary heart disease, has reached enormous proportions, striking more and more at younger subjects. It will result in coming years in the greatest epidemic mankind has faced unless we are able to reverse the trend by concentrated research into its cause and prevention.

How do we go about reversing this trend? Where should this concentrated research begin? For research, I say start with the relationship between stress and sexual problems. For reversing the trend, let us together analyze what we know about coronary heart disease—what are the most common "risk factors" we can (and most definitely must) avoid? Next let us examine my thesis that satisfying sex can save your heart and life. And lastly, let us see how my simple four-, then five-point plan can help you adapt to a much-needed new mode of living.

Going back to *Medicine for Moderns* for a moment:

It is far more important that the sex impulse be recognized and treated fairly than any question of morality. A person who satisfies his sex impulse in what society likes to call immorality, and has no further trouble with it is far better off than the moral person who becomes obsessed with ideas of cleanliness and godliness, in compensation for sex urges which he or she refuses to recognize, resulting in invalidism, and even insanity. Too much morality is probably worse, psychologically, than too much immorality.

Too bad we didn't pay more attention when a man as brilliant and dedicated as Dr. Slaughter stated this so long ago.

Now let's attend to the basics. Doctors know the immediate cause of a heart attack *medically* speaking: the arteries leading to the heart gradually narrow and become clogged; a blockage forms, preventing the heart from getting enough blood; if the blockage is complete, the heart stops, and the patient is dead. In other words, in most instances what we call a "heart attack" really is a disease *not* of the heart, but of the coronary arteries that lead to the heart. But few people realize that this hardening process, which accounts for the narrowing, begins in early life—as early as childhood, say some experts—and progresses silently and relentlessly.

Coronary heart disease was once known as arteriosclerosis, which means artery hardening. Today, atherosclerosis is the term more popularly used. The reason is that *athero* means swelling and swelling is closer to the truth, since heart disease *begins* with swelling and proceeds to hardening of the arteries. Myocardial infarction (the death or damage of the myocardial area of heart muscle) is another widely accepted term.

Thus, what we tend to think of as one "fatal moment" —the instant of heart attack—has been building in the body for twenty, thirty, or fifty years. The most preventable stages occur *earliest* in the course of the disease; that is why it is most important for the coronary-prone to receive the earliest possible diagnosis.

CORONARY HEART DISEASE

In 1912, Dr. J. B. Herrick, a Chicago physician, like myself, was the first to recognize the concept of the narrowing coronary arteries and the blocking of blood from the heart as the specific cause of sudden, instantaneous death. But what narrows and clogs the coronary arteries? Why does this condition occur, and more frequently (till age sixty) in men rather than in women? And why, more often than not, in relatively young, Caucasian men living in urban areas? We're still not sure and are far from a definitive diagnosis; and further still from prescribing possible cures.

Dr. George E. Burch, editor of the *Cardiovascular Review 1972*, wrote:

> We have devoted more energy to basic and clinical heart research and patient care than has any generation in history. But where are we now? . . . The life span of the white American male seems to be declining. This may be a good moment in medical history to take stock, to ask ourselves what we have accomplished? Despite our efforts, 50% of our countrymen continue to die of heart disease. Diet, anticholesterolemic agents, heart drugs, and surgery have not lowered the incidence of ischemic heart disease. In fact, among blacks it is more prevalent then ever. . . . We have to keep reminding ourselves that our patients have minds and nervous systems, emotional problems, social and economic worries. . . . With a knowledge of our accomplishments and problems yet to be solved progress can be made.

I took especial note of Dr. Burch's reference to emotional problems, as I had read in a news item in the *Los*

Angeles Sun Times (September 1973): "Emotional factors were a precipitating cause in fully 76% of patients admitted to one large city hospital with heart disease. And in another recent study, 23 of 41 patients with heart attacks had experienced severe anxiety just before the attack."

I wholeheartedly agree with Dr. Burch that this is a "good moment in medical history to take stock" of our accomplishments and to change our approach entirely. Dr. H. J. Roberts, director of the Palm Beach, Florida, Institute of Medical Research, castigates (perhaps rightly so) the heart studies fixedly focused on cholesterol and diet alone as "among the most flagrant examples of Parkinson's Law in medical research. The Coronary Drug Project and the National Diet-Heart Study, which will examine over 100,000 men and cost over $50 million are ill-advised, unjustified, and wasteful of public funds at this time."

With the problems yet to be solved, progress can be made. But not if scientists stick with the old, outmoded concepts of disease and healing. If we are going to find the missing link in heart disease, research must change its emphasis. By concentrating on isolated physical risk factors, scientists are misinterpreting the real nature of the disease. If there is a common cause behind high cholesterol, smoking, overeating, high blood pressure, obesity, and other commonly accepted risk factors, it will not reveal itself in these isolated aspects. The common denominator in these risk factors lies in the total picture—*the whole man or woman, one's whole life*. Because of the emphasis on physical disease with a specific cause and a chemical, medical, or surgical cure, the whole person has been lost sight of. But a multifactorial approach to curing and preventing heart disease is self-evident. And the importance of including sex and stress is no less significant and equally self-evident.

This same thesis of treating the total patient was similarly expressed by Dr. Walter E. O'Donnel, a Gloucester, Massachusetts, internist who accuses the "specialized" experts who teach in medical schools of being "more interested in diseases than in people. They see the patient as a collection of organs or systems rather than as a living unit. The patient is divided, sub-divided, and fractionated. One team studies the glomerular filtration rate, while another frets over thyroid function, and a third ponders the mysteries of our hapless patient's cardiac conduction system. Theoretically, somebody puts all this—and the patient—back together again when it's all over. Actually, this seldom happens."

In defense of why scientists continue to put emphasis on isolated physical organs and systems, it is only fair to say this did make sense at one time. During the first half of the century, for example, the chief concerns of medicine were fighting off deaths from infections, the healing of wounds, or removing a diseased part of the body. Until 1950 or so, science continued to make spectacular advances in this pursuit—virtually conquering most major killers, including childbirth deaths, tuberculosis, poliomyelitis, and many types of pneumonia.

But there haven't been any major medical advancements of note lately. In spite of the miracles of modern antibiotics and drugs, or the newly developed surgical procedures, sickness has not decreased. Our hospitals are overflowing and our medical costs are spiraling, but we are not, as a nation, healthier. Indeed, the overall American death rate and life expectancy figures (for the male sixty-seven, for the female seventy-five) place us *twenty-fourth in the world!* Something must be done, and soon.

Orthodox medicine, it seems, has reached a dead end. And since the organic approach, which cured the diseases of yesterday, will not meet the demands of today and tomorrow, I am forced to the conclusion that resolving our current health problems lies in a radically new psychological and sociological approach to medicine as a whole.

More and more doctors, I find it encouraging to say, are ready to (or are about to, judging from innumerable medical journals) change their views of disease and health to accommodate our present crisis. There is an increasing realization that to be an effective physician one must know the social trends and pressures that affect a particular patient. Most physical illnesses are admitted to be at least partly psychological. The major causes of death—heart disease, cancer, and stroke—are labeled "stress-related" even by our most conservative medical spokesmen. Our more progressive doctors now proclaim that no disease—and most particularly, mysterious ones like heart disease—can be understood unless we know how the hapless victims feel emotionally; what makes them joyous or dejected, confident or confounded, relaxed or irritated. Frank Slaughter hit this one solidly on the head, too, when he said: "Emotions cause widespread damage to organs, crippling millions of people every year through the twin pestilences of high blood pressure and coronary heart disease. Here lies the proof, not only that emotional tension causes disease, but that *it actually can kill*" (italics added). Can the case be stated more bluntly?

Meanwhile, heart disease continues to increase, as we have seen—600,000 deaths in 1972, an estimated 650,000 in 1973. Heart disease accounts for more than half of the deaths in the United States. This means that you can take all the others, add them up and they won't equal the incidence of this monstrous killer. Isn't it clearly time to conclude that the medical profession has been off base in its emphasis in heart research? More and more people are beginning to think so. And isn't it clearly time, too, to do something drastic about it in the face of a catastrophic crisis?

As I have constantly repeated, there is, alas, no simple single cause of heart disease. There are only the factors that have been statistically associated with it, the risk factors. I have already pointed out that the bulk of medical research in recent years has focused on trying to identify and control these factors, hoping in this way to prevent heart disease. None of the single or collective attempts has worked so far. Moreover, this research itself has produced puzzling contradictions and mysteries, suggesting strongly that somewhere in our knowledge of heart disease there is a *missing link*.

But let us not be accused of throwing out the baby with the bath water. It behooves us still to apply carefully every known fact—or even suspected fact—about risk factors. It also behooves us to examine all of the risk factors in toto, plus a few carefully chosen potential missing links I shall propose, so as to keep tracking down the nation's number one medical enemy.

RISK FACTORS

Heredity: On the surface, so far impossible to prevent and the most difficult to control and understand. For a long time it has been medically accepted that heredity plays a vital part in longevity. People point to their aged ancestors as proof that they come from "hardy stock." So, too, in the realm of heart disease, if your father died of a heart attack, the chances of your having the same fate are statistically high, particularly if you are a male. If your father died very young—under forty—the cards are quite possibly stacked even more heavily against you. There is evidence that some people inherit a tendency to high blood cholesterol levels, and consequently they are more prone to early development of atherosclerosis. But there is new hope. In an excellent book, which I highly recommend to my readers, *Freedom from Heart Attacks* by Dr. Benjamin F. Miller and Lawrence Galton, there is an informal question and answer session with Dr. Daniel Brunner, one of the most distinguished cardiologists of the Bedouin experiment in the Israeli Negev desert. The very first question he answers is evidence that our current environmental factors are more of an influence than our genetic backgrounds:

Q: Dan, what would you consider to be the most important findings coming out of Israeli research? Take an overview.

DR. BRUNNER: Perhaps most important of all, I'd think, is that environmental factors are so crucial. Certainly there are hereditary influences. There are rare people with genetic backgrounds that make them extremely likely to develop coronary heart disease; there are also the rare ones so resistant that it is almost certain they will never develop it, no matter what. But the overwhelming majority of people—possibly more than 90 percent —have genetic backgrounds such that they will develop the disease given sufficient exposure to disadvantageous environmental conditions. It's not their heredity that makes trouble inevitable for them; the fault lies with environmental influences.

Look at the Yemenites—a beautiful demonstration that environmental influences overwhelm any genetic ones. Here is a people virtually isolated from the world for thousands of years, living the life of Biblical times. Bring them into the Western world, free of coronary heart disease to start with, with none of the biological indications considered risk factors for CHD. Gradually, they begin to develop the risk indications. Their genetics haven't changed, only the environment. You can even speed the process up, make a radical change in a major risk factor—cholesterol level— in just five months by, in effect, force-feeding them a Western type of diet.

Q: And that gives us hope . . .

DR. BRUNNER: It certainly does. If we're not doomed to early CHD trouble by our genes but by environmental influences which we can modify, we're not inevitably doomed at all.

Q: The Bedouin studies help prove the point, too?

DR. BRUNNER: Yes. We need more Bedouin studies. But among the Bedouins, too, CHD is virtually absent, so are the risk factors for it—except among whom? The sheikhs, the wealthy. Not because the sheikhs and the wealthy are genetically different from the common tribesmen. Their wealth and power allow them to indulge themselves in rich fare.

Diabetes: Certain metabolic diseases such as diabetes, hyperthyroidism, and hypothyroidism can damage heart muscle directly or indirectly. Adequate diagnosis and treatment of these diseases will either prevent or slow down such changes.

In 1956, Dr. Thomas Francis, Jr., and a University of Michigan research team persuaded 8,600 residents of Tecumseh, Michigan, to undergo complete physical examinations. The study showed a high frequency of coronary heart disease among the known diabetics, as expected, but also, and perhaps more importantly, that people with heart disease are decidedly diabetes-prone. A high blood sugar level, therefore, can be, and is, an important risk factor.

Hypertension: Another disease that increases the tendency toward heart attacks because it accelerates the atherosclerotic disease process is chronic high blood pressure. Men between the ages of forty and fifty-five with hypertension are three times more likely than those with normal blood pressure to have a heart attack and, even more, strokes. A U.S. Health Survey for 1960–62 showed that 29 percent of the population has high blood pressure; yet Dr. Jeremiah Stamler of the Chicago Health Research Foundation says that one half of the country's millions of cases are undetected and half of those that are detected go untreated.

Smoking: Men: Death rates from coronary heart disease are twice as high for smokers of a pack or more daily than for nonsmokers. Death rates increase with the number of cigarettes smoked, with the degree of inhalation, and with the starting age. Men smoking a pack or more daily died sixteen years sooner than the average nonsmoker. In one study by Dr. David Spain of New York, it was determined that, at the time of death, the average age of heavy smokers was only 47.4 years (with a range of from 35 to 62) contrasted with an average age of 63.2 (with a range of 61 to 69) for nonsmokers. Smokers who are physically inactive are three times as likely to have a heart attack as smokers who are physically active. Smokers who do have heart attacks increase their chances of survival twofold if they are physically active.

Women: In September 1973, in the *Journal of the American Medical Association,* Dr. Spain warned that heavy cigarette smoking leads American women to early graves from sudden heart attacks. Concentrating on women who had succumbed to coronary heart disease, he and his colleagues questioned their next of kin. Did the dead women smoke? How much? Did they have a history of heart trouble? The answers were astounding. Fully 90 percent of the victims smoked; 62 percent consumed more than a pack a day.

The average female nonsmoker died at sixty-seven; the heavy smoker died nineteen years earlier, at forty-eight. The heart attack death rate among women is approaching the high rate suffered by men, Dr. Spain found.

Obesity: In a discussion of the prevention and control of heart disease held by the American Public Health Association, Dr. Irving S. Wright emphasized that obesity *in itself* is not a cause of heart disease, or of hardening of the arteries. However, since obesity is usually accompanied by high blood pressure, high blood fats, high blood sugar— all coronary risk factors—the problems of being overweight are consequently of major importance.

Too much weight is of further concern, of course, to

cardiologists since it puts an excess burden on circulation, which in turn makes the heart do more work. It is of real concern to me as well if being fat is exaggerated to the point that it inhibits sexual performance and desirability or creates a distortion of self-image.

An American Cancer Society study of 800,000 persons recently showed that overweight people have three and a half times the number of fatal heart attacks and strokes of those of average weight. Most alarming are insurance statistics: they show a much higher death rate for coronary heart attack victims who are overweight. In fact, a study of the Society of Actuaries revealed that thirty excess pounds reduces life expectancy four years.

Drinking: Drinking, too, is a highly individual matter. It does not of its own have a special value, plus or minus, but it is prescribed by some doctors who believe it to be more desirable than a tranquilizer for relief of tension, since liquor does afford a sense of sociability and well-being when taken in moderation. Other doctors prescribe moderate dosages for cardiac patients for its ability to counteract emotional problems; the danger here is that excessive drinking acts as a total depressant.

Not a risk factor, then, unless done to excess (which affects the cholesterol level), heavy drinking frequently leads to neglect of a good diet, creating vitamin deficiencies that can weaken the heart muscle. The caloric content of cocktails must be of concern to dieters. Alcohol supplies 7.1 calories per gram. Many Americans receive from 10 to 20 percent of their total calories from drinking. (A case of how one risk factor affects another could be made out of the fact that smokers invariably smoke most heavily when drinking.)

Lack of exercise: It is now generally accepted that physical work or exercise can be a major beneficial factor for much that ails us, including coronary heart disease. Exercise, too, has beneficial effects on most of the other risk factors—for example, it helps diabetics, lowers blood pressure, decreases blood levels of fats, inhibits smoking, and aids weight control and prevents obesity.

The degree of exercise for good health is an individual thing you must work out for yourself. To show its importance, let's just consider one form of recommended exercise—walking. If you decided today to walk for an extra hour every day, you probably would burn up 250 more calories a day, which is over 90,000 calories a year. Since to lose a pound requires burning up 3,500 calories, this simple decision could help you lose over 25 pounds a year.

To help you consider the many benefits of walking, allow me to recommend an utterly delightful book, *The Magic of Walking* by Aaron Sussman and Ruth Goode. Here's how they present their case: "Walking is the exercise that needs no gym. It is the prescription without medicine, the weight control without diet, the cosmetic that is sold in no drugstore. It is the tranquilizer without a pill, the therapy without a psychoanalyst, the fountain of youth that is no legend. A walk is the vacation that does not cost a cent."

In an article, "A Leading Physician Warns Runners," Dr. Harry Johnson, an authority on how to live longer, explains that an individual can expect a heart attack as a reward for jogging, expresses concern for this rising fad, and recommends moderation. He says: "If you're in good shape, jogging may be fine. If you're average—watch out. I'm strongly in favor of walking for exercise. If you walk as briskly as you can, you speed up your pulse, strengthen your heart and lungs and legs. In urban areas, where more and more of us are living, you can walk without attracting undue attention to yourself."

A new insight into the value of vigorous exercise, as opposed to light exercise, as protection against coronary heart disease (with its buildup of deposits in the coronary arteries that may lead to heart attacks) comes from a

British study by Dr. J. N. Morris and a medical team of the London School of Hygiene and Tropical Medicine. They reported in *Lancet* in January of 1973: "Of 16,882 business executives, age 40 to 64, who reported their exercise habits on a questionnaire, 232 have since suffered a first attack of coronary heart disease. Light exercise provided no particular advantage; but in those reporting vigorous exercise habits, the relative risk of developing heart disease proved to be only about one-third of that in other men."

Cholesterol: In 1912, the year that coronary heart disease was first diagnosed as such, a Russian investigator, N. Anitschkov, fed pure cholesterol dissolved in vegetable oil to rabbits and proved that it was the cholesterol that caused the damage to coronary arteries.

Today in the United States about 45 percent of the daily caloric intake—nearly half the calories we eat—is fat. The aim of the fat-control program recommended by the American Heart Association is to cut that percentage to 30 or 35 percent.

The American Heart Association Cookbook, published in 1973, tells the story of cholesterol simply and succinctly:

Medical research has shown that too many fatty foods can be damaging to the heart and blood vessels. . . . Fats are necessary elements of food, but excessive amounts can cause serious problems. The body handles fat in several ways: by burning it to produce energy; by storing it in tissues; or by silting it in the form of cholesterol along the walls of the arteries, the blood vessels that carry food and oxygen to all parts of the body. The silting of fats is part of the process called atherosclerosis—hardening of the arteries.

When there is too much cholesterol in the blood, it is likely to pile up along artery walls. So, people with high cholesterol levels are more likely to have heart attacks or strokes from blockages in the arteries.

Cholesterol is a risk factor, but the evidence isn't in, unfortunately, that lowering elevated blood cholesterol actually reduces the risk of heart attacks.

Unbalanced diet. A balanced diet is important for heart patients, as well as for everyone else. It should provide good general nutrition, with adequate amounts of proteins, minerals, and vitamins. An unbalanced diet can be a risk factor.

According to a noted nutritionist, Dr. Frederick J. Stare, chairman of the Department of Nutrition of Harvard University, in an article titled "You and Your Diet" in the November 1973 issue of *Reader's Digest,* half the people in the United States do not eat a balanced diet. The article explodes nine widely believed myths, all of which could account for half of our nation eating incorrectly. The answer is "False" to each of these statements: (1) Meat, potatoes, and two vegetables every day provide a balanced diet; (2) to get enough protein, you must eat meat at least once a day; (3) to lose weight, you must not eat bread, potatoes, or any fat; (4) adding a multiple-vitamin capsule to your meals every day will balance your diet; (5) you need three meals a day for a balanced diet; (6) meat has become so expensive that protein is the largest shortage in the American diet today; (7) everybody needs at least two cups of whole milk a day; (8) for older people, a balanced diet doesn't matter so much; (9) a balanced diet costs more than an unbalanced one.

The key to a balanced diet is simple. There are four groups of foods: protein foods, milk foods, cereal foods, and vegetable and fruit foods. Dr. Stare says: "If you eat the recommended number of servings from each group, your diet will be balanced."

Since the frequency of coronary heart disease varies so greatly between populations that eat different amounts and kinds of foods, diet, rather a balanced diet, which gives you food from the four basic groups, is most important in the prevention of heart disease.

The phrase *risk factor* itself owes its name to a federally financed study in Framingham, Massachusetts, without question the most famous and extensive study of coronary heart disease in this country. Since 1949 researchers have investigated Framinghamians' blood pressure, electrocardiograms, cholesterol levels, and smoking, eating, drinking, and other habits.

Since then two other study centers of note have been established in Albany, New York, and in Minneapolis, Minnesota. All three have established without question that the risk of a heart attack rises sharply with increasing levels of cholesterol. In the Framingham group of over 5,000, men and women with an average cholesterol level of 259 were found to have seven times as many heart attacks as those whose average was below 200; in Albany, three times; in Minneapolis, six.

Dr. Brunner in his Israeli studies found a national average cholesterol count of 264. Yemenites, who are virtually free of heart attacks, had an average cholesterol level of 159.

Many doctors, fed up with the emphasis on food, have looked into some of the puzzling aspects of diet and heart disease. When two California cardiologists, Dr. Meyer Friedman and Dr. Ray Rosenman, studied the eating patterns of forty-six normal American women and their husbands, they discovered what we all knew all along: women eat just as much fat as men, yet they still don't get heart disease to the same degree (but they are catching up fast).

A group of doctors headed by Dr. John Cassel of the University of North Carolina couldn't understand why their black patients were virtually immune to heart disease, whereas their white male patients were highly susceptible. When they studied the diets of the two groups in Evans County, Georgia, they discovered that even though blacks consumed more calories and more animal fats, they had lower cholesterol levels.

What it all boils down to is this: Heart attacks are associated statistically with high amounts of cholesterol in the blood. This in turn is associated with a diet high in unsaturated animal fats. But many people eat such a diet and do *not* have abnormally high blood cholesterol levels. And many people have high cholesterol levels but do *not* develop harmful fatty deposits on the walls of their coronary arteries. In other words, some people develop this arterial condition and live to a ripe old age, never getting a heart attack. Moreover, although the death rate from heart disease has soared during the past fifty years, Americans are eating no more animal fats than they did at the turn of the century. Our agricultural grandfathers ate even more butter, lard, pork, and eggs than we do today, and had less access than we do to year-round fresh fruits and vegetables.

Once again, there seems to be a missing link—vital, but missing. There is some other factor besides diet that causes cholesterol levels to rise, and coronary arteries to become diseased. And limiting our cholesterol intake does not sufficiently change the incidence of heart disease.

Even if lowering the cholesterol level helped more demonstrably, and even if changing the diet lowered cholesterol, many people wouldn't change their diets. Preaching abstinence has never been an effective healing method. As one of my patients told me, "I've already given up smoking and cut down on sugar and alcohol. If I have to give up my bacon and eggs for breakfast, and give up my favorite foods, steak and potatoes, I'd just as soon not go on living."

Some doctors advocate the use of drugs to lower cholesterol. Unfortunately, such drugs can be even worse for you than high cholesterol. A nine-year computerized national Coronary Drug Project, sponsored by the National Heart and Lung Institute and financed with $35 million appropriated by Congress, administered four types of drugs to 8,500 heart patients. It turned out that the drugs did indeed lower cholesterol levels, but at a great price. According to a recent report of the Coronary Drug Project, in at least one of these experiments the groups taking the drug (destrothyroxine sodium) had significantly more deaths from "cardiovascular causes" than the placebo group. When the results became clear, the experiment was abruptly ended. A similar experiment had been terminated earlier when it was found that men on the drug (in this case, five milligrams of estrogen daily) were suffering an "excess number of nonfatal cardiovascular events." Meanwhile, the Coronary Drug Project goes on experimenting with those of the original 8,500 patients who survived.

STRESS AND THE CORONARY-PRONE CANDIDATE

Two recent and highly encouraging trends in the field of heart research may provide the key to open the dark, mysterious doors of heart disease: the study of the influence of stress, and the study of the "typical coronary-prone personality." A later chapter deals in some detail with these studies, but for our immediate purpose here are the highlights of these findings. We know that sudden emotional shocks often precede a heart attack. And heart specialists have suspected that prolonged periods of emotional stress definitely contributed to the denouement of the disease. Until recently, however, there has been a lack of concrete proof of this theory. The critical turning point came in 1956 when Dr. Hans Selye, director of the Institute of Experimental Medicine and Surgery at the University of Montreal, published his stress research findings in a major breakthrough book called *The Stress of Life*. It illuminated to millions of professionals and laymen the way our glands react to stress, contributing to ulcers, asthma, and a wide variety of illnesses. Dr. Selye is the developer of modern medicine's stress concepts and author of hundreds of articles and books. Speaking at the 1973 annual meeting of the Million Dollar Round Table of insurance executives in Seattle, Dr. Selye said:

> Stress levels and the manner in which excessive stress affects each of us varies with our hereditary characteristics and environmental influences. Depending on this wide range of factors, stress can be manifested as a heart attack, mental exhaustion, high blood pressure, a simple headache or many other ailments. Your predispositions to certain disorders will, to a large degree, decide your specific warning signals and means of avoiding undue stress.
>
> No one can live without experiencing some degree of stress all the time. You may think that only serious disease or intensive physical or mental injury can cause stress. This is not so. Crossing a busy intersection, exposure to a draft or even sheer joy are enough to activate the body's stress mechanism to some extent.
>
> Does this mean that we should avoid stress whenever possible? Certainly not! Stress is the spice of life. Being associated with all types of activity, we could avoid it only by never doing anything. Who would enjoy a life with no runs, no hits, no errors?

Dr. Selye stated that nothing is more healthful than finding constructive outlets for one's talent and energy. He cautioned that each individual must discover his own stress level. "If you chase a turtle to run as fast as a racehorse, you'll kill it," he said. The same holds true for anyone who pushes himself beyond levels his body can properly endure. Dr. Selye is fond of quoting a small verse he wrote: "Fight always for the highest possible aim/ But never put up resistance in vain."

The four guidelines Dr. Selye presented in a session called "Stress and the Salesman" were: 1) Stop to Realize Everyone Suffers Stress; 2) Start to Recognize Early Stress

Symptoms; 3) Stop to Reorganize Eventual Stress Situations; and 4) Start to Relate Effectively to Significant Stress. How I wish he had added a fifth—Start to Relate Sex to Stress. Dr. Selye says that one useful approach to stress-related problems is "simply talk it out. Sharing your pleasures doubles them; sharing your problems halves them." A reciprocal case can easily be made for sharing sexual pleasure satisfactorily with a participating, appreciative partner.

Whenever you face a threatening situation, your adrenal glands pour out secretions that prepare your body to fight or run. Fats, including cholesterol, are also temporarily released into the blood to provide energy. The blood pressure and pulse rate go up. If you do something to work off this energy, if you fight, run, shout, do push-ups, or make love, the hormones and fats are used up and the blood pressure and pulse go back to normal.

How does stress affect the heart and blood vessels? Many men under tension drink, smoke, or overeat. They are often too tired and depressed to exercise. In this way, tension increases the risk factors associated with heart disease. But constant tension has a more direct effect on the circulation and heart: it can cause permanently elevated blood cholesterol, and it can make the blood clot more easily. Experiments have shown that under chronic stress the cholesterol level remains high—even if the person eats a low-fat diet. Studies have shown that the blood clots faster in an emotionally tense person. This may save a man's life in time of physical combat, but in civilian life it can be, unfortunately, a fatal clot in an already narrowed artery.

Numerous experiments have shown that fatty foods in themselves don't raise the cholesterol level, but that fat *combined with stress* does. One study went even further. Conducted by Dr. Henry I. Russek, a New York cardiologist and consultant to the U.S. Public Health Service, this project demonstrated that a high-fat diet is not dan-

gerous itself, but depends on the "catalyst of stressful living." (Russek also believes this works in reverse: stress is
more dangerous when combined with a high-fat diet.) Of
all the risk factors in heart disease, he declares, "none appears more decisive than psychic stress."

Animal experiments show that heart attacks can be
produced in rats *solely* by subjecting them to stress, without changing diet, drugs, or any other risk factor. Scientists have also reported that after the trauma of trapping
and caging, baboons often have heart attacks. In animals
in the Philadelphia Zoo, disease of the coronary arteries
has increased tenfold during the past ten years, though
diet and other physical factors have remained constant.
Experts blame this on tension caused by increased population density and caging.

It appears that the "X factor" in heart disease is not
cholesterol, after all, or any of the other traditional culprits, or even all of them combined. It is simply everyday
stress.

But what does that mean? Stress has always been a
part of life. Our ancestors faced war and persecution, fam-
ine and pestilence. Is our life today really more stressful?
Did a pioneer clearing the wilderness and hunting for his
food face less stress than today's commuter fighting the
subway crowds? What new stress exists in modern life
that accounts for the soaring heart disease rate? Is there
some change in social structure that parallels this change
in our health problems? We will discuss many stress situations in later chapters, but let us hope that future research will reveal much more about what kind of pressures
in today's world most disturbs the typical heart disease
victim.

Heart disease is much more prevalent among men of
a certain physical type. Studies have proven over and over
that the muscular, deep-chested, heavily built, square-
jawed man—the mesomorph—is at least twice as vulnerable
to heart attacks as the tall, skinny ectomorph. As early as

1944 the famous heart specialist, Dr. Paul Dudley White, asked: "Why should the most robust and apparently the most masculine young male be particularly prone to coronary heart disease?"

The key is in the words "apparently most masculine." Investigators who went beyond the externals to analyze the personalities of these hardy-looking specimens discovered that not only do they look more masculine, but they try to live up in every way to society's definition of "masculine." They try to be "he-men" or "supermen."

But there are contradictions and puzzles in personality studies as well as in every other aspect of coronary heart disease.

Studies carried out by the Massachusetts Coronary Research Project indicated that male coronary patients indeed do tend to look particularly masculine, but when investigators studied their "psychological components of masculinity," they discovered that, deep down, these patients were less "masculine" than other men. They showed more feminine reaction patterns than a control group of noncoronary males who were similarly quizzed.

Similar findings emerged from various studies into "Heart Disease and the Psyche" sponsored by the National Heart Institute. These indicated that coronary candidates tend to be anxious and tense; they are unconsciously trying to cover up their underlying need for love, tenderness, and dependence. They "rarely indulge in restful satisfactions," they "fail to act out their emotions," and they avoid "affectional involvement with other persons." Summarizing these findings, Dr. Mary Sherman suggested that "coronary disease may be viewed as an alternative to certain personality disorders, particularly for those culturally not permitted to be weak or to fail to compete successfully." In other words, some men unconsciously "choose" a heart attack rather than show their weakness and vulnerability in more obvious ways, such as weeping, being passive, or being emotionally dependent upon another. Thus, a man who has no hang-ups about showing his need for love is less likely to become a coronary candidate.

Perhaps the poets and mystics who identify the physical heart with the emotion of love know something science is just beginning to discover. Perhaps words and phrases like *heartache, heartfelt, coming from the heart,* and *a broken heart* are more than metaphors.

The most thorough, well-financed, and best-known personality study today is the "Type-A Type-B" test program conducted by Dr. Ray Rosenman and Dr. M. Friedman in San Francisco. In 1960 they interviewed 3,500 men between thirty-nine and fifty-nine who had no symptoms of heart disease, and classified their personalities into two categories. The Type-As were intense, driven, and aggressive; they had a sense of time urgency that made it hard for them to relax. The Type-Bs were more easygoing and could enjoy fun and pleasure without always worrying about getting ahead. Over the next twelve years the doctors observed the health problems of these men as they got older. So far, the Type-As have developed two-and-a-half times as much coronary heart disease as the Type-Bs (about three hundred cases have developed in all).

Cardiologists have concluded that a "coronary personality" is the most valid risk factor, and that to prevent heart disease these personalities should be identified early in life and protected from the environmental factors that increase their vulnerability to heart disease.

The purpose of this book is to introduce you to a new thesis for the prevention of heart disease. It is not my intent, however, to dismiss or downgrade any other of the established or supposed coronary risk factors. Each of these, in my theory, must be kept in line with the total physical being—that is what I mean when I say that a multifactorial approach to prevention is needed. Your life may depend upon an interaction of all the risk factors that you read here. I cannot urge you strongly enough if you know yourself to be coronary-prone, if you have already had heart problems or an attack, or if you recognize yourself in this book as the Apollo (male) coronary-prone type or the Atalanta (female), to learn all that is scientifically or medically known about each of these. It is impossible for me to diagnose specifically for you without a thorough investigation of everything about you. You can, however, learn to recognize symptoms in yourself. You must be completely honest with yourself.

My recommended procedure for doing so is a simple one. But don't let its simplicity stop you from doing precisely what I ask. Take a piece of paper. Draw a line down the middle, putting a plus sign on the left side and a minus on the right. List all of the coronary risk factors and write down what part they play—plus or minus—in your physical makeup. Be guardedly suspicious of each one as though your life might depend upon it, because in truth it may. Remember the final result for you will be seeing in just what jeopardy you are.

I could easily state: Stop smoking. That is the best possible medical advice and, if not the best, the safest from my point of view. But I am not going to do this because my experience has taught me (as I will discuss later) that preaching abstention often loses a patient. If he or she continues smoking, he ducks me, lies to me, or worse, feels guilt-ridden—a condition, I am convinced, that can be more damaging than the smoking itself. But you know yourself and how much you smoke and depend on tobacco as a stimulant. You know also its side effects. You must control your habit in relation to your own specific smoking problem, by cutting down or cutting out.

The same would be true had I chosen alcohol as an example. Again, it would need a highly individualized diagnosis. One of my patients gave up alcohol recently but continued to smoke like a chimney, as he had for many years. He found new and strong side effects from smoking that liquor had offset unbeknown to him. I mention this only to show further the interdependence of each of these factors. One has to be taken into consideration vis-à-vis the others, and changes can and do occur.

Dr. Benjamin F. Miller, a professor of preventive medicine, ended his brilliant book *Freedom from Heart Attacks* with a chapter entitled "If You Want to Give Up Cigarettes." The final paragraph was titled "To Smoke or Not to Smoke?" I have a completely different question to propose that seems to me much more to the point and imperative for the coronary-prone. The question is not whether to smoke or not to smoke; the question is not whether to gratify this or that oral pleasure; the key question to life and continued healthful living is: *to love or not to love?*

The next chapter will examine the particular kind of stresses that are affecting Americans today. Then, after a more detailed look at the reasons today's medicine is failing to help the victims of heart disease, we will return to the question that matters most: How can the potential coronary heart disease victim change his way of life to increase his chances of having a longer, happier, healthier life?

Future research into coronary heart attacks will be futile if we continue to ignore these two significant points:

(1) Coronary risk factors are most dangerous when they are accompanied by stress. Since heart attacks result from the interrelationship of many factors, prevention may not depend on any one factor, such as diet, cholesterol, exercise, smoking, drinking, weight, heredity, and so on, *but on a combination* of any or all of them.

(2) The importance of sex as an antidote for stress and therefore the major role that sex can play in the prevention of heart attacks.

Since it is far more important at this juncture that you hear my complete arguments for these two propositions, I shall only briefly introduce here the first four points of my plan for a new mode of living. They will be dealt with fully in a later chapter, along with the most important fifth point. The four points are:

One: Love—the key.

Two: Home—to paraphrase: "Wherever the heart is."

Three: Partner—the one you love, the one who affects everything in your life, especially your relations with others.

Four: Faith—a man or woman without faith isn't alive.

2

WHAT'S
HAPPENING
TO
MEN?

IF YOU'VE BEEN WARNED THAT YOU HAVE HEART TROUBLE, or if you already have had a heart attack, or if you recognize in yourself some of the symptoms or personality traits of the coronary-prone, then I must talk turkey to you. It should be just as though you were a patient sitting in my office and I knew this to be undeniably true of you. It is my job as a doctor to keep you alive, as well as healthy and active. That is why you would come to me in the first place. It is also my self-adopted obligation to see that you live your life to the fullest and enjoy it more abundantly. I have a natural reticence about preaching abstinence, as it is too often ignored and therefore self-defeating in that it lowers your morale if you fail to take my advice, and it creates a division between us.

Many patients aren't willing to pay the price. A patient would rather smoke that desperately longed-for cigarette, eat that tempting dessert, down that extra dry martini or highball, and stay sedentary when it comes to suggested exercise—in short, sit this one out. Such is the compelling force of ingrained habits.

I prescribe sex to you. In fact, lots more sex, with the only qualification—presuming you are physically fit—that you must be free of guilt or anxiety. I am hopeful that when you are sexually fulfilled, your resistance to that aforementioned cigarette, sweet, one-for-the road, or continued lassitude will be reinforced. Your need won't be quite so desperate. Sex can be a great consolation and a satisfying substitute.

Because I am concerned with the totality of your person, I propose sex as a starting point worth putting in working order. But if you know yourself to be coronary-prone, you cannot afford to ignore any of the other risk factors previously described or told to you elsewhere. I am prescribing sex on the assumption that you are going to put those other risk factors in check, and my prescription is going to help you control them because you'll be leading from strength. Too often life takes over and runs us without our knowing it. Now is the time for you to pause and get back in the driver's seat so that you are not caught unsuspecting with a sudden heart attack that may or may not give you a second chance.

Here are three of my own patient profiles to illustrate a point. The last time Tom G. tried to make love to his wife, as well as two times before, he couldn't. He's terrified of trying again. He might fail. He wonders if he could be impotent for life at the age of fifty-six.

Ted S., fifty-one, seemed healthy except for a few minor complaints—a backache, insomnia, and shortness of breath. He certainly didn't feel ill enough to require medical attention—until he suffered a stroke.

Nobody is sure what was bothering forty-eight-year-old Norman T., but he had been tense and preoccupied for quite some time. A few days ago, only a month after a complete physical examination found him to be in good health, he had a sudden fatal heart attack.

Physical disorders, sexual problems, and premature deaths are striking American males in frightening and increasing numbers. And that's just the surface picture. Men are going through a deep emotional and psychological upheaval as well. Although the changing role of women is attracting more national attention in the press today, the male role is also changing—and the change is painful; its psychological effects are staggering.

The physical and psychological pressures on American males accelerate to a dangerous level when they reach middle age. You can see the danger most clearly by looking at their health records.

Male life expectancy, after increasing for about a hundred years, began leveling off by 1950. And now it is *declining,* while that of women continues to increase. The gap between man's life expectancy and woman's is now about eight years and is gradually increasing. In 1950, women outnumbered men by 1 percent. In 1975 the difference will be more than 4 percent. If the trend continues, it is conceivable that we will become a nation dominated by old women.

A century ago, it was common for a man to bury two or three wives who had died in childbirth. Today the situation is very different; most women outlive their husbands, and more would outlive a second were there enough men to go around.

The single biggest man-killer is heart disease. But more men than women also die from acts of violence, accidents, strokes, and many other diseases. There is evidence that the physical health of the average American male begins to deteriorate long before he ever reaches his prime. Disorders such as ulcers, arthritis, hypertension, constipation, prostate trouble, as well as heart disease, occur at younger and younger ages. For example, prostate trouble once considered an old man's disease, now exists in many men over forty and in some in their thirties. Ulcers, too, now occur in men in their twenties, and even in children.

It is, moreover, during middle age that things go from bad to worse. The Mayo Clinic recently issued a disturbing report indicating that 83.3 percent of the men in their executive health program had "significant diseases." The 569 men in the program, averaging 49.5 years of age, had been given repeated medical examinations during a 20-year period. The results: only 95 of the men were free of major health problems. Obesity was the most common denominator: 165 men were fat. High blood pressure or coronary artery disease afflicted 135 men; 123 had polyps of the colon or rectum (considered potentially malignant); 100 had musculoskeletal disorders such as arthritis or rheumatism. Malignant growths were found in 46 of the subjects, and potentially malignant growths in a significantly higher number.

These men were successful executives who had once enjoyed normal health, who had access to the best medical care and the best living conditions. If they represent our well-cared-for, affluent, mature American male population, it is time to take a close look at the conditions that are making man an endangered species.

Why are males subject to such physical disabilities? Some experts say that it is because they are under far greater occupational stress and societal tension. Some say it is because men, unlike women, have fewer emotional outlets. One public health doctor put it this way: "A woman can release her tension through tears, but her husband must act manly and choke his back into his coronary arteries. And some people believe that it is women who are driving men into early graves."

An extreme view? Perhaps, but there is no doubt that men are reacting with physical symptoms to the anxiety produced by today's changing sexual roles. Some of the symptoms—impotence, homosexuality, compulsive eating, drinking, and smoking, for example—are inherently emotional. Other health problems have a more indirect relationship to the libido.

There may be more than coincidence, for example, in the fact that the nations with the highest incidence of male heart attack—the United States and Finland—are nations where women have rejected traditional sex roles. In both countries women's rights have been major social and political issues in the 1960s and 1970s. Moreover, according to World Health Organization figures, the countries with the lowest incidence of heart attack are Japan and France—both famous for the femininity of their women, and both countries where it is socially acceptable for a man to seek solace with a mistress or geisha.

THE SOCIAL BACKGROUND

The sexual distress of today's male is understandable. Modern man has been trained in such contradictory and confusing ways—just as he has learned one role, he is asked to adjust to another.

Men begin their lives deeply dependent on a female. The strong mother figure has, in recent years, been too often combined with a rather distant father who was preoccupied with trying to make a living. Everything important to the small boy—meals, toys, clothes, family activities—is run by Mom. At school, female teachers reinforce the image of female power and authority. Down deep, no man can escape the irrefutable fact that his life is in the hands of women.

During adolescence, boys must learn to push this image into the unconscious. They must convert to the idea that authority, strength, and power belong to the male, and dependence, softness, and compliance to the female. This prepares them for their next role: pursuer and seducer of the female. They learn to act dominant, accepting the male sexual ethic of "get all you can," as well as the male work-succeed-compete-achieve ethic.

While they are pursuing, getting, taking, and achieving (or at least trying their damndest to), they are preparing for their final role: that of the husband, who is expected to protect, care for, provide for, and sexually educate a wife.

But history has played a dirty trick on the man who was brought up this way. Right under his nose, the sexual double standard has broken down. Woman has become liberated—not only politically and economically, but also sexually. The modern woman doesn't necessarily want to be pursued, protected, or even provided for.

In the days when women had no sexual rights, their sexual behavior caused no problems for men. A woman was expected to submit; she didn't have to be aroused. But today the man is expected, even obligated, to give her pleasure. He has to worry not only about his own erection, but about her orgasm. His own sexual image is no longer based only on what he does and feels, but on the response he evokes in her. If he fails, the blow to his ego is far more shattering today, when women know what they want, than it was when "nice" women weren't supposed to care.

Some men see this as an improvement. "I think it's more wholesome and healthy this way," says thirty-year-old bachelor Ron A. "I like women who are independent and a little aggressive and open and honest about sex. It's cheaper, too—girls today aren't gold diggers."

But most men are ambivalent. They find honest, aggressive women somewhat frightening and even threatening. "The first time a woman said to me, 'If you can't make it, put on your clothes and go home,' I decided I'd rather have an old-fashioned girl. I don't like a woman to make a fool of me," says twenty-six-year-old Herb M. Many men, like Herb, long for the good old days when women depended on men for their social status, their security, their fulfillment, and their very lives.

Some—including superchauvinist Norman Mailer— have said that man's first mistake was making childbirth relatively safe and painless through medicine. As women no longer agonized and died in childbirth, they no longer feared men as the agents of their suffering and death. Man's power declined further as he lost control over woman's impregnation; pills, coils (intrauterine devices), and legal abortions allowed women the revolutionary idea that they could be in charge of their own sexual lives and reproductive organs. At the same time, population experts began spreading the word, and motherhood declined in popularity. Women began to do such unwomanly things as earning their own living by choice, hitchhiking, going to law school, crusading for abortion, and now looking at nude male centerfolds. Scientific studies showed that many women are multiorgasmic and thus sexually superior to men. Men began to take lessons from sex therapists in how to satisfy their wives. And as Mailer observes, many a man "bowed out to the vibrations of his superior," an electric vibrator.

In 1967 a Temple University sociologist, Robert Bell, predicted that an increase in women's interest in sex would cause serious psychological problems for men—especially men who are not highly interested or skilled in sex. In a speech before the American Medical Association, Bell said that he had observed that in a growing number of marriages the sexual desire of wives surpassed that of husbands. "It is possible that in the near future there will be an increasing number of problems in marriage centering on the lack of sexual satisfaction of the wife. The results may be far more serious for the sexually inadequate or uninterested male than they were for the unfulfilled female of the past." His prediction has come true. Women have become more sex-oriented, and men less so.

One symptom of this trend has been observed in recent years by hundreds of physicians, psychologists, counselors, and sociologists: the incidence of impotence has been rising. It is possible, of course, that impotence is actually no more widespread. But there is no doubt that many more people are discussing it and seeking help for it.

Ralph B., who is now in his early forties, is a typical example of the semi-impotent male. For twenty years Ralph has had trouble with erections, but things have gotten worse recently, driving him to seek medical help.

"In college I could make it with the town girls, but not the college girls I dated. While I was in the army in Japan, there was no problem. The Japanese girls I knew there concentrated on getting me all worked up and everything was great. When I first got home, I didn't have trouble finding girls. Lately, though, women have been giving me a rough time. Instead of sympathizing with my problem, they think about themselves. The last girl friend I had got mad and walked out. She said sex with me was a drag."

There are thousands of Ralphs today. Many are married, some blaming their impotence on their wives. Some are resigned, trying to accept the situation. But none is happy.

Impotence in a forty-year-old is nothing new. What is new is the rise of sexual dysfunction among even younger men. Steve, for example, is in his early twenties, married, and impotent. As lovers, he told me, he and his wife had a satisfactory sex life, though Steve admitted that "I've always been afraid I wouldn't be able to satisfy her. I always felt I wasn't quite enough of a man for her." After six months of marriage, he became impotent whenever she approached him sexually. He began to avoid sexual contact with excuses of work, illness, and so on. When he approached her, she'd respond vigorously. Invariably he would be unable to maintain an erection. No organic basis for his impotence was found by medical examination.

Another trend indicating that men are having increasing trouble with sex is the large number of young women who are consulting physicians and counselors about the sexual inadequacies of their lovers and husbands. You see this trend in the letters to advice columnists in the young women's magazines: ten years ago there was always a letter that asked, "Should I or shouldn't I?"; today there are more that ask, "Why can't he?"

Judy, for example, is a bright, bubbly nineteen-year-old engaged to a graduate student. "We love each other, and we love to make love, but he always ejaculates right away," she complained to me. "I thought it would get better with time and practice, but it's been a year now, and he's just the same. That's not the kind of sex life I want. I can't marry him if he doesn't get help."

In a current *Archives of General Psychiatry* study entitled "The New Impotence," three New York psychiatrists reported an increase of sexual dysfunction among their young male patients.

Many young men, they noted, resent being used as a "tool" for the satisfaction of a demanding woman. Their impotence or premature ejaculation is an expression of hostility and rage against women for exploiting them. Others are fearful and depressed from fears of not being able to perform adequately, wondering, "Will I have to maintain an erection in order to sustain a relationship?" This, Dr. George Ginsberg and his colleagues suggest, indicates a reversal of roles since the days when women acquiesced to sex in order to hold a man. Dr. B. Lyman Stewart, in researching impotency, reported: "Functional impotence of the human male is more common than in the past. Furthermore, the incidence of this affliction may continue to increase unless there are more drastic changes in our society. The Women's Liberation Movement . . . is another example of the desire of women to dominate men. In the end it will probably increase the incidence of impotence."

Other psychologists and physicians have observed a similar trend. A Chicago psychologist told us: "Among teenagers I counsel, I've noticed a definite shift in the past ten years. Girls are no longer inhibited and hung-up about sex; the boys are. The girls complain that the boys aren't aggressive and sexy enough, and the boys complain that they can't live up to what the girls want from them. Boys today are haunted by the fear of not being good sex partners. Many of them would rather avoid sex than face the test.

"Among mature couples there's a similar problem. Many men, down deep, believe that a 'nice woman' is not sexually aggressive. When she is, they unconsciously punish her by impotence or disinterest."

Today's victim of "the new impotence" no longer sees sex as a simple pleasure, but as a challenge. He no longer sees a woman as a passive erotic object to be enjoyed and exploited, but as a partner who is just as important as he is and who is capable of judging, rejecting, and exploiting him. This may be healthier than the double standard of the past, but it is certainly not healthy for men who interpret it as a threat to their masculinity. It is certainly not healthy for men who react with impotence—and, as is the subject of this book, with far more serious health problems.

It is true that the women's liberation movement is growing simultaneously with the increase of impotence among relatively young men. But the cause-and-effect relation between the two is open to question. In other words, female liberation is not necessarily the *cause* of male impotence. In fact, it may well be the other way around.

Just as many people join the political left, not because they are radicals or communists, but because they are dis-

illusioned with the status quo, many women join the liberation movement not because they are militant feminists,
but because they are disillusioned with men. Many women
become militant feminists because their men are sexually
inadequate.

"My husband was a bore," said one young woman who
now lives in a feminist commune. "He was so wrapped
up in his job that we didn't have time to grow or learn
to be whole persons. All he ever did was work, watch
television, drink—and occasionally try to make love."

Today there are increasing numbers of women who
find men boring and immature. Years ago Marya Mannes
observed that countless men stop growing when they start
working. After college they read only material relating to
their jobs; in the race for economic security, status, and
prestige, they cut themselves off from the wide range of
human experience without which no man achieves maturity.

Preoccupation with the rat race, sexual problems, and
drinking problems among men are driving more and more
young women to discovering the satisfactions of greater
equality in the world and greater sisterhood with other
women.

Even women who are against the female liberation
movement are disillusioned with men today. One woman
in her thirties told me, "I used to be a pussycat—and I still
am—but how the hell can you purr to a rat?" (When I
asked her why he was a rat, she said, "The rat race made
him one.")

Behind the sexually sophisticated swinging woman
is her dissatisfaction with men. This trend was revealed
dramatically at a recent symposium on swinging, which I
moderated. After a discussion by a panel of sexologists, the
symposium was thrown open to a free discussion and the
audience was invited to submit any questions anonymously
in writing. Many questions came in, ranging from "What
is English culture?" to "How does a girl say no to another

girl when she's not sure?" All questions were answered satisfactorily except for one which threw the group into an angry, confused discussion and was never answered at all. It was this: "Why do the fellows find the girls 95 percent satisfactory and the girls find the fellows only 50 percent satisfactory? What is wrong with the fellows?"

THE MIDDLE-AGE CRISIS

The health and sex problems of the adult male come to a head when he reaches middle age. This period is often compared to adolescence: all the turmoil and uncertainty is there without the strength and resiliency of youth. Or as one man put it, "I still don't know where I'm going, but now I'm more than halfway there."

Sexual anxiety among older men has been the subject of high tragedy and low comedy for centuries. But today the typical pattern—boredom with an old marriage, waning physical power, fear of old age and dying, and the hormonal imbalance of middle age—is intensified by the threat of changing sex roles.

For example, just knowing that he's growing old. It happens to everyone, of course, but it's usually hardest on men—especially a man whose image of himself depends upon his vigor, strength, and hard-won accomplishments. Because of our society's emphasis on masculine power and aggressiveness, men find it harder than women to accept the decline in physical powers that comes with age. It is harder for a man to be weak or inadequate in any way, because men are supposed to be strong and virile.

By the age of forty or fifty, most women have accomplished the life tasks of marriage and child rearing. They may be depressed by the emptying nest, but they also have a feeling of fulfillment that nothing can take away from them.

A man's sense of fulfillment is more elusive. By middle age he may have become professionally successful, but he must still keep striving. He is still expected to rise up the ladder, for there are plenty of younger men pushing from behind.

Some men react by trying to knock themselves out harder than ever to get ahead. ("If I don't make it to the top soon, I never will.") They know that if a man loses a promising job in his forties or fifties, he may never get another with the same potential. It is no wonder that middle-aged executives have a particularly high incidence of work-connected neurosis and anxiety. I see it every day.

Some men react contrarily and lose interest in their work. They begin to wonder if their quest for success is really worth all the trouble. Arnold G., for example, sold his advertising agency when he was fifty-six, left his wife and three kids, emptied his bank account and bought a yacht, determined to realize his dream of sailing around the world while he still had the strength.

The man who sticks with his job has retirement to dread. And to a man who has been defined and valued through his work for forty or fifty years, retirement in actuality represents rejection and uselessness. The prospect of being a "former" executive, teacher, salesman, and a "present" nothing often is terrifying. Especially if life outside the job is empty and unfulfilling—which is usually the case if he's been devoting most of his energy and interest to his work.

The biggest problems for the middle-aged man are unquestionably the ones that take place within the walls of his own home—particularly his bedroom. The children are bad enough. Living with rebellious, ungrateful adolescent children is no picnic. And having them grow up and leave home early is often worse. Many aging fathers refuse to admit that their children are no longer children. They cling to their "little girl." They are unconsciously envious of their sons. Conflicts with children, especially sons, are common for fathers who are facing the middle-age crisis.

But the marriage itself is usually the biggest problem of all. Statistics show that the divorce rate, which rises at about the fifth year of marriage, peaks again around the twentieth year. The main enemy of the aging marriage is not conflict and disagreement, but boredom or disinterest. One man described his marriage as "a bad habit that's too much trouble to break." As children depart and the couple is left alone with each other, unconscious dissatisfaction often degenerates into hostility and eventually hatred.

Chicago newspaper columnist Dr. Joseph Trainer has pointed out that the divorce rate among middle-aged couples would be even higher if so many unhappy marriages didn't end in a premature heart attack on the part of the husband. For it is at this time in a man's life when he is most vulnerable.

"Just when men are beginning to question themselves, their goals, and their futures, just when they are beginning to need close emotional relationships—this is when they often recognize, with painful clarity, the emptiness of their own marriage," one marriage counselor has commented.

A fifty-five-year-old salesman recently complained, "I feel lonely and I am bored with my wife, and I know it's mainly my own fault. During most of our marriage I took everything from her, without giving much back. She was wrapped up in me, and I was wrapped up in my work. Gradually she found other interests. Now I'm ready for a fulfilling, deep relationship—but, thanks to me, there's nothing there."

The emotional and physical turmoil of middle age is something legions of men are unprepared for. They know that women go through menopause and are apt to behave unpredictably, but they don't realize that men, too, go through the equivalent of menopause—the male climacteric.

Dr. Hans Selye, famed endocrinologist and author of the stress theory, has pointed out that the male sex glands begin to deteriorate in the twenties, and the deterioration speeds up during the forties. As the testes gradually manufacture less and less testosterone, the resulting hormonal imbalance influences many bodily and emotional functions. Some men suffer from symptoms not dissimilar to those of menopausal women—impairment of memory, fatigue, insomnia, depression, sharp changes of mood, hot and cold flashes. And almost all men notice a change in sexual functioning. A study of forty males aged thirty-five to forty-five conducted by six researchers at Yale University indicated that concerns about sex—fear of declining virility and dwindling attractiveness—were a problem for almost all of the men studied. Some degree of diminished sexual potency always occurs in middle age. As a man grows older, he simply cannot have as many and as intense erections and ejaculations in as brief a period as he did when he was twenty. This in itself is no great moment— but some men interpret it as such, especially those who tend to rate themselves by their sexual prowess in terms of numbers of conquests or orgasms.

One way that many men react to their less intense physical potency is by becoming highly erotic emotionally. Unfortunately, the wife is the last person to benefit. She is less appealing, while every other female in sight seemingly becomes irresistible. The climacteric male is often intensely romantic, sentimental, moody, and totally unpredictable. He falls in love at the drop of a hat. He often makes an idiot of himself over a young girl.

And then there are "the dirty old men." Sexual adventuring and philandering among middle-aged men is common. Some develop bizarre sexual interests. They may start collecting pornography. They may spy on lovemaking couples or expose themselves to young innocents. Or they may find they like boys better than girls.

In his study of the sex lives of older men, author Stanley Frank declared, "It is alarming how often mature men who never before have shown a predisposition for sexual deviations suddenly succumb to them rather than face the reality of physiological changes in middle age."

He cites the story of a successful New York surgeon who shocked his colleagues when he left his wife of twenty years to live with a young homosexual. Later his wife told friends that he had been haunted by fears of impotence for the past few years.

Perhaps the most unhealthy reaction to the emotional and physical pressures of the climacteric is giving up sex altogether. I find a great many men—especially those who are a bit hostile toward women anyway and who find it humiliating to fail at sex—conveniently become celibate at the first excuse. They gradually stop associating with women—even their wives. They spend more and more time drinking and playing cards with the boys. They often over-eat. They develop many psychosomatic symptoms. They grow old quickly and spend their remaining time sitting around as if waiting to die.

As Masters and Johnson have pointed out, the best aphrodisiac for older people is frequent sexual activity. The amount of testosterone an aging male's testicles produce is far less important for his potency than what is in his heart and mind. The theory that frequent intercourse prolongs potency has been confirmed in the cases of men who were castrated as a result of injuries. Even when the testicles were completely removed, many men were able to have complete and satisfactory intercourse because the pattern of sexual excitement and orgasm was firmly established in the nervous system. *It's all in the mind;* just as some men become impotent after a vasectomy or a psychological trauma, some men remain potent even after castration.

The famous heart surgeon Christian Barnard quotes the following verse as his jocular answer to the many men who frequently ask him how they can prolong their lives;

Be early to bed and early to rise.
Take noncompetitive exercise.
Avoid all stress,

Take care not to eat
Butter or eggs or cream or meat.
That it's bad to be male has been clearly proved,
So have your testicles removed.

But the man who gives up normal, healthy sex is, in effect, giving up life. The man who continues a rich emotional and sexual life stays young. Every aging man who has discovered himself rejuvenated after a love affair knows this. Many people of other cultures have known it, too, as chapter 4 will show.

3

WHAT'S
HAPPENING
TO
WOMEN?

ONE OF THE CHIEF CONTRIBUTING FACTORS TO HEART disease in men today is that the woman's role is changing, and men have not sufficiently awakened to that knowledge. The awakening, when it comes, is one of shock, and men, unable to cope with the change, leave themselves open to distress.

Indeed, many of today's modern women are groping for an answer to their own riddle, not fully aware themselves that, as their environment changes, as their husbands' roles change, they, too, must shift with the times. Too many of these women do not know themselves, and they, therefore, cannot possibly be helpmates to their husbands.

They patently have not learned how to adjust to new pressures and demands.

Furthermore what is often expected of them is not what women want in order to be content. They are unhappy and dissatisfied because they are living roles they feel they are being forced to play. Since they are disillusioned and do not know how to handle this, they overcompensate in other ways.

One night I received an urgent phone call from Harold A. to "come quickly. Something has happened to my wife!" I hurriedly went to their apartment, which luckily was nearby, and carefully examined his wife, Sylvia. She was hurt; there was blood coming from her head, and she was moaning and only semiconscious.

After I had taken care of her minor head laceration, she was conscious enough to talk to me. From the smell of alcohol on her breath, and a long history of dealing firsthand with alcoholics and alcoholism, including writing a book about it, I knew she was heavily intoxicated.

I tried to assure Harold that there was nothing to worry about. She had hurt her head in a fall brought on by too much drinking. Harold, fifty-six, and Sylvia, fifty, were Orthodox Jews, and, to say the least, my diagnosis was a shock to him. I knew what thought was going through his mind—*Shikker iz a Goy*. "Only Gentiles get drunk."

It is not surprising that when a woman is found unconscious her husband will suspect the cause because of past warning signals. For example, she has high blood pressure or experiences dizziness, or she is in a diabetic coma. Her husband usually knows that background and is more or less prepared for the unexpected. But to a religious Jew, it was a shock suddenly to learn his wife was an alcoholic.

When Sylvia recovered, she confessed. "I love my husband, yet I'm lonely because he is too busy with his job. He works hard, and he is tired when he comes home.

All he does is watch TV and fall asleep. He's too worn out for sex. I have two lovely sons, but I'm still lonely. One son lives with his wife on the West Coast. The other gave me two beautiful grandchildren, and they live in the suburbs near me, but I must conscientiously call my daughter-in-law first to see if it is convenient for me to see them."

Because of her loneliness, Sylvia did the worst thing possible. She associated herself with her neighbors who were in the same misery. Every afternoon they met for cocktails in a local lounge just to see new people. She was a conservative woman, not interested in cheating on her husband, nor in drinking. She merely wanted to be with people and to talk, and she soon realized that alcohol relieved her.

She found an outlet for her loneliness: the bottle. Alcohol became her new companion to relieve that empty feeling. But worse yet, she turned to her new love when she was alone at home, and, like an adultress, she hid her "lover" in the closet. Soon she began to have blackouts, the first true sign of alcoholism. Without knowing it herself, Sylvia became a hidden alcoholic, and the tragedy of it was that her husband didn't know it, he never even suspected.

Today's woman is in transition, no longer relegated to defined roles such as those played out in family games of her grandmother or great-grandmother decades ago. Modern woman, in her quest for a new awareness of herself and her environment, is being beckoned from the depths of the dark ages and lifted to a present-day renaissance. The journey for some is rough and rocky. Others never reach the destination.

All women are affected, singles and marrieds alike, and woman's relationship to herself, as well as to men, is the key to sex and its healing power.

TIMES ARE CHANGING

In his book *Future Shock,* Alvin Toffler warns us that between now and the twenty-first century, millions of ordinary, psychologically normal people will face a crisis because they are not prepared to cope with the sudden changes of our times. He emphasized that we are creating a new society—not a changed society, and, "unless we understand this, we shall destroy ourselves in trying to cope with tomorrow."

Man is changing his role as his environment changes, and, yet, where women are concerned, today's man, in his drive to achieve his own material success, often does not understand what's happening to the female. What he doesn't realize is that without a normal family life—in the case of a married couple, which guarantees love and sex and personal well-being for both parties—a man is placing his heart in jeopardy. If his wife is not content, she cannot possibly give him this important medicine, and they both lose.

According to many observers, despite women's liberation and sexual enlightenment, the scope of female sexuality has remained ambiguous. And it grows more so because her attitude toward sex is changing so rapidly.

We are familiar with the changes and goals of the women's liberation movement, but we are not sure of modern woman's role and desire in reference to sex and love. For example, during the last two decades we have seen the ambiguity of the modern woman in reference to love and sex. Before the liberation movement, the emphasis was on love. A woman would give sex to get love.

Then suddenly sex was important. Woman wanted sexual fulfillment. After gaining this freedom and engaging in unlimited sexual experimentation, she now seems to want love again. The uncertainty of her sexuality creates a sense of fear and insecurity, especially when she gets older. She may be confronted with "love-anxiety" which could be a crucial factor to her own and her husband's health, heart, and happiness. To evaluate her love-anxiety, we can classify woman in three ways:

(1) The lonely wife who wants sex and love but feels trapped and can't get it; (2) the lost woman who is a liberated female, can get sex, but is lost in a sexual wilderness without the capacity to love; and (3) the Aquarian woman who wants sex and love and knows how to get them.

Although the three women I have illustrated are prototypes, they derive from real women, though very few in fact will fit these classifications precisely.

THE LONELY WIFE

The lonely wife, as illustrated by the case of Sylvia A., is a traditional, old-fashioned woman. She hasn't changed from her appointed role taught her by society—to be a housewife and mother—but the world has changed around her, forcing her to become something she doesn't quite understand, and she rebels inwardly.

Her grandmother was as limited as she is now, but her grandmother did not face loneliness after she reached the age of fifty, because she assumed a different role as mother-in-law and grandmother. She was busy because she was still called upon to help—baby-sitting, cooking, whatever. She prevented the "I'm-going-home-to-mother" syndrome by assuming the role of marriage counselor. Right or wrong, she was busy, and her greatest satisfaction was in being a grandmother.

Grandmother's role was facilitated by the fact that, in all probability, she lived in the same community all her life, as did her relatives and friends. If she wanted to visit them, she did, without having to telephone for an appointment first.

Our ancestors knew each other. They knew what to expect of their mates because they grew up together with similar social standards, customs, and religion. Each person had a defined role, and each knew what it was. The wife cooked, cleaned, and cared for the children. The husband ruled over her and the household, and it was the accepted custom. The husband was never shocked because he knew what to expect of his wife. Nothing was hidden, not even alcoholism.

To our grandparents, marriage was an obligation, and love and sex were a bonus. They fell in love and married, but they weren't falsely romantic, expecting life to be filled with sunshine and flowers, love and sex. If the latter could be found in their lives, it was an unexpected gift.

Today, in our transient, on-the-go society, men and women meet as strangers. They aren't familiar with each others' backgrounds; and they marry too soon, before they really have a chance to know each other. When they become bored and lose interest in each other, they develop the greatest fault of marriage—*they lose communication,* and they again become strangers.

Whereas marriage was a tradition and an obligation, today, modern average Americans delude themselves that marriage will not only solve their premarital problems but will lead to perpetual bliss. When they find out their expectation is a mirage, the marriage is finished.

Dr. David Mace, a noted marriage counselor, stated in his book *Marriage East and West* that couples in the East are happier than those in the West. "They don't marry primarily for happiness, but to fulfill their family and social obligations. Any happiness that marriage brings is, therefore, accepted as a gift and not as a right."

Men and women in the Western world today do not marry primarily as an obligation, and they don't have to, but they have not sufficiently gotten to know each other before choosing to become life partners. The result is often disappointment, disillusionment, and shock.

To some women, marriage is an introduction to a new suffering, that of loneliness. Marriage for them is a germ of loneliness. The lonely wife suffers because she doesn't realize the necessity to change, to move with the situation. Her husband suffers because he doesn't know her role is changing. He does not realize that, once the children are grown, she may no longer be the satisfied person she once was, because she has not prepared herself for the eventuality.

THE LOST WOMAN

I have found that the majority of middle-class and upper-class American girls are more mature, more intelligent, and more cultured than the modern male; and, in many respects, superior to the stereotyped European woman—more intellectual, more dependable, and more dedicated. They are not as unfathomable, unpredictable, or fickle as the European female. Despite their superiority, many possess a certain sweetness, candor, and innocence not usually found in the non-American woman. I have also observed that they are more demanding and more spoiled than any other female in the world.

The stage was set early for the American woman's demands. In the pioneer days there was a shortage of women, and this male-female imbalance remained for a long time because more men immigrated to the United States than women. That was one of the reasons she was more favored, protected by law, customs, and so forth.

The European scene provided a different background. Ravaging wars and male emigration put the remaining men in great demand. The women tried to please them.

Despite the American wife's selfishness, she was a blessing for the American male, for she helped him in every respect—in his work, profession, business, as an inspiring companion, good housewife, mother, and, above all, she was his mistress. Truly we can say that she was the woman who helped the American male create a home and a country that in the eyes of the non-American is considered second to none.

To the majority of couples, home really meant "home sweet home." For the happy wife, home sweet home was a paradise. Of course, there were many unhappy wives to whom home was an asylum, but still preferable to spinsterhood, divorce, or widowhood.

Then the serpent reappeared and whispered to the modern Eve. To the happy wife he said, "Home is not a paradise, you delude yourself." To the unhappy wife he said, "It doesn't have to be an asylum. To make your own 'home sweet home' not an asylum, you must eat of two fruits of the tree of knowledge. The first fruit will make you aware of the importance of your equality to man. The second fruit will help you understand the importance of orgasm."

To which both women answered: "God wants me to suffer in pain and for man to be my master." The serpent argued, "Surely God couldn't want you to have pain in childbirth or He wouldn't have given you anesthesia. Surely He no longer wants child rearing to be a burden, otherwise He would not have sent baby-sitters, public nurseries, prepared foods, and diaper service into your lives. Surely He doesn't mean for you to lean upon man any longer, because He has enabled you to make your own living. You no longer have to be subservient to man; you are his equal, if not his superior."

Modern Eve found this advice very tempting and ate the forbidden fruit. Some truly liberated women were able to achieve both goals—equality and orgasm—without hurting man. But the lost woman failed to achieve the latter part of her goal, at least, because she was not sophisticated enough to understand love and sex. The reason for her problem is that she could not adjust to the paradoxes that filter through sex today. These paradoxes are a result of sudden changes in our time. Our ancestors did not suffer from these paradoxes because they took sex for granted and lived up to the standards of their times, whether those standards were permissive or repressive. The paradoxes arise when standards are in flux.

But somewhere between then and now came the sexual revolution, and, like every revolution, it didn't enter peacefully but took the American bedroom by force. Because of its suddenness, many got lost in a sexual wilderness.

Dr. Rollo May, author of *Love and Will*, describes three paradoxes. One paradox, he says, "is that enlightenment has not solved the sexual problems in our culture . . . the challenge a woman used to face from men was simple and direct—would she or would she not go to bed? . . . but the question now is can she or can't she?"

A second paradox, says Dr. May, is that the new "emphasis on technique in sex and love-making backfires . . . the emphasis beyond a certain point on technique in sex makes for a mechanistic attitude toward love-making, and goes along with alienation, feelings of loneliness and depersonalization."

The third paradox, Dr. May goes on, is that "our highly-vaunted sexual freedom has turned out to be a new form of puritanism. Our contemporary puritan holds that it is immoral *not* to express your libido."

I have observed another paradox, a fourth, which affects the lost woman—she doesn't know what she wants. Women liberationists, such as Gloria Steinem and Germaine Greer, know what they want, and they belong to different organizations that represent their individual goals and desires. The majority of women liberationists are independent and don't need marriage, but the lost woman wants both independence and marriage—she wants the impossible.

Unlike the lonely wife, she is not trapped; she is free, independent, but not totally emancipated. She is lost in that sexual wilderness without the requisite capacity for love. She seeks power and position in her life, but she also wants to be just like a man, and, in some respects, she wants to be superior. To achieve her aims, she competes with him as a rival and in doing so she emasculates him. She destroys his libido, and it is then that she is in trouble, because she now senses that she needs love and sex.

Like man, she wants and often demands sexual fulfillment. She is more sexually assertive, more aggressive, and more demanding than her grandmother, but she is less satisfied because she has not yet learned how to handle her sexual freedom.

The flapper knew where she stood. She wanted a home, husband, and family. The lost woman is confused. She is told she is better off single; she is indoctrinated with the idea that the joys of motherhood are a myth. The man who mates with this woman is in trouble because she is not capable of making love joyously and is not capable of loving.

Fortunately, the lost woman only constitutes a minority of the sexual revolutionists or women's liberationists. Thanks to the majority of considerate, compassionate, wise, and understanding women, a new type of woman is emerging.

THE AQUARIAN WOMAN

The Aquarian woman is a truly emancipated female who is liberated from the paradoxes that surround our sex lives. She is free of internal anxiety or guilt. She frees herself from mechanical sex and from the idea that it is fashionable or her moral duty to go to bed with every man, and, unlike the lost woman, she knows what she wants.

Between now and the year 2000, we will approach the age of Aquarius, the age of reality and awareness, an era which will replace the romantic, religious, and unrealistic age of Pisces. Unlike the old culture, it will give preference to openness over secrecy, cooperation over competition, personal rights over property rights, and sexuality over violence.

The Aquarian age will bring with it a new attitude toward marriage, emphasizing liberty and individualism, not double-standard religion and tradition. Emphasis will be on realistic love, not on romantic love. Marriage will not be a prison but a partnership, which gives the partner freedom to find fulfillment of his or her needs and desires, and an institution that allows both to live as personalities rather than just stereotypes of wife and mother and husband and father.

This third category of woman, whom I have chosen to call the Aquarian woman, is not restricted to the zodiacal sign of Aquarius. The Aquarian woman can be a woman of any of the twelve signs, but she is a very special person. What she represents is the emerging female of the coming Aquarian age, which is symbolized by truth, freedom, individualism, equality, and the brotherhood of man.

To understand the Aquarian woman we must realize that she is an individual, independent and free.

The Aquarian woman wants to change her role, not only through the tactics of the women's liberation movement, but through an awareness of the needs of her individual self.

Her relationship with her husband is a new partnership based on universal brotherhood, and it is a partnership that aims to build a healthy home and a better society.

She is the pioneer of the era, and she believes that to achieve a satisfactory and meaningful relationship between parents and children, between man and woman, and between man and man, we must try to live up to the Aquarian principles of truth, freedom, equality, individualism, and the brotherhood of man.

Man will begin to think less in the terms of "my masculinity demands that I always take the lead, and I'm always in control of the situation." The Aquarian woman will begin to think less in the terms of "I've got to be more aggressive so I can avoid being pushed around by men." Now they will be content to compromise. Both sexes will joyfully relate honestly and fairly to each other.

But love in the Aquarian age will not be totally free of the possessive, destructive, and turbulent aspects that characterize old-fashioned sex. Human nature is complex, and no human relationship can ever be simple. The confusion about what sex is for, however, gradually will be resolved.

With the disappearance of guilt and taboos, sharing pleasures and becoming intimate with another human being will seem a sufficient end in itself. Sex will continue to mean more than an orgasm; the magic of intimacy has a spiritual dimension even if the intimacy lasts only an hour.

Some things never change. Love and sex have always been mysterious, and the Aquarian woman is an inspiring enigma because she has her private world. She is a new kind of sexually liberated woman who feels free to give and accept sexual pleasure as an equal. She is not a sex object, but a partner in pleasure.

The Aquarian woman is feminine and she wants to be. She doesn't need to use marriage to solve her problems. She does not need to marry for security and sex, and, unless she feels she can support them and rear them properly, she doesn't want to bring children into the world. But once she gains maturity, she can have it all if she so chooses.

When she finds the right man, she may be willing to give up or modify her career if it becomes necessary, to be a good wife and mother. But first she must have that career, and she may, probably will, keep both. She'll never be lonely because she has her career *and* her man.

She will always have her career because, as a single girl who didn't rush to get married, she had ample opportunity to develop her talent or occupational capacity. She

will always have a man because she is sexually sophisticated, and has learned how to make love. She doesn't suffer
from love-anxiety because she is a disciple of the goddess
of love who believes, as Dr. Alex Comfort emphasized in
his book *The Joy of Sex,* ". . . playfulness is a part of love
which could well be *the major contribution of the Aquarian
revolution to human happiness"* (italics added).

The. Aquarian woman can help not only our troubled
men, but our troubled country. Recent events indicate that
the modern American males who control our nation lack
wisdom and determination to solve our crucial problems,
such as crime, alcoholism, and drug addiction.

Modern Americans planted the flag of the United
States on the moon. Can they inspire the world, as their
forefathers did, to accept the principles their flag represents—liberty, equality, and fraternity? In other words, are
American men ready for the new age? In the light of the
abundant evidence, they are not. They need the wisdom,
the determination, and the devotion of the Aquarian
woman.

I have studied thousands of American men and
women, and I have come to the conclusion that the
Aquarian women are more broad-minded, more tolerant,
more just, and more humane than the majority of American
men. Unlike many women, they do not want to rule or
destroy men; they want to be equal to them, not only as
colleagues and parents but also as citizens to create a
better world.

Michelle and Karen are good examples of the Aquarian woman. Michelle was brought up in a puritanical, religious atmosphere and married primarily because it was
expected of her. So, too, were sexual relations with her
husband for the purpose of producing children. She admitted to me that her sex life with her husband had never
been satisfying but, she said, "I couldn't complain because
I was made to feel that it was my duty; it was part of my
religious duty."

Finally, Michelle developed the courage of her convictions. She was not happy; she was not content; she was bored and no longer in love with her husband. She was, she realized, hanging on to a marriage only because she was afraid—afraid of what her family and church would say if she got divorced. Life, she concluded, was too short for such an existence, and she came to believe that "God gave us minds and the ability to seek happiness. God had not made my marriage; it had been the decision of two earthly beings who didn't know each other before they decided to marry." She determined to obtain a divorce even though she still had some inward feelings of guilt and misgiving.

"I didn't date for a while," she told me, "and when I did it was only once or twice with the same person and that was it. Then I fell in love with Jerry, but we were both jealous and possessive and leaned too much on each other. Eventually I outgrew him emotionally, so I started dating other men. But Jerry and I ended our relationship as friends.

"I wanted to experiment sexually and to meet new people, to reevaluate my priorities. I went to a nude encounter session, and it did help me. I learned from it, and it was the beginning of my feelings of freedom."

Michelle is an Aquarian woman. She's not afraid of getting older because now she has her career, she feels secure, she is socially popular, and she believes in the brotherhood of man. She told me that she holds no grudges against her former husband, and she points out that she ended her relationship with Jerry as friends. "Man is not my enemy," she told me, "he's my friend."

Michelle is an individual, and she needs some time to herself. "Sometimes I appear to be cold and detached and inconsiderate," she said, "but it's because I need the time to be myself and for mental rejuvenation. I want to be a person before I'm a wife and mother."

Michelle is a seeker of the new, and if she is capricious

it is because it's difficult to know what she will do. If a man understands and appreciates this new woman, her unpredictable or unexpected moves can only bring excitement and challenge. It is the best guarantee against boredom. However, if her man does not know her and cannot figure out her moves, one thing is sure. In the spirit of brotherly love she will never harm him, but will part with him as a friend.

Michelle is not afraid of being unmarried as she approaches her mid-thirties because she still believes in her own power. She *can* have a man, and she will never get old.

It is usually when she reaches her thirties or is moving into middle age that the Aquarian woman achieves maturity and sexual sophistication and success in her career and enough money to make her independent. When this happens, she will be more rewarding to a man than any young, immature sexpot. She has no anxiety about aging because she is acquiring the things she wants.

Our other example of Aquarian woman, Karen, a foreign correspondent, described herself and her goals to me in a letter. She said, "Dr. Scheimann, I will not be pressured by society into getting married. I love men, but I want a career first. I want to feel a sense of security and achievement on my own, to gain a deeper maturity, which I don't feel I yet have, and only when I have achieved some measure of success, will I feel adequate enough to form a successful marriage.

"I would like to make sure that the love I give and the love I get are permanent, and I will do my part to make it last, but I know there are no guarantees of that. It scares me a little because I'm basically old-fashioned. I want a man to love forever, although, I admit, I'm not looking for utopia. I know there isn't any such thing, but I also know that if two people love and respect each other you can come pretty close to it.

"When I do marry, I want to continue my career. I

doubt that I would be satisfied not using the talents I've built up, and I feel that the type of man I'm looking for will want me to continue. I've seen too many of my friends marry girls who never grew, while their own life-styles and careers boomed. Many of them are divorced now, and others are living in a state of hell.

"There are relatives and friends who constantly bug me about getting married. I look at them, remembering innumerable conversations where they have complained to me that all they seem to do is clean house, change diapers, fix meals, never get taken out to dinner, and worry about the fact that 'he came home late again last night.' I feel sorry for them. They have nothing else to occupy their minds.

"These same people have looked at me and said, 'Oh, you're so lucky,' and, yet, they want me to drop everything and join them in holy wedlock. If I would give up my career, they'd be overwhelmed with glee. Sometimes I think they are sadistic, or maybe just a little jealous. Well, I can understand that. Sometimes I feel a little jealous of them, too, but it's usually short-lived because I know, in time, I can have both worlds—career and marriage.

"I do think I'm lucky, but I worked for whatever luck I have. My career takes me all over the world; I'm getting into fields and beginning to enjoy success from both a satisfaction and money standpoint; I have met and dated some of the most interesting and successful men in the world and I think they find me interesting too.

"When I meet the man I will marry, and I do want to marry, I want to bring something to the marriage besides a body, and I want him to be someone who is interested and interesting. He doesn't have to be a gigantic success in monetary terms, but he must have a sense of self-satisfaction in whatever he has chosen to do just as I must be self-satisfied in what I'm doing. Only when we are both sure of ourselves, our capabilities, and our relationship to each other will we be able to enjoy a happy, sharing marriage.

"I was brought up in a puritanical setting, too, and I admit I still have some hang-ups about sex, but they're just about gone. Maybe I'm finally gaining some of that maturity I need before I'm ready to settle down. I've been through the sexual experimentation stage, and, now, I want to be one woman for one man as long as we both care for and about each other. But if it doesn't work out, I know we can both find someone else. I no longer believe that two people should make each other miserable forever."

Karen is almost an Aquarian woman. She knows and admits she is not yet fully mature enough for marriage, but she has acquired the other things that are needed before she makes the step. Once she has discovered the key to that final phase of maturity, she will be a fascinating woman.

A NEW SYMBOL

In the women's liberation movement of the 1970s, the emblem used is composed of two symbols. The smaller is a clenched fist signifying militancy. The larger is the sign of the planet Venus. Perhaps the emblem has a prophetic message: militancy should be a minor part of a woman, her identification should be more in keeping with the goddess of love. A truly liberated woman should be a disciple of Venus, whose purpose is to attract, to love, to express beauty and harmony.

The new Aquarian woman is perhaps not as romantic as the woman in the Piscean age, but she is the realistic and highly civilized woman of the future. However, in some respects, she is primitive and a woman of the past. Like the ancients, she worships the goddess of love, and, as a primitive, she believes in the healing power of sex.

4

SEX
AND HEALTH:
THE
ANCIENT
WISDOM

I WISH IT WERE OTHERWISE, BUT THE SIMPLE TRUTH IS
that the power of love and sex to heal, strengthen, and rejuvenate a man or a woman has not been scientifically or
systematically investigated. It seems to be a medical mental block. Perhaps healing sex never will be considered
respectable enough for research by computers, in laboratories, and under prestigious foundation or government
grants. Sex is suspect. But millions of people once believed
in the power of sexual love, including the most respected
leaders—the chieftains, high priests, kings, emperors (not
to mention a host of gods and goddesses). This awareness
of the power of love to sustain and lengthen life has not

entirely died out I am glad to say. And, as we will see later on, there is increasing evidence today that an active and satisfying love life can do more to prevent certain diseases than all the tools of modern science have yet been able to do.

In many ways our primitive ancestors were far ahead of us. For example, we are only beginning to realize that many illnesses are self-curing. Those that rest and time won't cure, the placebo factor (a reassuring word, a harmless pill, or a twenty-dollar checkup) often will.

The ancients were experts at psychosomatic medicine—it was the most effective kind they had. Since they (like us now!) couldn't get a doctor to make a house call, they had to rely upon the healing power of nature itself. And they augmented this power with magic, ritual, and religion. Whatever made them feel better was considered good medicine. The early medicine men achieved cures that would by today's standards seem miraculous and that are impossible to explain by our scientific methods.

Early man also knew a great deal about sex that we now ignore. He knew enough to use it for his well-being instead of suppressing it until it became a source of conditioned anxiety and guilt. He sensed instinctively what twentieth-century scientists are still reluctant to discuss: that sex could help man stay vital, fit, and strong.

Naturally, primitive standards of health were lower than ours. Just being alive, reasonably comfortable, and out of immediate danger was good enough for man during his first few hundred thousand years.

In a life filled with terror and mystery, anything that was warm, or comforting, or pleasurable was regarded as highly therapeutic. Sex was one of the few ready and reliable therapeutic activities. It was an essential part of primitive life—not merely a means to procreate, but to make life enjoyable and constructive. So, for thousands of years before modern science and religion came along to tell him how wrong he was, early man observed rites and customs based on the simple assumption that sexuality represented life and longevity along with the power to comfort and cure man and his community.

Most of these early uninhibited sexual practices have been interpreted by scholars as aboriginal attempts to increase the tribe's fertility. But these customs also made the tribe more compatible, more cohesive, and more vigorous. We don't know for certain to what extent these primitive sexual practices made the tribe healthier in specific terms of disease, infant mortality, and longevity. But we do know that for thousands of years most of the world's population believed in these instinctive copulative customs and practiced them happily as an aid to health and well-being. In that sense, they worked.

Sexuality, like all natural forces, was invested with sacred meaning and significance by the ancients. It didn't seem shocking then, as it does now to so many of us, to think of the universe as saturated with sex. The ancients believed, for example, that thunder was the voice of God and that the rain was his semen. According to anthropologist John Allegro, the early Mesopotamians believed that, when it rained, "somewhere above the sky a mighty penis reaches an orgasm that shakes the heavens . . . the divine seed shoots forth and is borne by the wind to earth."

The penis represented the force of life, creation, power, and strength. Many names of our ancient Greek and Near Eastern gods reflect this. John Allegro says that "Jehovah," for example, though usually politely translated as "Father," is actually based on a Sumerian word meaning "mighty penis." The god Baal got his name from "bore," which also means penis. And you can guess why Hercules was called "the Club Bearer."

Though phalluses abounded in primitive religion, female sexuality was also worshipped. A female had an apparently magical power over a man's body; she could cause his penis to move by her very presence. This must have seemed like sorcery to the male, who probably felt as ambivalent about it then as he does today. Menstrual blood, like semen, was considered sacred (unfortunately the Old Testament refers to a menstruating woman as "unclean") and endowed with healing powers. Some modern doctors believe that the placenta actually has a remarkable healing power: for example, it can cure burns better than any other dressing.

Female·frigidity was not a problem in those preguilt-and-shame days. It didn't exist. In most ancient cultures, women were considered to be as highly sexed, if not more so, than males. When the Greek deities Zeus and Hera asked the blind seer Tiresias, who had lived both as a man and a woman (the same Tiresias, by the way, who gave Oedipus the bad news) whether the male or female enjoyed sex more, Tiresias according to the legend replied, "Of the ten parts of coitus, a man enjoys one only, but a woman's senses enjoy all ten to the full."

Perhaps one reason that frigidity didn't exist was that virginity was not a virtue but held in contempt. When one anthropologist asked a Congolese native for a word to describe the state of virginity, the closest the tribesman could come was "mental defective." In some societies it was considered nearly criminal for a girl past puberty not to participate in group sex. Celibacy was uncelebrated.

Many curious customs revolved around how, when, where, and by whom the defloration of young girls should take place. Although it was sometimes done by strangers or a high priest (not infrequently with a sacred wooden phallus), the honor usually fell to some member of the girl's family. (In some "hillbilly" places, apparently, this tradition still persists—at least in story: an oft-repeated joke has the rural bridegroom reject his virgin bride because "if she ain't good enough for her home folks, she ain't good enough for me.")

Just as with any uninhibited sex, defloration rites and contempt for virginity also usually were written off as fertility superstitions by scholars. But starting sex as early as possible was a means of keeping the tribe not only fertile, but happy. Lots of sex and lots of babies kept them feeling in harmony with their environment—one definition of health.

In almost every early culture sex became part of regularly repeated group ceremonies. Often the local sorcerer, medicine man, or shaman was in charge of these rituals. Usually they took place outdoors, at planting or harvest times. Most anthropologists explain these orgies simply as attempts to increase crop production by example—that primitive men and women felt that they must periodically remind nature how the process of reproduction works.

The best-known expert on primitive rites, Sir James G. Frazer, warned that we must not think of these as "mere outbursts of unbridled passion." They were "deliberately and solemnly organized as essential to the fertility of the earth and the welfare of man."

True, the people did believe that human sex corresponded to fertility in nature. Some of them probably did believe that they were doing it for the good of the crops. But it was assuredly for their own good as well. It gave them a healthy outlet for tension and anxiety while it united the tribe in its identification with nature.

Originally, the more complete the sex act, the better. In one Central American tribe, couples were to abstain from sex for four days before planting time. Then they were to indulge their passions to the fullest extent. This may indeed have helped the crops—we have discovered that plants do indeed react in the presence of human emotions and actions. And it probably didn't hurt a primitive couple's sex life either. Similar advice is given by modern sex therapists who tell couples suffering from sexual dysfunction to abstain for a while, get to know each other in other ways, then try copulation again with copious expectations.

As centuries passed, the community orgy, outdoors

or in, was a tribal ritual performed not only seasonally, relating to reaping the harvest and to crop fertility, but also at times of social crisis, trouble, or change. This covered an increased number of occasions, including births, deaths, weddings, funerals, preparation for battles, celebration or mourning following battles, change of leaders, initiation of adolescents into adult society, and so forth.

These feasts, therefore, were religious only in the broadest sense. They were recreational and therapeutic. They were regular means of comforting, strengthening, and reinvigorating the tribe. In other words, they were good medicine, most pleasant and palatable, too.

Whether a ritual takes place in the village square, in the open fields, or in church, it allays anxiety. So does sex, when there is no guilt. After an approved, synchronized outburst of emotion, people feel refreshed, released, ready to start all over or, conversely, to refrain for a respite. Erich Fromm in the *Art of Loving* has put the latter in more scholarly terms: "After the orgiastic experience, man can go on for a time without suffering too much from his separation. Slowly the tension of anxiety mounts, and then is reduced again by the repeated performance of the ritual."

The emotional excitement and release engendered in these ceremonies broke down the barriers between individuals and made them feel, if but temporarily, part of the collective whole. The festivities of the flesh increased tribal loyalty and unity.

The orgy was refined by the Greeks and Romans (the Saturnalia was originally a winter festival, the Bacchanalia a harvest rite), but eventually, with the advent of sin and sexual guilt, such activities went hurriedly underground. Except for pale, apologetic imitations at Mardi Gras, May Day, and Oktoberfest, orgies and group sex didn't become popular again until the swinging scene and youth cultures of the 1960s and 1970s.

Primitive people had not been taught that fidelity is

a virtue and adultery a sin, so they ignored the former and indulged in the latter. Sharing sex partners was sanctioned not only a few times a year, at ceremonial orgies, but as an accepted way of life. It was an important part of the relationship of tribal brotherhood and sisterhood. It not only kept everyone interested, busy, and content, but it strengthened and stabilized the community.

Multiple marriage was an accepted institution among the ancient Semites, as well as in India, Northern Europe, Africa, and Australia. According to anthropologist Robert Briffault, it was universal among the early North American Indians.

There were many variations. Among one Alaskan tribe, there was a periodic general exchange of wives throughout the village. The custom of sexual hospitality was widespread, too. A tired traveler was refreshed with food, rest, and his host's wife or daughter.

Missionaries scolded the Cherokees for changing wives three or four times a year. One missionary wrote in wonderment: "They consider that the Good Spirit formed them to be happy, and not to continue together unless their tempers and dispositions were congenial." Apparently the belief that sexual happiness keeps people alive and well longer than boredom and disinterest or discontent was beyond the comprehension of the Victorian-bred missionary.

Apparently jealousy was just not a problem to these early wife-swappers. The need for variety and rejuvenation was more important to our early ancestors than the urge to possess. Only after people settled down to farming and village life did it become important to know which buildings, which cattle, which women, and which children belonged to whom.

Wayland Young, in his *Eros Denied*, has commented, "Cultures can be divided into two classes: those which, when they see a baby, say, 'Let's bring it up,' and those which say, 'Whose baby is that?'" Which, in the long run, is the healthier attitude? Sexual jealousy is, therefore, associated with the concept of "private property."

Of course men and women didn't stop rejuvenating themselves with fresh new partners, but it became increasingly hard for the average citizen to get away with it.

The next few thousand years of history brought magnificent achievements. The level of cultural and material attainment soared. But for the natural, primitive, erotic side of man, it was decidedly downhill. We concentrated on overcoming our embarrassing primitive heritage. Instead of worshipping nature we tried to conquer and deny her. Instead of freely using our sexuality for our own well-being, we tried to control it, leering and winking whenever it refused to be contained.

Civilization couldn't destroy the erotic side of man completely (not that it didn't try), but it pushed it into the darkest, most remote corners of life, separated from the important things like business, politics, and human health (sexuality has an important influence on all of these).

Today some of us think we have succeeded in conquering nature, but nature seems to be ready to wreak its vengeance. Many people rightly suspect that "it isn't nice to fool Mother Nature," and they are trying desperately to make friends with her again. The back-to-nature movement, the liberating effect of the pill and of two world wars and other historical forces have combined to bring sex back to center stage.

Some people are even making a religion of sex once more. For example, the attitudes and customs of the contemporary youth culture are remarkably similar to those of our primitive ancestors. Premarital sex is mandatory, virginity is ridiculed as valueless, female sexuality encouraged, and nudity abundantly evident.

More important, many young members of the counterculture feel a mystical connection between sex and nature. Sex seems to make them feel in harmony with their environment; it helps them "get it together." As one nine-teen-year-old youth so aptly put it:

> To me, nature and balling are the two most beautiful things. Making love outside makes me feel united with everything in the world. You can feel the love-vibrations all around you. It's beautiful . . .

Group sex is on the rise again. Many young people are rebelling against the impersonal atmosphere of our cities and the isolation of a nuclear family. They are trying, in effect, to return to the tribal relationship of a primitive society. Many of them live in communes and many participate in group orgies. Some have group marriages. As with the primitives, sexual jealousy or possessiveness is not sanctioned or encouraged. The bond formed by sexual sharing, the feeling of unity and belonging, is supposed to transcend jealousy. A young commune-member expressed it this way:

> We don't see how anything we do with our bodies can be bad. The establishment has been killing each other and exploiting each other for centuries and they call us immoral because we say sex is beautiful. Man, it's even more beautiful when you're with a bunch of people you love. Sometimes we have problems, but we'll never go back to the old way.

Unfortunately, it's not easy to carry this off in the midst of today's pressures. Two thousand years of emphasizing chastity and fidelity can't be tossed aside in two days or two decades. The primitives didn't have to worry about sin or guilt. Neither were they hassled by laws, custom, religion, or by parents, teachers, and clergymen.

It's difficult to return to nature when you're living in an urban pad in the East Village or Haight-Ashbury (it's even hard on a rural Vermont farming commune). Many kids think "back to nature" means never brushing your teeth, combing your hair, or seeing a doctor. But as long as their environment is full of refined foods, dirt and smoke, and disease germs, their health will suffer.

The pressures are too intense and the escapes too readily available to expect kids to resist the temptation to seek instant relief and happiness. Many do it through drugs.

The youth counterculture today suffers from epidemics of hepatitis, VD, and drug addiction with all their side affects.

Does that mean the ancient wisdom is wrong? Is there any evidence that primitive sexuality had a good effect on health and longevity? Conversely, among the primitives, did sexual promiscuity and lack of hygiene lead to disease epidemics? They did not. In fact infections and chronic ailments hardly existed at all before large cities and major trading centers exposed the people from one culture to the germs of another.

There are a few places in the world today where people have not been exposed to civilization and still live as our Stone Age ancestors did. Most people assume that these primitives are unhealthy and short-lived. Not true— except where the tribe has been exposed to civilization. *In the truly isolated places, disease is almost unknown.* The isolated Australian aboriginal tribes, for example, are among the healthiest people in the world, ranking in longevity, infant health, and general fitness with the upper-class American or Swede. René Dubos, in *Disease and Health,* reports that the primitive, isolated Mabaan tribe of Africa is healthy to an extent that would be "remarkable in the most medically pampered society." Similar societies exist in the jungles of South America, the islands of Oceania, and in isolated mountains in Asia.

As Dubos so correctly comments, "A civilized environment is not necessarily the healthiest one."

In one group of South Sea Islands, the population was almost destroyed by diseases brought by European explorers. Only fifty years of isolation (and no doubt its reversion to its ancient sex culture) saved it from extinction.

The Marquesas Islands were discovered in the late eighteenth century by Englishmen who remained, officially for the whaling trade, but really because of the beautiful women and the sex-as-religion culture. After a few years, venereal disease and other infections spread among the natives. The Europeans left, taking their doctors with them, but leaving the sin-and-guilt message of their missionaries. The population dwindled from thousands to a few hundreds.

Anthropologist Wilmon Menard described his first visit there:

> Women became barren because of multiple venereal diseases introduced by civilization's contaminating contact. Strong men ailed, coughed away their life's blood—and died. The once populated valleys became a series of ghost villages . . . I was profoundly shocked by the almost total extinction of these once almost perfect specimens of Polynesians.

But happily during the last twenty years a miracle has occurred. The young people began to revert to their erotic heritage. Constant indulgence was encouraged and the influence of missionaries downgraded. Sexual activity began at around fifteen. Menard reports that there is almost no jealousy or competition, and no emphasis on fidelity. If someone resists seduction, he is accused of being *mikinare*—influenced by missionaries. Today there are six thousand natives in the Marquesas, more than half of them under twenty. And there are virtually no chronic diseases on the island.

Other evidence has emerged during this century that indicates as well that too much civilization can be a bad thing, and that man cannot be truly healthy if his erotic nature is thwarted and denied. Today there are some signs of a return to the ancient wisdom. This doesn't mean that monogamy will disappear or that there will be open barbaric orgies in suburban backyards. It does mean that more and more people are turning away from orthodox science, back to their own basic instincts as the best indicator of what is healthy for each individual.

It was at the turn of the century that the new emphasis on sexuality began in a most unsuitable setting: the Victorian Age. Prudery reached giant proportions then: in the truly polite homes even the furniture legs were dressed, and the works of male and female authors were kept separated on the bookshelves. And certainly no respectable family library contained a single volume by that scandalous upstart Sigmund Freud.

Freud was not the first doctor to notice that people who got sick often had severe sex problems. For centuries people had been "wasting away with grief" and "dying of a broken heart." But Freud was the first to make this a subject for science instead of for poetry. He put it all together (in one hundred volumes) and made it official. His theories became the basis of psychiatry and the foundation of psychosomatic medicine. Freud reminded us of what our ancestors knew: that physical affection is as necessary for health as breathing and eating, and that you can get sick from a disturbed sexual conscience. Or, to put it in more Freudian terms, he demonstrated that when sexual desires are repressed into the unconscious, they often show up, not only in dreams and accidents and psychological upsets, but in organic disease.

For years many right-thinking people thought Freud was a crazy "dirty-old-man" who saw sex in every innuendo or inkblot. Today, however, he seems rather tame. Recent insights into human sexuality seem to suggest that not only was he on the right track, but that in truth he didn't go far enough.

For example, people scoffed when he said that most of our dreams have a sexual basis. Today's sleep researchers have discovered that almost all men have constant erections when they dream (the equivalent state in women is, of course, more difficult to demonstrate).

One of Freud's most shocking theories was that children, even little ones, have active sex lives. Most people found that a singularly repulsive idea. But today we know that the need for body contact and erotic pleasure begins in the womb and doesn't end till the grave. And it pervades most of life in between. In fact, I see increasing evidence that *physical contact and affection literally can be a matter of life and death.*

Fifty years ago, for example, thousands of babies in hospitals and orphanages died mysteriously every year, in spite of receiving excellent physical care. Doctors investigated and finally instructed the nurses to cuddle the babies for a half hour a day. Among the cuddled babies, this disease, called marasmus, virtually disappeared.

If you find it difficult to believe that babies feel so strongly about cuddling that they'd just as soon die without it, watch a nursing baby sometime. He will continue to cling, mouth, and suck the breast long after his stomach is full (he gets all the milk he needs after the first five or ten minutes), until he falls contentedly asleep.

Animal experiments have also shown that touching, stroking, and sex can do wonders, and that taking them away *can kill.* Baby mice and kittens who are not licked and patted enough sicken and sometimes die. In a famous experiment, Dr. Harry Harlow studied monkeys who were deprived of physical contact with other monkeys during infancy. The ones who survived grew up to be withdrawn, hostile, homosexual, sexually inhibited, and unable to mate normally. In another experiment, newborn monkeys were given two mother substitutes—one made of terry cloth and warmed by an electric bulb and the other with a food-giving bottle. The infant monkeys preferred softness and warmth to food.

A breed of superrat has been developed simply by

giving them extra doses of stroking and handling in infancy. When adult, these rats are able to withstand stress that gives other rats heart damage and ulcers. Adult animals when deprived of their mates have been known to refuse food and starve to death. On the other hand, old male rats live longer when caged with young female rats. Most animals who live unusually long are very active sexually. This is interpreted to mean that they are sexy *because* they are healthy—but I believe it could well be the other way around.

Adult humans, too, thrive on love and fail without it, although their reactions and habits obviously are more difficult to observe than those of babies or animals. Population studies show that almost everywhere in the world married people live longer than single people, while the longevity rate of divorced and widowed people drops drastically. In Great Britain alone, the heart attack rate is 40 percent higher among widowers than among married men at the same age. We also know that an unusual proportion of previously healthy widows and widowers deteriorate rapidly and soon follow their spouses to the grave.

Doctors have frequently observed that very sick and very old people, many of whom feel abandoned, respond magically to a human touch. Commenting on the relationship between health and the feeling of being loved, psychotherapist Sidney Jourard has noted: "There have been many informal observations of people, previously limp, lackluster, dispirited people, who increased in muscle tone, integration of personality, and resistance to illness, once they were told they were loved. . . ."

It isn't fashionable, alas, to make detailed, extensive, expensive studies on the emotional causes of good health. But there have been a few investigations that indicate that certain diseases, including tuberculosis and pneumonia, are related to *the loss of love*—not simply to invasion by specific bacteria.

The tuberculosis bacillus is everywhere in the civilized world, but some people get sick from it and some people don't. In the 1920s, when TB was still rampant, a few doctors investigated its cause. They asked a group of patients some questions, compared them to a group of nondiseased people, and concluded that TB occurred much more frequently in people who (1) have an inordinate need for affection, and (2) have recently suffered a break in their relationship with a loved one.

Studies of the fatality rate from pneumonia during the early 1940s (just before penicillin) indicate that the disease occurred chiefly among lonely people who came to city hospitals, and that the patients who had few visitors and human contacts had a much higher death rate. This was attributed to general ill health, but later research in psychosomatic medicine has shown that loneliness itself can precipitate the disease. One physician, A. H. Schmale, found that of forty-two patients admitted to a general hospital during a three-week period, forty-one had recently had a disruption in an important relationship.

The healing power of love and sex has always been a more popular idea in story, song, and folklore than in science and medicine. But in the search for new methods to increase longevity, the contemporary scientist should tap the power of sexuality. The relationship of sex to human longevity is an ancient theme. The primitives knew instinctively that they probably would live longer if they had something to live for. Since they didn't have many other forms of recreation available, sex was inevitably what kept them going. They equated aging with sexual decline, and sexual vigor with overall rejuvenation and health.

Unfortunately, we who are more civilized tend to spend our prime years making a living and struggling for power and glamour. By the time we start worrying about our longevity we have often lost sight of what life is really about. We try to stay alive by seeing our doctors when we get sick and by taking the right vitamins and antibiotics. Those who can afford it search for increased longevity through the surgeon's knife, a pill, or an injection, rather than through a change in the way of life.

The orthodox medical profession today flatly denies that there is such a thing as "rejuvenation." Yet recent discoveries clearly indicate that if any physical factor can make a tired old man feel young and fresh again, it is the hormones secreted by his sex glands. The most radical and successful of today's attempts at rejuvenation confirm the ancient view: *the sexual force is the key to an overall increase in health and longevity.*

Rejuvenation formulas are not new of course, nor did they all concentrate on sex. In the Middle Ages, alchemists recommended to their aging clients medicines containing gold (considered a general cure-all), the blood of children (to revitalize tired blood), snake meat (vipers were supposed to have the secret of rejuvenation), or all three. Later, daily but limited doses of lethal arsenic were recommended to prolong life and vigor.

But after the function of the endocrine glands was discovered, doctors began to recognize that many symptoms of old age—fatigue, arthritis, loss of moisture in the skin, mental decline, increased susceptibility to colds, and so on—might be caused by reduced amounts of hormones secreted and sent out through the body by the glands, especially the sex glands. In the nineteenth and early twentieth centuries, rejuvenation efforts usually involved some method of getting fresh young testicles (from animals, of course) and transferring their power to tired, old—and usually rich—men.

One of the first to try this was a French physician, Charles E. Brown-Sequard. For years he had been fascinated by the possibility that an old man could be rejuvenated by the hormones of a young animal. Then, in 1889, at the age of seventy-two, after he had long been failing in health, he shocked the Paris Biological Society by announcing: "Today, after only the third injection of an extract from the sex glands of young bulls, everything has changed. . . . I recovered the strength I possessed years ago. . . . Today I was able to visit Madame Brown-Sequard."

Soon thousands of French doctors were injecting testicular extracts into their impotent or aging patients. Some appeared successful. For others, however, the rejuvenation lasted only a few weeks, until the injected hormones were used up. Later researchers claimed that there could not have been enough hormones in the extract to make such changes, and that Brown-Sequard's rejuvenation was due mostly to the power of positive thinking.

Around fifty years later the surgeon Serge Voronoff went even further: he actually transplanted the testicles of apes onto aging men. In an article written for the *Encyclopaedia Britannica*, Voronoff wrote:

> The only remedy for aging is to graft a young testicle, whether that of a young human being or of an ape . . . so as to increase the vitality of all the cells which are weakened but not yet atrophied and therefore still able to renew themselves and thus effectively to rejuvenate the whole organism.

The effect of his operations was temporary, but to his patients apparently even a few weeks of renewed vigor was well worth the huge expense (as well as the considerable indignity). The operations became so highly sensationalized and Voronoff so wealthy that the medical profession eventually ostracized him.

By far the most successful of today's experts in rejuvenation is Paul Niehans of Switzerland, whose "cell therapy," while not accepted by orthodox medicine, has supposedly cured and rejuvenated thousands, including, in their final years, Pope Pius XII, Konrad Adenauer, the Aga Khan, Somerset Maugham, and other celebrities.

For about $2,000, Niehans injects his patients with cells from sheep fetuses or from the endocrine glands of mature animals. The cells must be very fresh—used not more than an hour or two after the animal is killed. Niehans claims that fetal heart cells can cure a failing human heart, that brain cells can revitalize the brain, and so forth. He believes that "there exists a relationship between longevity and the endocrine glands, in particular the sex glands" and that cell therapy is the way to tap this power. Many of his patients agree. Others say the technique is a hoax, and that any "rejuvenation" is due to the placebo effect (if the patient thinks it helps, it will). There is still no definitive proof one way or the other. But surprising numbers of the rich, famous, and ailing still flock to Switzerland for cell therapy.

Today even respectable, orthodox doctors treat aging men with injections of testosterone. The treatments are prescribed for impotence, but surprisingly often an overall rejuvenation takes place. Recently, hormone implantations have been developed with an effect that lasts for months. For some men, this artificial source seems only to replace the natural source of testosterone, resulting in further atrophy of the testicles from lack of use. For others, however, the artificial boost is just what they need to start their own machinery functioning again.

Of one thing I am certain: current attempts at rejuvenation by any kind of medical therapy are not only unreliable, but very expensive and limited, therefore, to the very rich. The effect of frequent sexual intercourse can in many cases bring about the same results. Of course intercourse's reliability as a rejuvenator depends on various other things—the combination of partners, their needs, attitudes, and overall relationship. But I would point out it is readily available to one and all and what's more—it's usually free.

Unfortunately, do-it-yourself rejuvenation isn't as easy for us as it was for our primitive ancestors who hadn't yet developed taboos and inhibitions. For them, doing what came naturally was socially approved. For us, a shot of hormones seems more tangible, more scientific, and far more well bred than stirring up our sex glands. Why should we go to the trouble of changing our values, emotions, and habits when modern science promises instant cures?

This attitude is encouraged by physicians who publicize the pills and shots and operations, but have nothing whatever to say about the effect of sex on health. As a result, the infections and epidemics that can be cured by injections or a pill are disappearing, but chronic, incurable diseases are ignored by the one discipline that should investigate them and apply its findings—the recalcitrant medical profession itself.

5

SEX
AND
HEALTH:
MODERN
MISCONCEPTIONS

THREE QUOTATIONS COME TO MIND TO SET THE STAGE FOR
this chapter: "No animal shows the ambivalence toward
sexuality that marks the neurotic human being"—Dr. Alexander Lowen. "Of all the most highly energized needs of
man, the only one that is not necessary for his survival is
the one that gives him the most trouble"—Ashley Montagu. And someone who remained anonymous said even
more tellingly: "Why are we so screwed up about screw-
ing?"

Where did we go wrong? How did a function that
was once a simple source of pleasure and self-renewal become a serious source of anxiety and guilt? Why do so

many people, including far too many doctors themselves, think of sex as weakening, corrupting, and dangerous—in short, unhealthy? And why, too, in the most affluent, technologically advanced nation the world has ever known, has the science of medicine failed to accept sex and failed to use it as an instrument to increase human health and happiness?

To answer these questions, we'll first have to look at two major influences on our current view of sex and health: religion and medicine. We have learned from both that human nature is basically sinful, that sexuality is its worst sin, and that, if sex has any influence on health at all, it is a harmful one.

Western religion, of course, was the first source of the sex-is-sin point of view. As we have seen, religion per se isn't necessarily antisex; some religions not only accept sex but glorify it. Before they were westernized, the Hindus, Buddhists, and Taoists of India, Japan, and China fully accepted sex and incorporated it into religious life. But to anyone reared in our Judeo-Christian tradition, the idea of sex being united with religion is shocking. From the beginning, Christianity told us that the lowly flesh is inferior to the lofty spirit. Sex represents the base, animal, hellish side of man as opposed to the spiritual, superior, heavenly side.

We have all learned that Adam and Eve made God angry. And that the punishment for their sin was terrible: not only did God send Adam and Eve out of Paradise, but, in effect, he sentenced them to death by not allowing them to remain immortal. Millions of children for hundreds of years have gotten the Biblical message: sex is dangerous.

During the early centuries, the Christians actually tried to get rid of sex entirely. (The Shakers have done precisely this. Every member of the Shaker commune is supposed to remain celibate; the sect is kept alive by new recruits from outside the community.) Chastity and the love of God were the highest goals to which man could aspire; sexual love and earthly pursuits were the lowest. This wasn't Christ's idea, nor that of his earliest followers with the possible exception of Saint Paul, but his later followers became obsessed with stamping out sex. By the fifth century many were enthusiastically castrating themselves to prove how pious they were. Around the same time, Pope Gregory the Great told his flock that if you are alive, you are automatically sinful because your parents sinned when they conceived you. The best one could hope to do about original sin was to avoid repeating it. Celibacy was the answer.

This attitude toward sex didn't help the status of women. To avoid their attractions, many men actively envisioned women as repulsive and shameful. Clement of Alexandria, a third-century churchman who was relatively liberal for his day, encouraged this. "Every woman," he announced, "should blush at the thought that she is a woman."

Over the years, this attitude took its toll. The glorification of celibacy led to a decline in the population of the Western Empire. The defeat of Rome by the barbarian Huns from the North has been blamed on everything from decadence to lead poisoning, but one scholar, Dr. Richard Lewinsohn, claims that the antisex doctrine was responsible. "Unless we assume that the innumerable treatises in favor of asceticism were mere literary efforts and that no one except a few thousand monks and nuns ordered their lives after them, one is forced to conclude that sexual abstinence did more [than corruption] to bring about the downfall of Rome."

But the lusty barbarians, though gaining an empire, gradually lost their ancient traditions. In a few centuries they too became converted to Christianity and to the idea that sex is sinful.

During the Middle Ages women remained symbols of temptation and danger to body and soul. Motherhood was their one sacred function. In his *Eros Denied*, Wayland

Young quotes a typical medieval warning against associating with females: "Woman pollutes the body, drains the
resources, kills the soul, uproots the strength, blinds the eye
and embitters the voice." No wonder celibacy seemed
safer.

The medieval obsession with witches is another example of the fear of female sexuality. Many witches were
young and attractive women accused of casting spells on
upright men, as well as having intercourse with the devil,
eating babies, and other bizarre outrages. Even today,
calling a woman a witch is one way to refer to her as
sexually repulsive.

Today it seems a bit beside the point to criticize the
church for its philosophy of sex and health; after all,
orthodox religion is certainly no longer the dominant force
in society it once was. But it has left its mark on the
practice of modern medicine.

The influence of religion on medicine is one reason
why we still have an epidemic of venereal disease—an
epidemic that, as we will see in the next chapter, could
easily be wiped out. And religion is the reason why most
doctors still refuse to consider sexuality relevant to health
and disease. Today's medical science reflects the philosophy
of yesterday's religion—not only in its sexual puritanism
but in its philosophy of what a human being is.

Our view of human anatomy, for example, is based on
the Christian idea that the body is a house with a soul
living in it—religion concentrates on the soul and ignores
the body; modern medicine does the opposite. They both
assume that the body and the psyche are separate and
distinct, ignoring their interaction. After all, don't we have
separate specialties—psychiatry for the mind and medicine
for the body?

Even today, despite Freud and psychosomatic medicine, many doctors see the body as a machine. It functions
well when all parts are well fueled and in working order,
and it becomes diseased when a part wears out or becomes
broken or is invaded by a foreign organism. Whatever

can't be observed by sight or special tools is not scientific and doesn't count.

The well-known British surgeon William Osler said around the turn of the century, "One finger in the throat and one in the rectum makes a good diagnostician." And many doctors still agree with that. The fact that human beings care much more about matters that cannot be seen or touched—things like politics, beauty, loneliness, hate, fear, love—is ignored by science. Like religion, science represses human passions.

In 1942, in the shadow of World War II, Philip Wylie wrote his controversial *Generation of Vipers,* in which he attacked many "gods" of our society, including science.

Man's physical senses were extended enormously by science. . . . No other attributes of man were, in any way, either extended or vitalized by science. Man's personality, his relations with other men, his private ethics, his social integrity, his standards of value, his love of truth, his dignity or his contentment, were not even potentially improved by the scientist. . . .

A few suits of clothes, some money in the bank, and a new kind of fear constitute the main differences between the average American today and the hairy men with clubs who accompanied Attila to the city of Rome. The behavior of Attila's boys has been duplicated by millions upon millions of Nazi soldiers and laymen, in detail. They are Western men, remember,—scientific and Christian, like ourselves. . . . Each had studied science and each had gone to church—and yet each was able to embrace rape, murder, torture, larceny, mayhem, and every other barbarous infamy the minute opportunity spelled itself in the letters acceptable to him.

Have science and religion done any better by mankind since Wylie wrote this? If you think about Hiroshima, air and water pollution, the assassinations of the sixties, the atrocities of Vietnam and the hostilities elsewhere in the world, you'd have to say no.

Science is supposed to be detached and objective, making no moral judgments and ignoring the injunction, "Thou shalt not kill." But in the realm of sexual behavior, science has been strangely moralistic, supporting the injunction, "Thou shalt not enjoy sex." If medicine were as objective as it is supposed to be, it would treat sex just as it does the other natural functions, like digestion, respiration, and circulation. But it never has. Medicine is for all practical purposes as antisex as religion.

During the nineteenth century, for example, most physicians strongly supported the "sex-is-evil-and-dangerous" point of view. This led to some astounding medical errors. Devastating examples of this can be found in the book *The Anxiety Makers*—a book devoted to this subject.

A hundred years ago, doctors warned patients never to have intercourse during menstruation, pregnancy, or for many months after childbirth; children born from such an act, they said, would probably be diseased or malformed. Overindulgence, doctors claimed, was weakening and could even be fatal. A man has just so much sperm and sexual energy, they explained, and the more he uses, the sooner it is all gone. Therefore, middle-aged men became impotent because they were too sexually active during their youth; they should have saved themselves. Today we know that just the opposite is the case: the more sexually active a man is in his youth the longer his activity is likely to continue.

The *Physiology of Marriage*, written in 1866 by an American doctor, William A. Alcott, warns against excessive frequency of coitus, suggesting it be restricted to once a month. British doctors were a bit more liberal; they suggested once every ten days. Dr. William Acton, a prominent London physician, wrote a popular book on the subject that expressed the accepted theory of the period. Acton stated, for example, that he was consulted by a man suffering from loss of semen, weakness, inaptitude for work, and loss of sight in one eye. "In answer to my further

enquiry he stated that since his marriage he has had con-
nexion two or three times a week. . . . This one fact, I was
obliged to tell him, accounted for all his troubles."

Just about the worst thing a man could do, of course,
was masturbate. An editorial in the *New Orleans Medical
and Surgical Journal* in 1854 stated: "In my opinion, neither plague, nor war, nor smallpox, nor a crowd of similar
evils, have resulted more disastrously for humanity than
the habit of masturbation: it is the destroying element of
civilized society."

The list of devastating consequences of the habit is
awe-inspiring. In *Sex, Man and Society*, Benjamin Rush,
a nineteenth-century American doctor, is quoted as saying
that masturbation produces "seminal weakness, impotence,
dysuria, tabes dorsalis, pulmonary consumption, dimness of
sight, vertigo, epilepsy, hyponchondriasis, loss of memory,
fatuity and death." (He forgot to mention hair growing on
the palm of the hand.)

A French doctor, Claude-François Lallemand, quoted
in *Eros Denied*, claimed that he could always spot children
who masturbate—"they are thin, pale and irritable, and
their features assume a haggard appearance. . . . Habitual
masturbators have a dank, moist, cold hand, very characteristic of vital exhaustion; their sleep is short, and most complete marasmus comes on; they may gradually waste away
if the evil passion is not got the better of. . . ."

Doctors recommended various cures for the evil passion, including ice-cold baths, sleeping on a hard mattress,
and that old favorite, sleeping with the hands tied behind
the back.

The doctors rarely mentioned the possibility of women
masturbating. That's because no decent woman would
ever do such a thing. A nice woman didn't even have
orgasms, according to Dr. Acton, who declared, "I should
say that the majority of women (happily for society) are
not very much troubled with sexual feeling of any kind."

The *Married Lady's Companion*, a popular American

book of the period, advised women that sex could produce "hypochondriacal affections, hysterics, fevers and death." Therefore, "everything which may have a tendency to inflame this passion ought to be cautiously avoided."

If a woman should show signs of enjoying sex, then doctors were ready to treat this disorder. Many advocated surgical removal of the clitoris and even hysterectomies to help females get rid of those "troublesome feelings."

What kind of effect did this medical attitude have on a population already confused and guilty about sex? We're not sure but we know it certainly didn't improve matters.

When advice or treatment by a doctor actually produces harm in patients, the resulting condition is called an iatrogenic disorder. It is clear that, during the nineteenth century, at least, sexual anxiety, frigidity, and impotence were aggravated, and in some cases caused, by medical advice. If we add to these sexual problems the stress-related diseases that often go along with sexual dysfunction, the list of iatrogenic disorders becomes alarming indeed.

The sad fact is that many of today's doctors are still living in the nineteenth century in regard to their misconceptions about sex. They may be excellent at surgery or bonesetting, but their moral, emotional, and ideological barriers are rigid.

For some years now, a few leaders in the medical profession have been concerned about this problem. A 1966 editorial in the *Journal of the American Medical Association* stated:

> To some, sex is the ultimate area of privacy, and hence not appropriate for study and evaluation. No scientific criteria can justify such a conclusion. It is no more reasonable to teach students the anatomy of the reproductive organs and ignore the way these organs function during their ordered activities than it would be to study the anatomy of the stomach but disdain any knowledge of motility, secretion or disease under various kinds of gastric activity. . . . Perhaps one reason many physi-

cians have abdicated their role in providing sexual advice is recognition that their knowledge is deficient.

There was some favorable response to this editorial; for example, the journal *Medical Aspects of Human Sexuality* was formed for the purpose, according to its editors, of helping doctors "meet the need for better ways of understanding and managing the sex-related problems of patients."

Nineteen sixty-six was also the year when Dr. William Masters and Virginia Johnson published *Human Sexual Response*, which contained the results of their laboratory studies of sexual behavior. Masters and Johnson tried to be as scientific and serious as possible, but some of their methods shocked and outraged both laymen and medical colleagues (Masters and Johnson observed intercourse and masturbation, and used volunteers—not only married couples but single people and prostitutes). One doctor criticized Masters for violating sexual privacy. Another accused him of violating "all the proprieties, traditions, and accumulated wisdom."

But in spite of the controversy, Masters and Johnson have insisted that sexuality is the proper concern of medical doctors. They have stated, "It would probably be ultraconservative if we said that at least half of all marriages are contending with significant degrees of sexual dysfunction. . . . We are talking about sex as a natural function, but the medical profession has never treated it as such."

As directors of the Reproductive Biology Research Foundation in St. Louis, Masters and Johnson are currently making an exhaustive study of sexual dysfunction and methods of curing it. The information they have gathered has been available to doctors for years. In 1965 they published details of their counseling procedures in a doctor's handbook. But few doctors read it, and even fewer were prepared to follow its recommendations.

But as Dr. Masters recently told an American Medical

Association Conference on Medicine and Religion held in San Francisco, doctors had better become prepared. "As the public becomes increasingly comfortable with the subject of sexual response, those professions dealing with the problems of human sexual interaction will be swamped by the legitimate demands of a long-suffering society for relief from the destructive influences of sexual inadequacy."

Today the Victorian era is long gone and we are supposedly in a period of enlightenment and freedom. Sexual activities (unspecified) between consenting adults are now legal in many states. Some churches have taken liberal stands toward homosexuality, cohabitation, divorce, and other aspects of sexual behavior. Everybody it would seem is joining the sexual revolution—except doctors.

Today high schools, even some elementary schools, have courses on sex education. I have met many high school students who learned about sex during their regular course of studies, but I have met very few medical students who have been taught about sexuality in universities. Recently in an open interview with seventeen interns and medical students, of the entire group only three said they had any formal instruction on sex following high school.

Before 1960 not one medical school in America offered a course in sexual functioning. Yes, they taught anatomy and reproduction, but not how sexuality is related to other bodily functions or how it is related to emotional factors. Still today no more than half of our medical schools go beyond naming the parts and describing the process of reproduction.

There have been a few studies of sexual knowledge and attitudes of medical students. The results are dismaying. A 1959 study by Dr. Harold Lief of senior medical students in five Philadelphia medical schools showed, for example, that one-half of them still believed masturbation is a cause of mental illness. And one-fifth of their instructors believed it, too! Dr. Lief also pointed out that doctors tend to be sadly uninformed about sex; he said it was partly because the "closed environment of medical school, with its long years of study, gives them little opportunity to experience real life."

In a later study conducted by Leo Shatin, Ph.D., a series of multiple-choice questions on sex was given to eighty medical students at New Jersey College of Medicine and Dentistry. Most of them chose the wrong answers most of the time. For example, forty-seven of the eighty chose the wrong definition of "wet dream," and fifty-nine did not know the cause of wet dreams. To the question "Is a sexual climax necessary for a woman to get pregnant?" forty-three students answered yes. Forty-six answered that syphilis is incurable; seventy said yes, that the sex desire of women declines with menopause; and thirty-three said yes, that a menstruating woman should be considered "slightly ill."

To see how the medical students compared with other groups, the same test was administered to law students and to a random sample of twenty-one-year-old men with two years of college. The scores of the medical students averaged .2 points lower than the law students, and only 4.5 points higher than the twenty-one-year-olds.

One doctor, Sherwyn M. Woods, of the University of Southern California School of Medicine, Los Angeles, has observed that "the vast majority of medical students exhibit behavior appropriately described as inhibited: a significant number are still virginal, anxiety and conflict are frequent. The findings that medical students are highly deficient in knowledge of human sexuality and highly anxious and troubled in their own sexual lives have serious implications for the clinical practice of medicine."

Many doctors are simply embarrassed by sex. They don't want to bring up the subject, and they hope their patients won't. They have plenty of sensible reasons, saying, "I'm a doctor, not a marriage counselor." "My patient's sex life is his own business, not mine," or "My patients would be embarrassed if I asked them about such a delicate and private subject." Yet this delicacy doesn't prevent doctors from prodding and poking every body orifice and asking detailed questions about other "private" functions.

Frigidity, impotency, masculinity crisis or male climacteric are closely related to the patient's sex life. Since any of these could cause, or be responsible for, a patient's physical ailments, a patient's sex life is patently a doctor's business—even more so if he is an internist or cardiologist. In 1968, Dr. Ira B. Pauley conducted a survey of physicians' attitudes and experience in dealing with their patients' problems. He found that psychiatrists and obstetrician-gynecologists obtained a sexual history more often than specialists in internal medicine and general practitioners. This is an unfortunate gross negligence, because the same survey revealed that about one person in every ten who consulted a physician was considered to have a significant sexual problem.

Most patients who have sexual problems do not visit a psychiatrist if only because they can't afford it; a gynecologist treats only women so that rules out men; the resultant truth is that the majority of patients still visit their own general practitioner with such problems, with the exception, perhaps, of an internist if they develop severe stomach and chest pains.

Despite their disinterest in sex many doctors will try to help their patients if they complain of frigidity or impotency, but the advice they give all too often just reveals their ignorance. Many doctors still believe the myth that impotence is an inevitable consequence of aging. "You're supposed to slow down when you hit forty" or "What do you expect at your age?" are common reactions to patients' complaints of impotence.

When Marvin C. went to his doctor for a regular checkup a few days before his fiftieth birthday, he was told, "I want you to start taking things easy. You're not a young man anymore, you know. If you want to keep on playing golf three times a week, use an electric cart to get around." When Marvin asked about sex, the doctor said, "Be careful—don't push yourself too hard."

A few months later his wife told me, "Ever since that doctor told Marvin to slow down he's been worried and tired. He acts like an old man." She paused, then burst out, "He *is* an old man. He's even afraid of sex now!"

Marvin is on his way to a full-blown case of iatrogenic impotence.

In an article published in *Medical Aspects of Human Sexuality*, Dr. Robert C. Long commented, "Family physicians, pediatricians, obstetricians, gynecologists, and internists encounter patients with sexual problems almost daily. Unfortunately, these physicians have had little or no formal training in the field of human sexuality. This results in feelings of inadequacy and discomfort."

And Dr. Harold Lear said, "An important consideration is the damage done to patient's sexuality because of what doctors do *not* say. Doctors tend to overlook or ignore the sexual implications of their patients' diseases."

Doctors Wilbur Oaks and John Moyer have observed that psychological factors, and particularly sexual factors, play a vital role in their patients with high blood pressure. "Some of the very definite symptoms they complain of— vertigo, headache, weakness, fatigue—can be linked directly or indirectly to sexual problems."

Ignoring sex is especially damaging in the case of patients who are recuperating from major surgery or serious illness. Most doctors counsel such patients on diet, drugs, alcohol, smoking, rest, sports, and occupational stress—but not on when or how to resume sexual activity. This gives patients recovering from heart attacks, hysterectomies, colostomies, or other operations the impression that they cannot have sex at all any more.

Dr. Nathanial Wagner, a Seattle psychologist, has commented on the great amount of research that has been done on the reaction of the heart to various activities such as jogging. "We've even studied the heart's reaction to walking on the moon. But data on the heart in the bedroom is almost nonexistent. Yet to most people with cardiovascular difficulties, sexual activity is an important aspect of daily living. It's certainly a more common one than handball or walking on the moon."

An intelligent, humane doctor should discuss sexual rehabilitation with every coronary patient. Patients recover much more rapidly when they are encouraged to become active and to resume a happy, normal life.

When the doctor fails to mention sex at all or warns against it, many patients immediately think of the stories they've heard about men dying during sexual intercourse. Some doctors still believe in and promote this myth.

The fact is that anybody who dies during sex would have died anyway, whether he were playing golf, watching television, or digesting a heavy meal.

It is fear of a fatal heart attack that often leads coronary patients to give up sex unnecessarily. A study of sexual activity among men who survived and recovered from heart attacks revealed that two-thirds of them cut down on sexual activity even though there was no physical reason to do so. A percentage of these patients, therefore, became permanently impotent for no good reason.

Psychologist Nathanial Wagner reports that 10 percent of all men who have had a heart attack become impotent—*and not because of their physical health*. "This must be considered to be a fear response," he concluded, "and it probably could be alleviated with adequate counseling." In 1962 Dr. Edward Weiss, one of the few physicians who was directly interested in sex and its relationship to heart disease, warned us that "very often after heart attacks the patient is instructed by his doctor 'to take it easy' in regard to sexual intercourse, so that he approaches the act of intercourse with considerable anxiety. The same is true for his wife, who already may feel that she has been in part responsible for her husband's heart attack. In general where marital intercourse takes place in an atmosphere of a good, affectionate relationship with a healthy spouse willing to cooperate, *it is helpful rather than harmful to permit it,* once the patient has recovered from the acute phase of the illness" (italics added).

After a decade, some cardiologists are beginning to realize that Dr. Weiss was right. In 1972 two sex magazines, *Sexual Behavior* and *Medical Aspects of Human Sexuality,* published articles with similar advice concerning sex after a heart attack. In September 1973 a scientific medical journal, *The Consultant,* published an article advocating sex after a heart attack with a positive prognosis.

I believe in prevention, therefore we shall also discuss sex before a heart attack. And in later chapters I shall present a detailed, unbiased guide to sexual behavior before and after a heart attack.

A few years ago a forum on our national health was held at Sun Valley, Idaho. One conclusion of the forum was that Americans are "overdoctored, overhospitalized, and overdrugged." Americans would benefit more, participants agreed, by changing their life habits than by having more medical treatment after they get sick. We spend at least 10 percent of our income on medical care—over $70 billion a year. Yet this expensive care is largely wasted. It is not directed toward our real national health problems.

We need medical care that takes into account the relationship between social and personal problems and physical disease. We need a medical profession that can catch up with the psychic half of man. We need doctors who recognize that our anger and fear, our loneliness and depression, as well as our poor diets, lack of exercise, and poisonous environment, are making us ill. As long as we can't cure today's diseases, we will have to learn how to prevent them by changing our habits and attitudes.

More and more doctors are accepting the conclusion of the Sun Valley forum. They are beginning to give advice to their patients on how to live more sanely and soundly. They are at last recognizing the need for a new way of life but, unfortunately, the majority of these physicians do not include in their prognostication a plan for two of the most crucial aspects of living: sex and love. One can forgive a medical man, particularly if he's a puritan himself, on the grounds of ignorance, but I am hard put to it to find forgiveness for a physician who is silent if he knows the importance of sex and love in the scheme of things and fails to prescribe for both intelligently.

6

THE
FORBIDDEN
FRUIT

THERE'S AN OLD STORY ABOUT A WOMAN WHO ASKED HER doctor for a method to prevent venereal disease. "Drink goat's milk," he told her. "Before or after intercourse?" she queried eagerly. "Instead of," he replied.

This anecdote is intended to be humorous, but in its overtones it isn't really funny. It reveals the medical profession's static, time-honored approach to health problems that stem from activities traditionally related to the moral or religious sphere. When faced with venereal disease, drug addiction, alcoholism, smoking, or obesity, doctors say, "Stop doing it." They take the same attitude toward stress-related diseases: "We will conquer heart disease only if people stop smoking, stop overeating, start exercising more, and avoid stress." They might as well attempt to end lung cancer by urging people to stop breathing. Telling people to stop doesn't change their behavior; it only adds guilt and fear to the other risk factors involved. We have a right to expect a better understanding of human nature from our physicians.

Man has always desired most the unobtainable, that which is forbidden to him. Explorers dared the Himalayas because they were inspired by visions of the Forbidden City—Lhasa. For centuries men dreamed of fabulous treasures located in the most inaccessible spots on earth—El Dorado and Atlantis for example. They have climbed mountains, toiled across deserts, and hacked their way through steaming jungles in their untiring search.

A doctor must understand such longing. He must understand that man, particularly the coronary-prone individual, resents negative commands and is reluctant to obey them. This is especially true when the prohibitions apply to the oral and sensual pleasures of food, drink, and sex.

In Italy, for example, it is expected that a man will kill his wife's lover; even in the United States, "the unwritten law" almost guarantees that a jury will free a man accused of such a crime. And yet, the prospect of being killed doesn't end the lover's amatory adventures. The element of danger indeed enhances his enjoyment.

Most societies have not tried severely to limit sensual and oral pleasures. They have instead worked toward modifying or sublimating one or more of them through custom, law, and religion, while leaving others unregulated.

Most religions, for example, place a taboo on certain foods. The dietary laws of the ancient Jews not only protected them in the days when trichinosis was widespread, but made religion a part of daily life. Many Indian tribes think of one animal—their totem—as sacred and would regard eating that animal with as much revulsion as an American would cannibalism.

Alcohol, which all of civilization has witnessed in one form or another, has also been dealt with in a variety of ways. Some primitive tribes allow heavy drinking during religious festivals involving the entire tribe, but regard the solitary drinker with disgust. The Moslems prohibit alcohol completely, as do many religious groups in the United States.

When a society totally forbids one pleasure-seeking instinct, however, it is generally quite permissive about others. The Hindus and Moslems (except during the month of Ramadan) place few sexual restrictions on their male followers, nor do they probibit smoking or narcotics such as hashish and opium. The Victorians, who were extremely repressive about sex, indulged in gargantuan eating and drinking bouts that stagger the mind and sicken the stomach. Most societies have been wise enough to realize that some oral gratification is germane to humankind.

But in the United States it has been our unique misfortune in this century to have been the leader in the crusade against every basic human pleasure-seeking instinct. Legal restrictions, social sanctions, and medical admonitions have all been used to enforce abstinence. Moralistic judges, fire-and-brimstone preachers, and doom-predicting doctors have combined to forbid pleasure and to frighten us into renouncing enjoyment. They have taught us to identify sex, liquor, and now food and diet with disease and emotional problems. This scare approach does not work.

During Prohibition, "the Noble Experiment" designed to free the working class from the perils of Demon Rum, crime soared and more people drank than ever before. Bootleggers and gangsters became national heroes, and speakeasies swallowed up the nation's social life. The forbidden alcohol seemed far more attractive and glamorous than when it was readily available. We realized finally years later that Prohibition was a mistake and repealed the Eighteenth Amendment. Now it is time for us to realize that prohibition per se is a failure.

Alexander Woollcott of the famed Algonquin Round Table succinctly summed it up for many: "Whatever I like is illegal, immoral, or fattening." Strawberry cheese-cake or a banana split is no longer allowed to be an inno-cent pleasure; now they are risk factors for coronary heart attacks. Since we will not abandon our pleasures, however, we eat them anyway, and accept, however guiltily, the compounded risk.

This calculated denial of our natural instinct, this suppression of bodily pleasure, may explain the anxiety and guilt that is now so much a part of modern life. Unfor-tunately, our moral, political, and medical leaders are so conditioned to imposing moral values that we cannot expect much help from them.

The medical profession may be the most guilty. Some politicians are in the forefront of the legislative battle for greater freedom; some ministers are practicing a new people-centered theology; most doctors, however, still con-sider themselves the guardians of traditional morals.

This attitude can be illustrated by a couple I inter-viewed. They had attended a bacchanalian party until very late and had then stayed up for the remainder of the night in order to attend early Mass. "How can you go to Mass after an orgy?" I asked them. "We are good Cath-olics," they replied. "Swinging has nothing to do with our relationship to the Church. Why should we feel guilty? We don't cheat on each other; everything we do is by mutual consent."

"What about confession?" I asked. "Doesn't your priest condemn your swinging and tell you it's wrong?"

"He doesn't approve of it," they answered, "but he knows that we're good Catholics, that we never miss Mass, and that we are bringing up our children in the Church. He tells us that he prays for us, that God forgives us, and tells us in the words of Christ, 'Go, and sin no more.' "

When this couple developed gonorrhea as a result of their swinging, they went to a Catholic physician who was also a friend. He brings his personal moral beliefs into his practice and refuses to prescribe birth control devices and is a spokesman in the antiabortion campaign. He was horrified by their story and told them, "It serves you right."

A clergyman was broad-minded enough to realize that his condemnation of this couple's sexual habits would have no effect, so he concentrated on relieving any religious anxieties they might have had. The doctor, however, who should have helped them and reassured them, did his best to shame and frighten them.

Other tragedies have grown out of misguided preachments on the part of physicians. Dr. James L. Mathis, an assistant professor of psychiatry at the University of Oklahoma, told in *Medical World News* of a sixteen-year-old girl who sought help from her family doctor. Although she was greatly embarrassed and ashamed, she told him that she had engaged in oral-genital contact during a drinking party and asked him whether this meant she was perverted. Instead of telling her that such contact is quite frequent among adults and going on to give her advice appropriate for one of her years, he abruptly told her to seek psychiatric help. The girl, convinced by his attitude that she was indeed perverted, went home and killed herself.

Obviously, the "goat's milk" approach is a failure. People are willing to try "before" or "after" but reject the possibility of "instead." This pat approach has proved useless in combating the twentieth-century problems of obesity and venereal disease. Both these problems, like heart disease, reflect the emotional stress and loneliness so common in our country today. The medical profession lacks the insight into human nature needed to convert self-destructive behavior into healthy behavior.

Despite diet books, low-calorie foods, and diet pills, the adult and adolescent population of the United States is growing fatter and more badly nourished. One explanation of this paradox is that physicians have concentrated on the physical aspects of diet while ignoring the psychological needs that are causing compulsive eating.

The majority of doctors overlook the following factors:

1. Overeating is the result of a childhood association between food and love and usually continues into adulthood if the patient feels a lack of something essential in life. Overeating is, thus, an unhealthy response to emotional or environmental pressures.

2. Food is essential to life but starvation diets, which deny the basic satisfactions and sense of security that food conveys, can cause serious emotional, as well as physical, damage.

3. Advising compulsive eaters to control their caloric intake through willpower or drugs is as irrational as telling an alcoholic to stop drinking or a gambler to avoid racetracks.

4. Like others with emotional problems, the compulsive eater must be given support and encouragement rather than preachments.

In order to lose weight, the obese patient must follow a balanced diet containing fewer calories. This, however, requires a strong motivation; all too often, persons who are sexually frustrated, lonely, or unwanted lack the necessary motivation for successful reducing. This is the reason I have advocated that overweight patients learn to relate to the opposite sex. When, for example, a fat and unhappy girl begins to learn more about men and sex and feels more comfortable with them, it becomes easier for her to stop her compulsive eating. These new interests bring satisfactions that help her to be content with a low-calorie diet.

There are times, of course, when an individual may be better off staying overweight rather than enduring the frustration and emotional strain that unsuccessful attempts at weight reduction can cause. In any case, the most important elements in the new treatment of obesity are prevention and persuasion.

For most people, weight put on during childhood and adolescence is almost impossible to lose, but later weight gains can be prevented with relative ease. Even if an adult patient is overweight, the physician can, through counseling, persuade the patient to control his diet and become more active, thus preventing further gains.

The widespread problem of venereal disease is at last beginning to receive the attention it merits. Authorities now confess that we are faced with an epidemic, not a minor social difficulty, but they cannot agree on how to solve it. The medical profession's approach to obesity reveals sins of omission, while its approach to venereal disease reveals sins of commission. Obesity is, quite simply, not being treated as efficiently as it might be; venereal disease, on the other hand, is actually spreading partially because of prudery and ignorance on the part of doctors.

Venereal disease could be eradicated, or at least pretty well controlled, through proper treatment. Two microorganisms are responsible—the spirochete in the case of syphilis and the gonococcus in the case of gonorrhea. Both are amenable to treatment in their early stages. Prompt reporting of the symptoms to a doctor and rapid administration of the appropriate drugs restore the patient's health quickly and easily.

Despite these well-known facts, many doctors, social workers, policemen, teachers, and parents think of venereal disease as a moral problem rather than as a medical condition. Infected individuals avoid treatment because they cannot admit to themselves or others that "nice people" contract venereal diseases. Shame and guilt take precedence over health considerations.

As a result, gonorrhea has become the most serious common infection in the United States today. It is the most frequent cause of acute abdominal pain in girls between fifteen and twenty-five years old. Syphilis too is on the rise.

The situation, on the whole, is worse today than we've

ever known it. This means an incredible toll in human suffering—more sterility, more pain, more blindness, more deformed babies, more insanity, and more shame, guilt, and hatred that stem from untreated and unnecessary venereal disease.

"If you go to a private physician, it's expensive and embarrassing," one social worker told me. "If you're under age they usually tell your parents. It's almost impossible to find the free VD clinics because they aren't advertised. If you do find one, it's in the worst section in the city. You feel dirty just walking into one."

In Chicago, for example, a city with several universities, the headquarters of the American Medical Association, and some of the finest hospitals in the world, a great many venereal disease patients can't get prompt treatment because no hospital or university clinic has a VD department. Because of this, the majority of medical students in the area see few cases of gonorrhea or early syphilitic lesions.

One Friday afternoon a patient walked into my office. "I need your help, Doctor," he told me. "I have a dose of gonorrhea and I have to be cured by Tuesday—when my wife comes home."

I examined him. He did indeed have gonorrhea, but I also noticed a sore on his penis. I told him that I didn't want to give him penicillin immediately because it would make a reliable test for syphilis impossible. Since he didn't have the money for a private clinic, where he could get a dark-field test, I sent him to the city's free VD clinic. He called me a few minutes later in despair.

"The clinic closed at five, and because Monday's Labor Day they won't see me until Tuesday. That'll be too late. What can I do now?"

Fortunately, he was able to borrow enough money from a friend to go to a private clinic, have the test, and obtain antibiotics. If he hadn't been lucky, his wife's health and, possibly, his marriage would have been jeopardized because he couldn't get rapid, free treatment in one of the world's greatest health centers.

Our current VD problem is an example of the way in which morals can defeat science. Although we have the technical means of eliminating this miserable, crippling disease, our psychological hang-ups prevent us from using these techniques effectively.

In the case of heart disease and other stress-related diseases, we face a similar dilemma. We can perform technical miracles—organ transplants, blood vessel repairs, changing body chemistry through drugs, and so on—but we cannot control the emotional factors that interact with the body and which influence health so profoundly. We can't see through the maze of physical factors and technical gadgetry to the problems that are really making us sick.

The modern physician must realize that the long-range answer to killing and disabling diseases is not treatment but prevention. Repairing damaged individuals alleviates the problem, but does nothing to lower the incidence of disease. When a disease cannot be cured quickly and easily by a drug or operation but stems from a whole pattern of behavior, the only way to stamp out the disease is not to let it start in the first place.

Dr. Paul Dudley White, for example, started a "children's crusade" to teach children to be diet- and exercise-conscious. Since the groundwork for later atherosclerotic disease is laid in the early years of life, he reasoned, early education and training can prevent disease in adulthood.

Prohibition and scare tactics do not work when dealing with youngsters. Teen-agers are exposed to a barrage of warnings about VD and smoking, and yet the rates of both are rising alarmingly among adolescents.

If we wish to protect potential victims by warning them while they are young, we must find another way. In the cases of drug addiction and stress-related diseases, this means teaching people from childhood not only how to eat and drink, but also how to love and how to live in our stress-ridden society. Doctors alone cannot accomplish this task, but they must participate in it; they must recognize at least that the present approach toward chronic diseases is short sighted and superficial.

We must remember the words of an old and beautiful Castilian song:

If I had a warm loaf of bread,
A glass of aguardiente,
And a maiden's kiss—
Bread, drink, and a kiss—
I would not fear the raging serpent.

This kind of attitude indicates a high tolerance to frustration and a low likelihood of developing stress-related diseases. Even though doctors tell us that bread increases our consumption of triglycerides and cholesterol and that alcohol raises our blood pressure, the Castilians have low rates of heart attack.

One explanation is that bread and alcohol become dangerous when they are accompanied by stress; also guilt and fear, instilled by the prohibitionist. Bread and alcohol are neutralized by the powers of a kiss—that is, love and sex, which reduce stress.

Prohibition and scare tactics not only add to the risk factors causing coronary disease, but can also cause heart disease themselves. The case of Frank O. is a good example of iatrogenic (doctor-caused) disease.

Frank was a relatively happy and healthy advertising executive in his fifties. One day he stopped in at a chest X-ray mobile unit. A letter informed him that he was free from tuberculosis, but suggested that he consult a physician about a possible heart condition.

Frank became frightened, and visited a doctor immediately. The physician studied the X-ray film and told him that he had an enlarged heart and that he was overweight. He also diagnosed high blood pressure (a normal reaction to fear and tension).

The doctor ordered Frank to quit smoking, lose thirty pounds, and cut down on fats and alcohol. Otherwise, he threatened, Frank was likely to get a heart attack. Frank was completely demoralized and found it impossible to follow these instruction. He became guilty and angry with himself, as well as frightened of the consequences. His wife started treating him like an invalid, and their sex life rapidly deteriorated. Soon thereafter he became impotent. Three months later he suffered severe chest pains and was convinced that he'd had a heart attack.

When I saw Frank, he was in a state of acute anxiety about his weight, his impotence, and, above all, his heart. His blood pressure was high, but not dangerously so. His electrocardiogram was normal, and an X-ray film showed a larger than average heart, but one that was, in my opinion, quite normal for his body build. It was clear that Frank was still in good shape, even though his life was falling apart.

I didn't scare him or try to forbid his normal activities. I gave him hope and advised only moderation. His condition, I told him, was psychosomatic and temporary. After talking to his wife, I assured him that his impotence could be cured in a few months with her help.

He found that moderation worked where total abstinence had failed. He could not quit smoking altogether, but he cut down from two packs a day to seven cigarettes a day. He found it difficult to lose weight, but he maintained his current weight without gaining. He did this by cutting down on fats, beer, and potatoes.

I persuaded his wife to develop her sexual power and to use it for Frank's benefit. This technique worked very well, and his impotence soon vanished.

Frank is now taking better care of himself—without undue anxiety—and is far more likely to stay healthy than he was before.

Physicians can't stop the epidemics facing us by using scare tactics. They are ignoring the fact that smoking, cholesterol, and overeating are far more dangerous when they are associated with stress. Compulsive eating, drinking, and smoking are symptoms or consequences of emotional frustration and, thus, cannot be cured by frightening the patient and may indeed be made worse by fear and guilt.

The best hope for stress-related diseases does not lie in gloomy attitudes and abstinence. It does not lie in careful measurement of each gram of fat and each calorie consumed, or meticulous exercise plans. It is not necessary to take away pleasure in order to preserve life. Pleasure is a boon to health, not a detriment.

Dr. Edward R. Pinckney, a consultant in internal medicine and a former editor of the *Journal of the American Medical Association,* says, "I believe that emotional stress itself—the way we react to life situations—causes more heart disease than all other risk factors combined."

I am convinced that coffee, cigarettes, alcohol, and rich foods in moderation are not harmful if they give pleasure. *Heart attacks strike those with too little pleasure in their lives, not too much.*

When asked in a question-and-answer column in the *Journal of the American Medical Association* how to prevent a heart attack in a coronary-prone patient, Dr. J. Hurst of the Emory University School of Medicine replied: "I do not know how to predict the occurrence of a coronary incident with great reliability. Even when we can predict the possibility of coronary incidents, I do not know how to prevent them. . . . Your question highlights our ignorance and emphasizes why we need more research."

7

SEX
AND
STRESS

IF YOU LOOK AT WHAT'S HAPPENING IN HEART RESEARCH today, you are tempted to conclude that the researchers are as puritanical as practicing doctors. Even the most enlightened ones—those who say that heart disease stems from emotional factors—still ignore the biggest emotional factor of all: sex. This chapter will add this factor. I will pull together what the stress-and-personality experts are saying and will try to complete the portrait of the coronary victim by filling in the missing pieces of the puzzle.

By now, all but a few of the most adamant diehards among heart researchers have given up trying to find a sole physical factor that causes heart disease. After thirty years of trying, no study, no matter how detailed and expensive, no matter how brilliant the scientists, has been able to pinpoint one important single cause of heart disease. Experts now emphatically agree that a single cause doesn't exist.

It's pretty clear now that changing diet, stopping smoking, and exercising simply hasn't worked. In spite of all efforts to spare heart disease victims through these methods, more and more men, at younger and younger ages, are dying of coronary heart disease.

Scientists know that men and women—young and old —in societies quite different from ours are largely free of coronary heart disease regardless of what they eat and smoke and how much they exercise. Until recently, black men and women were relatively free of the disease. Also, while deaths from coronary heart disease have soared during the past fifty years, the white male's habits of diet, smoking, and exercise have not increased in pace. All these facts have led medical researchers to look elsewhere for something to blame coronary heart disease on. And they have found two convenient scapegoats. One is called "stress." The other is called "the coronary-prone personality."

Stress gets the blame for everything from crime to cancer these days. But it still isn't clear exactly what stress means. No one seems to know why something that can be an invigorating challenge to one person can make another person sick. And no one has proven that a particular kind of stress is related specifically to coronary heart disease.

The biggest problem with blaming stress for coronary heart disease is that you can't isolate it and study it with the traditional tools of science. Stress isn't measurable the way calories and cholesterol are. Its existence can't be proved the way we can prove that a man is overweight or has high blood pressure. If a patient says, "I'm so upset it's making me sick," we have to take his word for it. If he insists, "I'm not disturbed, nothing is bugging me," we can't be sure he's telling us the truth.

Has stress been overstressed? Or do we just need more investigation into what it is and how it affects our bodies?

Those who say stress can make you sick have a lot of evidence going for them. There is no doubt any more that emotions do indeed affect the physical structure and function of the body. Every emotion you feel causes concrete physical, chemical and psychic reactions. Some of these can be observed and measured, proving that they are triggered by intense emotion. Others are more difficult to pinpoint.

One observed, stress-induced physical change causes stomach ulcers. Over twenty-five years ago two New York doctors began studying a patient with a peculiar problem. Because of a childhood accident he could not swallow food in the normal way, but had to be fed through a tube inserted in his abdominal wall. The doctors could watch the interior of his stomach through the opening. They noticed that every time he got angry his stomach lining became engorged with blood; when he was afraid, it turned pale. Under periods of strong emotion the stomach acids ate away at the lining, and raw, bleeding spots developed. Here before their eyes was proof of the correlation between emotional stress and stomach ulcers.

If it were possible to have such a window into our coronary arteries, we might observe a similar process. We might see that the sticky, clogging buildup along the walls of the arteries increases after or during certain emotional states. Just as our stomachs "knot up" when we feel scared and threatened, so do our coronary arteries—only we can't feel it (unless the circulation becomes blocked severely enough to cause pain).

But since researchers can't directly observe our arteries, they have to speculate. Their speculation is convincing. Everybody knows, for example, that strong emotions affect the speed and rhythm of the heartbeat. Doctors also know that fear causes blood vessels to constrict, which raises the blood pressure. Fear also results in an increase of adrenalin in the blood, which makes it clot more quickly. And it has been proven that fear and anger, in some people, at least, increase the amount of cholesterol in the blood.

These four products of stress—narrowed arteries, high blood pressure, the formation of blood clots, and cholesterol deposits in the arteries—are the immediate physical causes of artery disease and heart attacks.

All these physical changes are intended by nature to prepare the body for physical action. But today's equivalent of fear is worry. We don't face physical attacks from our natural enemies: we brood and fume about our bosses, our income taxes, our petty injuries. And the modern coronary candidate doesn't do anything physical to work off his raised blood pressure and burn up his cholesterol. All he does is stay sedentary and keep on worrying, which can make these biochemical changes chronic.

Those who still insist that physical habits, not emotional feelings, are responsible for heart disease, should be reminded that worry and irritation are often accompanied by smoking, overeating, overdrinking, insomnia, lethargy, and other unhealthy physical habits often blamed for coronary heart disease.

There really isn't any room for doubt anymore. Where the doubt comes in is in answering two crucial questions: 1) What particular kind of stress leads to heart disease? 2) What kind of person is most susceptible to this stress? If we knew the answers to those questions, we would know enough to win the biggest battle in our war against heart disease: prevention.

The question "What kind of stress?" has been under constant study of late. We ought to have a clear answer by now. But we don't. Why? Because researchers have looked in the wrong place for stress. Out of all the areas of our lives that might be sources of emotional disturbance—unresolved childhood problems, fear of aging, pressures of urban living, loneliness, boredom, economic worries, problems in a love relationship, and so forth—out of all these possibilities, almost all researchers have chosen only one: emotional problems associated with occupation.

Why do they choose this one area? This emphasis reflects the value system of many of today's business-oriented physicians. It reflects, too, their puritanism. And occupational stress is a fairly convenient subject to study and measure with the tools of scientific analysis. It takes little effort to get a man to talk about his work. People aren't embarrassed to complain about their demanding, stressful jobs—in fact, many are proud of it (few men, on the other hand, are proud of their problems in bed). For these reasons, most stress studies ignore everything but work. In the following review of some of the best-known studies, you'll see that the results have been inconclusive.

CORONARY CANDIDATES

One of the earliest studies of the relationship between occupation and heart disease was conducted by an English physician, J. N. Morris. He studied the coronary heart disease rate among a group of London bus drivers and compared it to the rate among a group of bus conductors of similar ages. The bus drivers had approximately twice as many heart attacks. Drivers, it was explained, have more responsibility and anxiety and fewer physical outlets on the job than conductors.

Dr. Morris then studied the coronary heart disease rate among many other occupations. He discovered that hairdressers, for example, have more heart attacks than shoemakers, and clerks more than gardeners. Interpretations of this varied; some thought the differences in heart disease rate should be blamed on the amount of physical exercise on the job; others thought it was solely the result of the anxiety involved. All this proves is that, once again, the experts don't agree.

In 1962 Dr. Henry Russek approached the study of occupational stress in a somewhat different way. He first drew up a list of occupations and had a panel of judges agree on which ones were most stressful. Then he sent out medical questionnaires to 1,000 men in each occupational category, asking about their history of coronary heart disease.

Sure enough, Russek found that the coronary heart disease rates were consistently higher in the occupations considered more demanding. Among doctors, for example, the harassed general practitioner had a much higher rate than the dermatologist (who rarely has emergency calls). The busy courtroom trial lawyer had a higher rate than the office-based patent attorney.

A comparison study by Dr. Russek showed that, in one hundred cases of coronary patients and one hundred healthy people of similar ages, 91 percent of the heart patients admitted acute job stress, while only 20 percent of the healthy people did so.

Unfortunately, Russek did not investigate the effects of a highly demanding job on a man's private life. It seems obvious that long hours, great responsibility, and stress and strain would interfere with marriage and other social and sexual relationships, thus creating another source of stress even more dangerous than the first.

Russek's work seems to imply that heart disease is more prevalent among those with greater responsibility and professional success. But the opposite conclusion emerged from a 1968 study by Dr. Lawrence Hinkle, involving 270,000 male employees of the Bell Telephone System. Dr. Hinkle found that low-ranking workers and foremen had *higher* coronary heart disease rates than executives of the same ages. Men with college degrees had

30 percent fewer cases of heart disease than those lower in the educational and occupational hierarchy.

A more recent study of 3,102 residents of Evans County, Georgia, conducted by Dr. John C. Cassel, came up with a still different slant on the relationship between a man's job and the health of his heart.

Dr. Cassel originally wanted to find out why white men have so many more heart attacks than black men. Among the 3,102 people he studied, black men had only half as much heart disease as whites, even though blacks ate far more animal fats and more had high blood pressure. When Cassel studied the occupations of these 3,102 people, he found one group of whites with as low a coronary heart disease rate as the blacks: the sharecroppers, lowest on the social-economic scale. White farmers were moderately prone to coronary heart disease. The most coronary-prone were whites who had moved up the economic ladder from farming to industry.

And what does all this prove? Does a Georgia share-cropper have such a relaxing, easy job that this alone can account for the differences in the coronary heart disease prevalence between white sharecroppers and blacks, on the one hand, and successful whites, on the other? It seems unlikely.

All these studies of occupational stress would be valid if the most important part of a man's emotional life were the part he spends at work. But that simply isn't true. What happens to the subjects studied by Drs. Morris, Russek, Hinkle, and Cassel when they get home from work? Are they able to release their fatigue and worry through a satisfying relationship with a loved one? Can they work off their tensions through sex, play, or laughter? Or are their bodily reactions to occupational stress—their raised blood pressure and increased cholesterol—intensified by additional frustration at home?

These are some of the questions still unanswered by studies of the relationship between stress and heart disease. Until they are answered, no useful conclusions can be drawn.

Occupational stress, after all, is nothing new. All through history men have faced danger and anxiety in their work. Some were crushed by it; some thrived on it. Man traditionally turned to the privacy of his home for a refuge, a place of comfort, a shock absorber. His emotional and sexual life served as an antidote for the bruises and scars he suffered doing battle with the world. Today a man may not slay dragons or battle with his natural enemies, but he still needs a shock absorber.

In my own practice I have found that men in highly stressful occupations are far less likely to develop ulcers, hypertension, heart disease, and other physical manifestations of stress as long as they are getting plenty of love, admiration, and pleasure in private life. A man may feel threatened, humiliated, and powerless at work, but if he feels strong and virile at home he can withstand such pressures.

One patient, Bernard N., has been coping with extreme occupational stress all his adult life in the cutthroat ready-to-wear clothing business. For thirty-eight years his happy home life was a refuge and revitalizer after the constant strain of keeping up his business in a deteriorating urban neighborhood. Then, when Bernard was sixty-six, his wife died. He was lonely and depressed. He found his work more and more difficult and exhausting. He became less and less active, he overate and gained weight. Finally, at the age of sixty-nine, he had a heart attack.

While recuperating in the hospital, Bernard met another patient, a widow ten years younger than he. They fell in love, married, and went to live in his home. Bernard went back to work. He recently told me, "I'm not lonely anymore. We are happy together. We even have sex together once a week. Now that I have someone who loves and admires me, I feel respected by my employees and customers again. Before, when I had to put the dresses back on the rack myself, I felt ashamed. I would get tired and have to sit down. Now it doesn't bother me, because I know I'm a big shot at home."

It is not stress alone that matters; it's what a man does about it. If he is able to release stress in a healthy, pleasurable way, he will feel refreshed and his body chemistry will return to normal. But sexual frustration added to his other frustrations can be a deadly combination.

Though most researchers are still too prudish to investigate the effect of sexual frustration on the human heart, they are more open-minded when it comes to the sexuality of animals. In a number of cases experimenters have tampered with the natural mating habits of animals, to discover that the animals—especially the males—developed heart and artery diseases similar to those in man.

For example, in the 1960s the National Heart Institute sponsored research on the relationship between heart disease and personality factors, using interviews with human coronary patients. Of course, the subject of sex was totally excluded. But one experiment in the series tested the effects of different mating habits on chickens. When male chickens were caged in groups of six or twelve, with two males for every one female, the male chickens had frequent myocardial infarcts (heart attacks) while the females did not.

Dr. Sylvia Sikes of the Nuffield Institute of Comparative Medicine in London traveled to East Africa to study the incidence of heart and artery disease among wild game animals. She discovered that the wild elephant is now highly susceptible to heart disease—in fact many elephants have been dying of heart attacks. Why? We can't be sure, but Dr. Sikes explains that the natural mating habits of elephants are altered when they are restricted to protected game reserves surrounded by human settlements, instead of the wild hills and thick forests they originally lived in. The elephants are frustrated. Heart and arterial diseases also occur in wild animals caged in zoos.

In a famous experiment, Russian scientists were able to produce coronary heart disease in baboons by arousing violent sexual jealousy in them. They took a male who had been living with several females in a large compound, and put him in a screened cage where he could still see his ex-wives. Then they put into the compound a vigorous young male who took over the sexual role of the first baboon, who witnessed the action helplessly. "This situation," reported the experimenters, "led to the most violent excitation expressed in rushing about the cage, furious cries and attacks on the wire netting separating the rival." Within five months the baboon had died of severe atherosclerosis.

I don't recommend this kind of terrifying and tantalizing experiment with human beings. But there are other ways to study the effect of sexual stress on the development of heart disease. Until somebody uses them, we have little reliable, accepted evidence other than the observations by doctors of what their patients (who already have heart disease) worry about. And many have pointed out that these patients seem to have an unusual degree of sexual anxiety.

Dr. A. J. Mandel of the University of California reported that his patients with coronary heart disease often had marital problems centering on sex. "We have seen the onset of impotence correspond with the diagnosis or onset of coronary artery disease. This, in itself, is one of the major precipitating causes of moderate to marked depression in males in middle age. Occasionally this will become the sole focus of the patient's complaints. . . . Frequently the patient and the physician are faced with the fear of death associated with sexual activity or the feeling of being already dead without it."

Heart experts in the Soviet Union, while not discussing sex directly, do emphasize the part played by domestic strife, as well as overwork. Eugene I. Chazov, Soviet Minister of Public Health, reported to UNESCO in 1972 that a study of heart attacks at the Myasnikov Institute of Cardiology revealed that the attacks were preceded by an acute emotional upheaval in 20.5 percent of cases, by chronic emotional tension in 35 percent, by prolonged overwork in 30 percent, and by physical effort in 4.5 percent. As a result, Russian cardiologists are emphasizing preventative measures such as cultural activities, travel, and other forms of recreation. "We attach great importance to human relationships," said Dr. Chazov. "The spirit of comradeship, tact, discretion, self-control, and respect for others are fundamental for the education of a healthy generation. They are also important in the prevention of cardiovascular diseases."

Although nobody seems to want to come right out and pinpoint sexual anxiety as the stress most responsible for heart disease, one recent study came close to it. Two Amsterdam doctors, H. Kits van Heijningen and N. Treurniet, believe that the situation preceding a heart attack almost invariably includes two kinds of stress: trouble at work and trouble at home. In studying thirty men under fifty-six who had heart attacks, they discovered that most were extremely hardworking and had suffered some sort of setback—a loss of income or prestige—in their work. This poor job situation was reinforced by a humiliatingly tense situation at home. As an example, the doctors cite the case of a patient who had suffered a heart attack while driving with his family on a Sunday afternoon. Weeks later, during psychotherapy, the patient admitted that just before the attack his wife had belittled him, laughing at him and comparing him unfavorably to her father.

Not every man, of course, will react to a belittling remark from his wife by having a heart attack. Not every man is in danger of heart disease if he is fired from his job, fights with his wife, or becomes impotent. Apparently stress does not always cause biochemical changes associated with heart disease.

Some men are able to avoid stress altogether. Some

find a healthy physical or emotional outlet. And some seem to be able to withstand stress with no ill effects.

But there are kinds of stress that are difficult to cure with a healthy, emotional outlet. They are appropriately called the "broken heart" and the "lonely heart."

During my fifty years of medical practice, I have learned that the most damaging psychological trauma and the greatest emotional stress are: 1) loss of the object of our love or disillusionment with our mate and 2) the sense of being unwanted.

Very often we can replace the job we loved and lost; if our boss slanders us or insults us, we can change jobs. We can even retire if we have enough money. But it is difficult to replace the object of our love, especially as we get older. When our beloved ignores us, or hurts us, it could harm the heart.

According to observers all over the world, married people live longer, especially if they have a feeling of belonging and a sense of being loved. Modern, middle-aged men are frequently alienated from their families and too often feel lonely and unwanted, especially if they are sexually inadequate.

Some people naturally have a high tolerance to loneliness or to the loss of a love object. In fact, these people often prefer solitude. If they are disappointed with a mate, they withdraw without any harmful effects. However, some hard-driving, egocentric, or male-chauvinistic persons will suffer if they have problems with their loved ones. This type of person works hard; consequently, often he is away from home. Although he provides well for his family as far as material things are concerned, he is not in residence enough to provide them with sufficient affection, support, and guidance. And, he may receive little, if any, affection from his family. He becomes isolated and lonely in his own home, with his own family as they turn to him less and less for their needs. He becomes even more isolated and frustrated as he grows older and his sexual potency declines. Many professionals believe that this type of person is a good candidate for a coronary.

CORONARY PERSONALITY PROFILES

The subject of the "coronary-prone personality" is one of the most controversial in the field of heart research. But it is receiving more and more attention. An increasing number of people are saying that, if we are ever going to prevent heart disease, we must stop concentrating on the disease itself and start concentrating on the characteristics of the man who gets it.

Middle age is too late to begin treating heart disease. During the Korean war, autopsies of soldiers killed in battle revealed that 75 percent of them, averaging twenty-two years old, already had signs of artery degeneration. Coronary heart disease begins early in life and develops for years before there are any evident symptoms; therefore, the best way to prevent heart disease is to identify the coronary-prone person while he is young and outline a lifelong prevention plan for him.

We must teach our children how to cope with the ruthless changing times. We must be aware that different personalities react in different ways to sudden changes. And, we must recognize these different personalities before it is too late.

Up to now, most studies of the coronary personality have been based on analyzing the characteristics of men *after* they become coronary patients. Seventy years ago the great physician William Osler described the typical patient as "a keen and ambitious man, the indicator of whose engines is always set at 'full speed ahead.'" In the 1930s, Flanders Dunbar made such a study and came up with a number of personality traits that are still considered typical of heart patients:

1. They work hard and seem to enjoy driving themselves without mercy.

2. They are rigid in life-style, functioning well as long as their life role is rewarding, but shattering easily if their defenses are cracked by illness or some other trauma.

3. Many had an early competitive relationship with their father, and as adults they are still striving to compete with authority figures.

4. They have strong guilt feelings about sex, although many are drawn to promiscuous behavior, resulting in moral conflicts.

Another approach to the coronary personality is based on studies of body physique. Your body build, it seems, has much to do with your temperament. And your temperament has much to do with your susceptibility to heart disease.

In the 1930s Dr. William H. Sheldon studied 4,000 male bodies and established that they fell into three basic types: endomorphs (soft and round), mesomorphs (hard and muscular), and ectomorphs (long and lean). Then he went on to measure their temperaments and personalities. He discovered that certain personality traits did indeed correspond to the physical types. The three types also differ in their susceptibility to certain diseases.

The typical tall, thin ectomorph, for example, is shy, introverted, and intellectual. He is sensitive to noise and distractions and seeks solitude when troubled. The ectomorph is often particularly prone to respiratory diseases and allergies.

The short and round endomorph is easygoing, relaxed, and cheerful. He loves good food, good drink, and sleep. He depends on social approval and turns to other people when troubled. The extreme endomorph is often fat and may suffer from diabetes, hypertension, strokes, and other disorders found frequently among the obese.

The mesomorph has large bones and joints and heavy, strong muscles. He loves activity, especially exercise and competitive sports. He often speaks loudly, is assertive and courageous, and when troubled tends to take direct action. He is more than twice as prone to coronary heart disease as are endomorphs and ectomorphs.

Boston physician Menard M. Gertler reports that in one group of ninety-seven coronary patients studied at Massachusetts General Hospital, none was chiefly endomorph, six were ectomorphs, and the rest were predominantly mesomorphs. In the population as a whole, this also holds true: ectomorphs are the least vulnerable to coronary heart disease, endomorphs slightly more vulnerable, and mesomorphs highly vulnerable.

A recent study by anthropologists C. Wesley Dupertuis and Dr. Lelio Franchesini shows that endomorphs and ectomorphs who do get heart attacks have a much better survival rate than mesomorphs. During the period of rehabilitation, "those with strong, well-muscled bodies . . . felt deprived of their normal activities as males and tended to resist efforts to relegate them to a passive role," said Dupertuis. They were "more reluctant to accept any limitations on the physical expression of their role as head of the household and breadwinner." They also had the shortest survival periods.

Since most men are not extreme mesomorphs, however, body build alone cannot identify the potential heart patient before he develops symptoms. All these studies of the coronary personality can also be criticized on the grounds that since they are based on men who already have the disease, some of the personality traits uncovered, such as anxiety and depression, may result *from* the disease.

A way to establish a more valid portrait of the coronary-prone personality would be to give thousands of healthy young men a battery of psychological tests, analyze their personalities, and then observe them during the next ten or fifteen years to see which personality type develops coronary heart disease. That's exactly what two

San Francisco cardiologists, Dr. Ray Rosenman and Dr. M. Friedman, did. They came up with what is up to now the most impressive, well-known, and controversial heart-personality theory yet: the "Type A—Type B" theory (described briefly in Chapter I).

After interviewing 3,500 men under sixty, Rosenman and Friedman classified about half of them as "Type A": hard-driving, ambitious, impatient men with a sense of time urgency and a preoccupation with getting things done. The behavior of many of these men, they found, was characterized by excessively rapid body movements, tense facial muscles, explosive conversation, and many unconscious body gestures.

The rest of the men were classified as "Type B." They were more relaxed, patient, slower-moving, and less competitive. Both groups had similar drinking, smoking, eating, and exercise habits. Yet over the next twelve years the Type As developed heart trouble at a much higher rate than the Type Bs. Of 300-odd cases of heart disease that had developed in the group since 1960, more than 70 percent of the victims have been Type As. Not only that, but even men with Type A personalities who have good heredity, low blood pressure, low cholesterol, and other good risk factors are more likely to develop coronary heart disease than Type Bs.

Rosenman and Friedman are convinced it is personality, not risk factors, that predispose a person to coronary heart disease.

But not everybody is as convinced as they. Some critics say that the A-B theory still doesn't explain why the coronary heart disease rate is soaring. A hundred years ago heart disease was rare. Weren't there any Type A men around then? Some doctors have criticized the methods used to determine whether a man is Type A or B, suggesting that a more complete battery of psychological tests be used. Other critics say that the description is highly exaggerated—most coronary patients do not exhibit the driven, tense behavior described in the study. Dr. Henry Russek notes, "We consider this description to be a caricature rather than a portrait of the average coronary patient."

But the biggest flaw in Rosenman and Friedman's study is this: in the most thorough and influential study of personality and heart disease ever conducted, an essential part of the personality is left out. The study tells us how the Type A man relates to his co-workers (he is competitive), how he functions during conversation (he speaks rapidly and interrupts often), during recreation (he hardly ever has time for it), and under pressure of deadlines (he is obsessed with meeting them). *But it does not tell us anything about his sexual and emotional nature.*

Yet sexuality is probably one of the most important differences between the Type A man and the Type B man. If Type A is a man who seeks power and prestige, he needs sexual power as well. A man who shows such a clearly identifiable driving, intense, achievement-oriented personality must surely manifest these qualities in his sex life—the one area of his life where physical and emotional action are combined. Sexuality is certainly a more significant aspect of a man's personality than how he talks during an interview or his clock-watching habits. And it is certainly more closely related to his health.

Dr. Friedman says, "Some A's *never enjoy a meal, never stop to taste the food or savor the wine.* They measure their lives in figures—how many units sold, how much income earned, how many tasks accomplished. Yet looking back a year afterwards they can recall none of these achievements. Quality, not quantity, makes life worthwhile."

But what happened to the joy of sex? If the Type A persons enjoy the pleasure of eating and drinking, they usually enjoy the pleasure of lovemaking. The advice that Dr. Friedman gives to the Type A man regarding his recreation reflects a puritanical and unrealistic attitude. Dr.

Friedman advises: "An A should learn to play for recreation and relaxation. When he plays golf he should take time to enjoy the outdoors, the trees and the clouds in the sky." He ignores the fact that the Type A person can also enjoy watching the girls in short skirts or short pants play golf.

An experience of mine proves this point. One bright sunny morning my wife and I decided to play a game of golf. It was a truly beautiful morning and the trees looked especially green and vibrant, and the white clouds were emphasized against a clear blue sky. My wife looked especially charming in her new blue and white dress. Everything symbolized spring, except me. Normally I am a late riser. If I do not have my eight hours of sleep I look even older than my years.

When our name was called, we were paired with two handsome men. I introduced us: "My name is Gene and my partner is June." (I prefer to enjoy my golf game instead of giving medical advice.) They too used only their first names—Bill and Tom. Bill was a typical Type A as described by Dr. Friedman, except he obviously loved women. Perhaps he found it a sacrilege for a beautiful woman like June to play golf with her "father" or some "old sugar daddy." He tried to make a date with her. June politely rejected him by saying, "I'm a happily married, sexually fulfilled woman because my husband [pointing to me] is a Hungarian bon vivant and a well-known sexologist. He is not as good a golf player as you are, but he plays a perfect game in bed."

Recently I discussed Dr. Friedman's puritanical attitude with several doctors. One woman colleague of mine gave me the most startling answer: "Dr. Friedman is justified. The European concept of the pleasures of wine, woman, and song is obsolete. Modern women are no longer the objects of pleasure."

In such magazines as *Sexology, Pageant,* and *Forum,* as a columnist and a writer I have expressed my liberal attitude toward the sexuality of the modern woman. Nevertheless, I am old-fashioned enough to advise every woman who is mature and independent that she can be a sex object if sex makes her happy and she can make someone else happy too. But I emphasize that *she should be also a love object.*

Ignoring sex is a venerable tradition in the medical profession, it would seem. One excuse often given is "We don't want to invade our patients' privacy." But when a man's health is at stake, when an epidemic that strikes down so many men remains unchecked, such an excuse just isn't acceptable.

Patients aren't as reluctant to talk about sex as doctors think they are. They may need some prodding but with the right approach—empathy, encouragement, compassion, concern—most men are glad, and often relieved, to talk about their sex lives.

During the last few decades I have studied the body builds, personality types, and sexual histories of many hundreds of men. Some of those I studied were patients, some friends and social acquaintances, some I met on trips, and some were medical colleagues. A number had heart disease when I first studied them, others developed it later, and still others have not developed it. All were willing to reveal their sexual histories and problems once they knew their confessions were in professional confidence and of concern to me.

Putting all these factors together, I have evolved a portrait of the coronary personality—one that includes the sexual dimension. No one man has all of the characteristics I include in my description, of course, but if a man has many of them and is also undergoing sexual stress, I would consider this a danger sign.

THE APOLLO TYPE

Many years ago Dr. Stewart G. Wolf of the University of Oklahoma said that the coronary man is like the mythological King Sisyphus. Sisyphus was condemned to spend eternity in Hades, pushing a large rock up a steep hill, only to have it roll back, and having to push it up again, never quite reaching the top. Like Sisyphus, said Wolf, the typical coronary candidate is constantly engaged in futile striving, never achieving his goal.

My description of the coronary personality is based on another figure from mythology: the god Apollo. Apollo was powerful, handsome, arrogant, and strong—the god of heroes, athletes, and champions. The epitome of masculinity, he would never submit to authority and he even defied his mighty father, Zeus. Toward his enemies he could be ruthless.

But Apollo had a gentle, sensitive side. He was also the god of sunlight—warm, loving, creative, and generous. And he was the god of music, poetry, dance; he loved beauty and luxury. He had the gift of prophecy, and as god of the healing arts was often consulted in cases of sickness.

Toward women, Apollo expressed both sides of his nature: the fierce and the sensitive. In spite of his power and magnificence, he had a fragile masculine ego. When he saw a woman he wanted, he pursued her and carried her off. But if he didn't receive the devotion and admiration he demanded, he could be harsh and cruel. Many of his love affairs turned out tragically. Since he was immortal, he survived them—but his modern equivalent is less fortunate.

The modern Apollo also has a two-sided nature. But under today's pressures to be successful and masculine he often overemphasizes his aggressive side, denying his warmth, creativity, and gentleness. If he has no outlet for these qualities, he can become sick. Most important, the modern Apollo cannot live without being loved. If he is emasculated, he dies.

Of the hundreds of men I have studied, I was most concerned with those of a generally mesomorphic build, who had the energetic, assertive personality that doctors today refer to as Type A. They were all somewhat coronary-prone, but some of them—the Apollo types—were far more so than average. (Of course, a large number in the study were temperamentally either ectomorphs or endomorphs—men who had neither the personalities nor the physical characteristics of the coronary candidate. But these men are not particularly prone to heart disease even under emotional and sexual stress.)

The extreme mesomorph is heavy-set, often built like a boxer. His hand is usually thick and muscular, and the index finger is often longer than the ring finger. He is not particularly sensual; sex for him is an athletic performance, a way to assert his ego. Under emotional stress he is more likely to feel rage and anger than rejection and anxiety. He is more likely to die of stroke than of heart disease.

The true Apollo type is often physically less massive than the typical mesomorph. His hand is firm and fleshy, the fingers rounded. Like the mesomorph, he is proud and dominating and has an urge for power, status, prestige, and action. He is a bit of a show-off and enjoys being the center of attention. But he is more complicated than this. He is extremely sensitive and somewhat aesthetic. He responds to beauty and he has an intuitive understanding of the needs of others. He is usually an exciting and sensual lover, as long as he has an admiring partner. He can be so charming, though, that most women don't mind concentrating on him. If his wife treats him as a king, he will make her a queen. But the modern Apollo—often without realizing it—is highly vulnerable emotionally and sexually. If he is betrayed or rejected, he is seriously hurt. If he makes the mistake of sacrificing his love life or his status in the outside world, he becomes a coronary candidate.

The story of Jason F. is an example.

Jason F. was a typical modern Apollo. He was a successful, middle-aged manufacturer earning $65,000 a year. Outgoing, generous, and charming, he seemed the perfect husband, father, and citizen. A lover of music, he was a regular patron of the opera. He also managed to enjoy an occasional discreet love affair.

When Jason was fifty-five his daughter married a young student, Walter. His wife urged Jason to give his new son-in-law a job, so Jason agreed. Much to his surprise, Walter turned out to be a brilliant businessman: within two years he doubled the company's profits. Gradually he began telling Jason how to run the business. Jason swallowed his pride and went along with Walter. But he was beginning to feel less important, both at work and with his family. And of course that included less sex at home. Around this time Jason took a business trip to Florida. There he met Sandra—twenty-two years old, uneducated, blonde, a Southern belle and beautiful. Jason fell in love with her. He wanted to give her everything, and she in turn adored and admired him. He asked her to return to Chicago with him and work for him. She agreed.

Jason found Sandra an apartment and gave her a secretarial job.

But a few weeks later Walter told him, "Dad, I don't care about your private relationship with Sandra, but she's a lousy secretary. She's not doing her job and it's bad for the company." Jason had to agree. He told Sandra, "I want you to become a topnotch secretary. I'll send you to the best business college in town for six months." Sandra hesitated, then agreed. Their love affair continued, though she was no longer at the office.

But just before it was time for Sandra to return to work, Jason received a letter:

Dear Jason:
I am writing to say good-bye. I must tell you that I have been in love with another man for the past three months. He didn't want me to give up the chance to go to business college so I couldn't tell you before. But now we are moving far away. I will always be grateful for everything you have done for me.

Sandra

Jason was totally demoralized. He felt betrayed. He was angry. His joy and zest for life disappeared. Six weeks after he received the letter, he had a massive heart attack. Jason survived, but he is still not his old self, and perhaps never will be.

All men need love, but some men need it more than others. An Apollo personality who has an inadequate outlet for his great emotional and sexual drive becomes a coronary candidate.

But heart attacks strike many others besides extreme Apollo types. The victims cover a range of personalities, physical characteristics, and occupations. Two groups in our society are distinguished by rapidly growing rates of heart attacks, and we will look at these groups next.

8

THE
VICTIMS:
APOLLO (Male)
AND
ATALANTA (Female)

As a doctor who spends a great deal of time at medical seminars and symposiums with other doctors, I have observed, to my profound sorrow and dismay, that my colleagues exhibit many of the characteristics of the coronary-prone Apollo type. In many respects these men are as powerful as Apollo—except in their sex lives. Therefore, I am going to take the liberty of using the modern American doctor as the prototype of the individual in our society who is most seriously in danger of an impending heart attack. I do hope my brothers in the medical fraternity will understand and forgive this license since it allows me to use case histories quite close to home. It helps, too, that in so many of these cases I have met and talked with their wives as well.

My approach is hardly meant to be disparaging to doctors—they are among my closest and most cherished friends. I commend their selfless devotion and deplore the personal price they pay. It appalls me and I write from the heart. However, I address all Americans, in diverse and unrelated fields, who fit the pattern I'm describing.

THE MODERN AMERICAN DOCTOR

In our society today there are two groups, male and female, who typify the Apollo personality: the modern doctor and the Apollo's female equivalent, Atalanta, the modern "liberated" woman. Both groups are experiencing mysteriously growing rates of coronary heart disease. And both are undergoing special kinds of sexual stress.

If you look just at the surface, the modern American doctor seems to have everything. He is successful, educated, affluent, respected in the community. Patients are in awe of him. Neighbors respect him. Little children admire him. Men envy him. Women fall in love with him.

But under this rosy exterior, there are signs of serious trouble. In the areas outside of his work, the doctor isn't doing so well. His marriage tends to be shaky, his personal life empty and unfulfilling. Although he has every reason to be healthier than most people, he is not. He is twice as prone to heart attacks as his European counterpart and *more* prone (at any age) than the highest-risk group in the world: white American middle-aged males. The man who seems to have everything is neither happy nor healthy.

Some of the modern doctor's problems stem from the widening gap between what his image used to be and what he really is. He used to be a god—but in the 1970s there are no gods.

Once it was easy for the doctor to live up to a godlike

image. The healer has always had a special, honored role in society. The earliest doctors were priests and magicians endowed with supernatural powers. Even up to the first half of our own century the doctor was glorified, respected for his scientific skill and, as a stereotype, loved for his kindness and compassion. The old-fashioned horse-and-buggy doctor was an American folk hero, a symbol of unselfish dedication to human welfare. This sentimental view of the wise, benevolent, miracle-working healer is pictured in the famous English painting "The Doctor," by Sir Luke Fildes.

Doctors in pre-World War II Vienna, then the world capital of medicine, were at their peak of prestige. The "Professor" (no one would ever call him "Doc") was revered by the people. He truly had the stature of the sacrosanct: he lived a noble, dignified life. He was not harassed by government regulations, tied down to the endless paperwork of insurance forms, threatened with malpractice suits, paid with fees as a plumber would be, but with "honorariums." He enjoyed the adulation and gratitude of his patients; he was a philosopher as well as a scientist, a patron of the opera and symphony, a lover of beautiful women—in short, an Apollo at his best.

But today Apollo has fallen. During fifty years of medical practice I have seen the doctor fall in the public's esteem from a pedestal to a footstool. The American doctor has lost the respect and love he once enjoyed. The public is growing ever more hostile toward doctors. This year thousands of malpractice suits will be filed. Angry patients accuse doctors of being callous, impersonal—and most of all, greedy. As a colleague recently complained, "At first I was a god. Now when my patient is sick, I'm an angel. When he has recovered, I'm human again. And when he gets the bill, I'm a devil."

Has the personality of the doctor actually changed during the last fifty years, or has only his image changed? What is today's doctor like as a person?

Doctors, of course, are individuals—as different from each other as ministers or engineers or members of any specialized group. But the medical profession produces unique demands and expectations, and doctors tend to acquire certain characteristics in common.

Every doctor I have ever known is motivated, down deep, by a need for authority and power. As a child, he dreamed of being a great healer. He would save lives, be calm and effective in emergencies, solve people's problems, earn their gratitude. The doctor wants power over the greatest forces we know: the forces of life and death.

When the aspiring doctor grows up and goes to medical school, he is in for a bit of a letdown. He must spend many years working and studying. He can't spend as much time drinking with the boys or making out with the girls as his contemporaries. It's a long, hard, tedious grind. Many doctors never forget it. Even when they have reached the top of the social-economic ladder, many never feel quite secure. No status is ever elevated enough for them.

Perhaps that's one reason many doctors tend to be materialistic and ostentatious once they make it. Today's doctors are a far cry from the self-sacrificing old-fashioned rural G.P. Today more and more of them like to flaunt their wealth. They are known for buying the fanciest homes, the snazziest cars, the biggest yachts. They like expensive forms of leisure. Doctors are known to be obsessed with golf, but they also like boating, skiing, hunting, and other status sports. They live affluently and show it off. In that sense, they are consistent with being Apollos.

Although doctors today are no longer revered, they don't want to give up their godlike status. In an article called "Humility and Compassion—Why Hast Thou Forsaken Us?" Dr. Richard Miller of Dayton, Ohio, wrote, "Young doctors of today have no humility. They set themselves up as medical gods who can do no wrong. . . . [The doctor] finds it easy to criticize, is unshakable in his opinions, and lives on an inflated ego believing he is the master of medical knowledge."

Today's doctor still has the arrogance, pride, flamboyance, and power-hunger of an Apollo. But he has lost his warm, imaginative, intuitive, pleasure-loving side. He has forgotten how to enjoy what is really important in life. And he has lost his magical power of healing. Today he depends on a battery of laboratory tests in order to make a diagnosis, instead of using his highly developed intuition. He follows the rules rather than his talent as a healer. If he sees a symptom he doesn't flatly recognize, he refers the patient to another specialist.

The modern doctor is a very vulnerable human. He has even lost the power to heal himself.

Despite all that's going for them—most doctors come from upper-middle-class backgrounds, where they have had the best of childhood care; only the vigorous could have made it through medical school and internship; they have far easier access than others to the latest medical knowledge and techniques—they are not particularly healthy themselves. In fact, they are more prone to psychological symptoms and stress-related diseases than men in most other professions.

An early study by Dr. Charles McArthur, a Harvard research psychologist, followed the careers of 268 college men, 47 of whom became doctors. By middle age the doctors were making an average income of $38,000; economically they were doing fine. But when this group was compared to a control group from the same socioeconomic background and was interviewed as to drug use, need for psychiatric treatment, marital problems, and other indications of emotional instability, doctors didn't do so well. In each category, physicians did much worse than members of the control group. Over a third of the doctors had a history of drug dependency and a third had required psychiatric treatment, whereas only about 20 percent of the controls had these problems. Seventeen percent of the doctors had been hospitalized for psychiatric symptoms compared to 5 percent of the controls. And almost half the doctors reported "bad marriages," as opposed to 32 percent of the controls.

The conclusion of the study was that physicians not only display more psychiatric symptoms than their contemporaries, but that their response to life's pressures seemed to turn their frustrations inward.

This conclusion is supported by the most important indication of doctors' poor health—their abnormally high rate of heart attack. When smoking was shown to be related to heart disease, a hundred thousand American doctors stopped smoking, and today doctors smoke less than other groups. Yet heart disease is still their leading cause of death. It causes a slightly higher percentage of deaths among doctors than among the American white male population in general.

Dr. Henry Russek observed that a study of doctors' obituaries since 1955 shows that there has been no increase in the average age of death among physicians during the past sixteen years. The fact that doctors now appear to die of coronary attacks at the same average age as before is a disappointing observation, since no group in our population has practiced greater abstinence from tobacco in recent years. . . . Although the mean life expectancy at birth for all persons in the United States is approximately seventy years, physicians as a group fall short of the mark.

Smoking isn't the only thing doctors have given up. Since the cholesterol controversy started twenty years ago, thousands of doctors have gone on low-cholesterol diets. The two best-selling diet books of our day, *Doctor's Quick Weight Loss Diet* and *Dr. Atkins' Diet Revolution*, were logically written by doctors. In their book, *How the Doctors Diet*, Peter and Barbara Wyden describe in detail the eating habits of twenty-two doctors and their families. A few random quotes will give you an idea of how seriously these doctors take their diets, and how little pleasure they now get from food.

"At one point during the period of his early research, Dr. Page almost never ate anything for lunch except a dish of cottage cheese with catsup."
"For a long time now she has bought butter only when there was company."
"Dr. Alexander gave up just about all visible eggs about nine years ago, though he will occasionally have an egg in a salad."
"I went to a dinner last night and had about half the portion of roast beef, no potatoes, all the vegetable, the roll dry, and I had one spoonful of the ice cream. . . . I *love* ice cream."
"We talk all the time about food."
"There are never days when I eat as much as I could."
"I feel sinful when I get a good steak."

But in spite of self-imposed dietary restrictions, the coronary heart disease rate among doctors is not decreasing, but increasing. According to Dr. Samuel Friedman, since 1931 coronary thrombosis has risen by 21 percent as a cause of death for doctors. And a study of "Health in the Medical and Other Learned Professions" by Haitung King, Ph.D., reveals some chilling statistics. Of the four "learned professions"—the ministry, teaching, law, and medicine—members of the medical profession die at the youngest age and have the highest rate of fatal heart attacks. The mortality rate (number of annual deaths per 1,000 persons) for American doctors has been increasing since 1950 and is now much higher than doctors' mortality rates in any of the other countries studied (England, Wales, Scotland, Denmark, New Zealand, and South Africa).

Why should American doctors be so prone to heart attacks? When they try so hard to stay healthy, why do they fail? Why is medical knowledge, abstinence from to-

bacco and fatty foods, and professional success not enough
to maintain health?

A sixty-four-year-old doctor who had suffered a heart
attack warned his colleagues to take care of themselves
as they grow older.

"Like most older physicians, I couldn't adopt the slow-
down that might very well have forestalled the heart
attack. Faced with the same professional expenses as
younger men, I couldn't justify settling for a lower gross
income. . . ." He went on to complain about dues in professional associations, rising office rent, and other expenses.
"Stress had to cause the attack," he explained. "My family
history shows no trace of heart disease and my wife and
I eat sensibly, neither drink nor smoke, and have long
worked out moderately on a bicycle exercise machine."
Although he referred frequently to money worries as a
source of stress, and though he explained his careful health
regime, he said nothing about pleasure, recreation, or fun.
Shortly after his warning to other doctors, he died from a
second heart attack.

At seminars, meetings, conventions, and lectures, I
see that many doctors are deeply troubled. Not only do
they no longer relate to their patients as human beings,
but they have difficulty forming loving relationships in
their private lives. They have forgotten their need for play,
pleasure, and love. An Apollo personality who concentrates
on work, professional status, and abstinence, and ignores
his other needs is without question in danger.

This problem can be seen most clearly in doctors' marriages. The divorce rate among doctors is high enough, but
their rate of unhappy marriages is even higher. The doctors' poor family life has been blamed on the long hours,
emergency calls, and other exacting demands made by
the medical profession. But today fewer and fewer wives
are accepting these excuses. They suspect that a man who
spends long hours away from home is not necessarily more

dedicated to his profession, but less dedicated to his wife. They are right.

The typical pattern of a disintegrating medical marriage goes something like this: the young medical student marries, and his wife subordinates her own interests to support him. He grows and matures while she continues to take care of his children and his domestic needs. As times goes on, he becomes less and less interested in her; she sees life passing her by and grows more and more resentful, often finding solace in shopping sprees or alcohol. Because she doesn't want to jeopardize her status as a doctor's wife, she is often afraid to rebel openly by making a scene or having an affair.

Doctors' special position in the community understandably makes them—and their wives—reluctant to seek professional help. Sometimes, although this is becoming less and less so, they will live in misery for years rather than undergo the social stigma of divorce.

Unlike his counterpart in other professions, a doctor who has a sterile relationship at home doesn't feel free to seek sex outside of marriage. As one colleague commented, "A lawyer can have an affair with his client, a businessman with his secretary, a college teacher with his student—but a doctor who has an affair with a patient is really asking for trouble." Only a minuscule number of doctors would ever give it a thought, or try.

The reason, however, may be more than professional ethics and discretion. There is some indication that doctors as a group suffer from impotence more than other men. A few years ago Dr. James McCary startled an American Medical Association convention in Denver by reporting that middle-aged and elderly physicians have a far higher rate of impotence than members of other professions of the same ages. Many of the doctors I interviewed admitted they had sexual problems. For some, it is a permanent state they feel they can live with. For others, like Dr. W., it is a temporary stage.

Dr. W., an orthopedic surgeon, was a typical Apollo —appealing, athletic, talented, and a bit arrogant. He played golf regularly. Music was a special love; he played the cello every other week with a string quartet. His wife was attractive and lively, and during their younger years they had maintained a good relationship.

He was treated royally at home, by his wife and daughter, and at work, where he was highly respected by patients and colleagues.

In early middle age Dr. W. was appointed head of his hospital's orthopedic department. His career blossomed as he enlarged and modernized the physiotherapy and re-habilitation services. He gave up golf, stopped playing the cello, and spent more and more time at the hospital.

Gradually, things began to deteriorate at home. His wife resented the fact that he was ignoring her; she became more and more demanding, and, when that didn't work, rebellious. Sex became unsatisfying, then infrequent, then almost nonexistent. One day his daughter ran off and married, against Dr. W.'s wishes. He had lost the devotion of both daughter and wife. (His wife later remarked to me, "When our daughter married, it broke his heart.") A few months later Dr. W. was stricken with a heart attack.

He recovered, and while recuperating he had plenty of time to think things over. He realized that the orthopedic department was doing fine without him, while his own marriage had been falling apart. He realized how important his marriage really was, and he decided to take a vacation with his wife as soon as he could.

Today Dr. W. and his wife are happy. He has taken up golf and the cello again. He and his daughter are reconciled, and his greatest joy is his two-year-old grandson. Now Mrs. W. says: "He truly feels like a king when his grandson comes to visit him and runs to meet him with open arms and yells 'Grandpa!'" He changed his life before it was too late.

Middle age is a time of crisis for many men. For doctors it is often a period when problems they have pushed out of their minds for years will no longer be denied. Doctors are not threatened with loss of professional stature like other men; at middle age they are at the peak of their income and professional status, with retirement a long way off. But the emptiness of their private lives and the loss of their sexual vigor can suddenly become a major threat. This is a common problem among doctors. Dr. Thomas Hacket of Harvard University described some typical patterns of behavior that occur when the doctor with a less-than-perfect marriage is struck with the "Male Menopause Syndrome." One is the "Gauguin Syndrome," named for the famous Frenchman who, at middle age, left his family and career as a banker, ran off to the South Seas to get away from it all, and became a celebrated painter. The doctor in the film *Carnal Knowledge*, who at middle age left his wife and tried to recapture his youth by marrying a liberated youngster, is another example of this type.

Another pattern, the "Scapegoat Wife Syndrome," occurs when a middle-aged man begins to feel unfulfilled and depressed and blames everything on his wife. If he's tired, it's her fault; he's overworked from supporting her. If he becomes impotent, it's her fault because she's shallow, boring, and not sexy enough. An Apollo personality who rejects his wife in this way will become old—and often sick —before his time.

A third pattern is the "Sacred Amulet Syndrome." Dr. Hacket explains: "Men who take great pride in their sexual potency, feeling it's an essential proof of their manhood, are usually very disturbed when they find their powers declining in middle age. . . . Then along comes a sexpot, usually a decade or two younger. . . . She's the sacred amulet, the Aladdin's lamp that has magically restored his youthful powers."

This reaction to middle age is typical of the dynamic mesomorph kind of personality. If he is unable to revitalize his marriage or to find a sexpot, he may find his sexual problems reflected in health problems, particularly heart disease.

Many middle-aged men suddenly feel the urge to "live it up a little" before it's too late. But until American males, especially the Apollo types, truly learn how to live, until they accept the life-giving part of their natures—their gentle, spontaneous, creative side, their sexuality—they will continue to die prematurely.

THE MODERN AMERICAN WOMAN

For many years medical men have pondered the mystery of why American men have heart disease more pronouncedly than women. After all, the two sexes have the same kind of heart and circulatory system. They are similar in heredity, diet, exercise habits, and medical care. But the coronary heart disease rate for men has been consistently rising, while women's, until recently, has stayed relatively low. During the 1950s the Massachusetts Coronary Research Project reported that men under forty are thirty times more likely to die of a heart attack than women. In those days a woman under forty without diabetes or an obvious health problem could be confident of not having a heart attack.

Scientists at first thought that the female hormone, estrogen, must be a protection against heart disease. There is still some evidence of this; women who have had both ovaries removed do have a higher rate of heart disease, and experimental female animals whose ovaries are removed develop hardening of the arteries. Regardless, after menopause, when estrogen production is sharply reduced, the women's rate of coronary heart disease increases, but it doesn't equal that of men till age sixty.

There are flaws in this theory. If estrogen alone were responsible for protecting women against heart attacks, then postmenopausal women immediately would have as high a rate as men. And men given estrogen would be immune to coronary heart disease. This is not the case. Today many doctors question whether estrogen is the answer. Women's relative immunity to heart attacks remains a mystery.

If it is true, as I have emphasized throughout this book, that sexual stress is an important and unrecognized factor in heart disease, today's changing sex roles should affect women as well as men. As the double standard disappears, as more women begin to experience the same sexual freedom and demands as men, their health problems should change accordingly.

After all, liberated women today are expected to perform sexually as equals to men. Inability to achieve an orgasm, while not as obviously humiliating as male impotence, will be extremely threatening to females.

The increasing numerical superiority of women over men and the breakdown of marriage add large numbers of single women to our population. Once, such women could move in with their married relatives and help with the children. Once they could find outlets in church work. But for the modern woman, these traditional roles are unsuitable. Today most single women live similarly to single men—except that they are more anxious, afraid of rape and crime, and fearful of being lonely and unwanted.

Female sexual frustration is nothing new; it has been causing psychosomatic symptoms in women for centuries. But the way they sublimated their frustration—by having babies and dedicating themselves to caring for a family—today is challenged as a valid role for women. The whole female role, in fact, is in question. Women today, while not yet under the same kind of sexual stress as men, are equally unsure of how best to express the sexual side of their personalities.

How is all this affecting the physical health of women? Is their heart disease rate actually changing? The answer is yes, frighteningly so.

A colleague of mine was recently shocked when, upon returning to his work at St. Joseph's Hospital in Chicago after a three-week vacation, he discovered that of the patients recovering from heart attacks in the intensive care unit, *almost half were women.* "It may be just an isolated example," he said, "but I've never seen such a disproportionate number of female heart patients before."

The director of the National Heart and Lung Institute, Dr. Theodore Cooper, corroborates the "unaccountably sharp" increase of heart disease among American women under forty-five. He told a 1972 American Heart Association symposium that hardening of the coronary arteries has increased 11 percent in women during the past seven years. "In the past," he noted, "we have concentrated largely on middle-aged men . . . but now we may have to concentrate more on women as well."

APOLLO AND ATALANTA PROFILES

Dr. David M. Spain, speaking at the American Heart Association convention in Dallas, reported that a study prior to 1967 of the ratio of men to women dying suddenly of heart attacks was twelve to one; a study of fatal heart attacks between 1967 and 1971 showed a ratio of only four to one.

Some clinicians have attributed this change in ratio to Women's Lib; they speculate that women who want to live like men take on the risks of men's diseases. I have observed that often enough women who identify with men drink and smoke as much as men. And Dr. Spain blames heavy smoking for the increased incidence of sudden fatal heart attacks in women.

Dr. M. F. Oliver too believes that heavy smoking contributes to coronary heart disease. At the annual convention of the American College of Cardiology in San Francisco in 1973, Dr. Oliver said that young women with coronary

heart disease have at least one of the following risk factors: high cholesterol, high blood pressure, heavy smoking.

But high cholesterol, high blood pressure, and heavy
smoking are only coronary risk factors *if they are associated
with stress.*

An increase in the suicide rate among working young
women suggests the stress they are now under in their
competition with men in business. Stress is also evident in
their increasing rate of heart disease. I believe that the
effects of stress in these women have occurred because
they have not had the opportunity yet to acquire tolerance
to occupational stress.

Can the women who get heart attacks today be classified as less feminine, more liberated than women who
don't? This is a difficult question to answer; but, there are
definite indications that professional women who are single, divorced, or widowed have a decidedly higher coronary heart disease rate than housewives.

Drs. Shigeaki Hino and Tomoaki Shinoda of St. Luke's
Hospital in Kyoto, Japan, studied 522 women treated for
heart disease. They found that Japanese women who are
now beginning to participate in professions formerly closed
to them are exposed to the same occupational stresses that
affect Japanese men. The incidence of heart disease in
Japan was previously seven times higher among men than
women; in the past ten years the ratio dropped to 3.7 to 1.
The growing amount of cholesterol in the Japanese diet
(which is fast becoming westernized) was also implicated
as a factor in the increasing evidence of heart disease.
Japanese women seem to be losing the protection against
heart disease that the medical profession has assumed all
women possess simply because they are female.

I have observed a similar phenomenon. The women I
know who have recently had heart attacks tend to identify
with men; they had developed rivalry and hostility. These
women are reminiscent of Atalanta, the beautiful huntress
of Greek mythology. Atalanta's father had wanted a son.

When she was born, he decided she was not worth bringing up and left her on a mountain to die. She was raised
by hunters and became their equal in hunting, shooting,
and wrestling. Her only interest in men was as hunting
companions, and she had no plans to marry. She also became swift-footed and was celebrated for her racing ability.
Eventually she discovered who her parents were and went
to live with them. Her father apparently was reconciled
to having her as a daughter because she seemed almost as
good as a son. When her father wanted her to marry,
there was no one to marry because she would have only a
man who could outrun her (apparently one way of avoiding an oracle's prediction to her of a disastrous marriage).

There are many modern Atalantas who reject their
femininity to compete with men. I remember two such
women especially well. One, Mrs. B., is a strong, dominating woman to whom love and sex were never important.
She became a partner in her husband's real estate business
when her son was old enough to be left with others. Soon
she was running the office and became her husband's boss
until his death. She became extremely successful. She enjoyed her work, her poker games, and her son. When he
married she moved in with the couple. She supported her
son, his wife, and later her grandson. Her daughter-in-law
resented Mrs. B. but could do little about it. Then her son
was killed in an accident and the daughter-in-law turned
her out of the house and refused to let her see her grandson. Mrs. B. felt unloved and unwanted and for the first
time was without a male object to love (or dominate). Two
weeks later Mrs. B. had a heart attack. She later told me,
"I know people think I'm tough, but I loved that baby.
Without him I had nothing to love."

Another woman I recall is Florence, an unmarried,
highly successful career woman. Florence is a true Atalanta.
She had never had a father's love. She is attractive, charming, and enjoyed the attentions of men, but she was fiercely
independent. Like Atalanta she could not accept men ex-

cept as equals. She had many affairs but rejected any man who became too possessive or dependent. She told me, "It always turns me off when they want to get married." Then she met a man who was different. At first she was fascinated and intrigued. Then she admitted to herself that at the age of forty-three she had fallen in love for the first time. Florence was used to getting what she wanted, so she proposed to him. He confessed that he was married. When she suggested that he get a divorce, he said, "This is just an affair. No one can replace my wife." Florence recovered well—on the surface. She seemed her old carefree, independent self. But before her forty-fourth birthday she had a heart attack.

Will the Atalantas among us become the newest coronary-prone group in our society? That depends on whether the power of love between the sexes is great enough to overcome our present sexual confusion and disruption.

For anyone—male or female, Apollo or Atalanta—who realizes that his sex life influences his health, there is hope. We have given the victims of heart disease a great deal of attention. It is time now to find out what we can learn from those who are not experiencing this disease—those who have healthy hearts.

PART TWO

THE HEALTHY HEART

*In Part One, "The Broken Heart," I spoke as
an angry man—angry because of the unnecessary suffering
and illness caused by sexual problems. In this
section I speak as a happy man—happy
because during my fifty years
of practicing medicine I have learned
the positive power of sex and love.*

*In Part Two I will show you what
we now know about the healthy heart—
that is, those groups in our society
who have very low rates of coronary
heart disease. Also, I will try to explain
why sex is a good medicine.*

9

MEN
WHO DON'T
HAVE
HEART
ATTACKS

A PROMINENT HEART SPECIALIST ANNOUNCED RECENTLY
that there is no evidence that the traditional methods of
treating heart attack patients are effective. Dr. Eliot Cor-
day, a researcher from UCLA, said that exercising, quitting
smoking, reducing cholesterol in the diet, and losing weight
may make the patient feel better without lessening the
risk of heart attack. Lately, more and more observers, like
myself, have concluded that emotions such as anger, hatred,
and unhappiness are the major cause of heart attacks, not
cholesterol, diet, or high blood pressure.

This has been substantiated by Dr. Wallace Ellerbroek of Sunset Beach, California, who believes that the

high cholesterol levels that play a role in heart disease are more the result of emotional disturbance than diet. He cited a study of Navy flight cadets that showed that on mornings when they were scheduled to fly their cholesterol counts were very high, ranging from 400 to 650. On other mornings, however, their counts were normal, ranging from 140 to 165. Dr. Ellerbroek emphasizes that miserable people have high cholesterol rates while happy people do not. He concluded, therefore, that control of emotions is far more important in preventing heart attack than sticking strictly to a low-cholesterol diet.

I have observed that persons who have marital and sexual problems are invariably miserable people and can't control their emotions or anger.

The people most likely to become heart attack candidates are victims of a society where the male/female sex roles have undergone dramatic shifts and where sex is consequently complicated and/or anxiety producing.

A study reported in the *British Medical Journal* examined a large number of men and women who had experienced myocardial infarctions before the age of sixty-four. Out of a group of sixty married couples, twenty-two couples stated that they had not had intercourse for some time before the husband's illness. Two couples, in fact, had never consummated their marriages!

But there is a positive side to the relationship between sex and health as well. Bad sex or no sex may increase the risk of a heart attack, *but good sex seems to keep you well.* Self-confidence, a sense of security, and a mature appreciation of sex have beneficial effects on body chemistry. The old-fashioned enjoyment of "wine, women, and song" is better for you than tranquilizers and an inordinate desire to achieve status and wealth.

Unfortunately, thorough studies of the positive benefits of pleasure have not been made. The medical profession is eager to study everything harmful, but sex and pleasure cause doctors some embarrassment. We still feel that pleasure is basically self-indulgent and sinful and that it "isn't supposed to be good for you." Any theory that claims health benefits from pleasure, therefore, must rest on speculation and examples rather than on statistical proof.

New theories are not easily accepted. We all know of Louis Pasteur, revered today as a great scientist and doctor. But he was considered something of a fanatic when he first evolved his theories. Despite his careful, scientifically controlled experiments, nobody wanted to believe him. This problem still exists.

Sigmund Freud, unable to support his theories with statistics, used the case history technique to prove his points and was attacked for being unscientific. The modern psychiatrist, of course, is armed with Rorschach (inkblot) tests, personality inventories, and computerized questionnaires to help him make his diagnosis. This, we are told, is scientific. We should ask ourselves one question, however: where would the modern-day psychiatrist be if Freud had not previously expounded his theories? The clinical methods used to "prove" Freud's theories were developed years after he began his work and are based primarily on his work. The theory must come first; the work of later years will document it "scientifically."

Furthermore, we have all learned to be somewhat wary of statistics. We know that they can be deliberately manipulated to give a false impression. Even if no desire to deceive is present, statistics can be misleading. The sample may be inadequate, based on too narrow a group for any conclusions to be drawn. An example of this could be taken from a *New York Times* article in mid-October 1973, when it reported a survey sent to 1,000 doctors in the state of California. It stated that 5 percent of *all doctors* voluntarily admitted to having had sexual relations with their patients. A startling, shocking statement. The truth is that a simple sex questionnaire was sent—at random, presumably—to 1,000 doctors (specialists as well as general practitioners) and 460 answered. *Of these* 5 percent admitted a sexual experience with a patient. (This runs more true to form of what I know about doctors and sex. I too could probably make a categorical statement: "According to a recent 'study,' over 50 percent of *all* doctors refuse to discuss sex at all!") But what do we definitely know? Twenty-three admitted sex—5 percent of those who answered, or 2.3 percent of those questioned. One wonders, was the sex volitional, occasional, continual, or was it occupational in a therapeutic sense? In any event this example shows how statistics can be misleading.

In addition, the bias of the observer may affect his analysis, quite unconsciously. If you were to ask two divorce lawyers, one a "male chauvinist pig" and the other a militant feminist, why there are so many unhappy marriages, you would get two very different answers. Their opinions would doubtless be misleading because, based on their professional experience, each would attract a different type of client or because each interpreted facts to fit preconceived ideas.

There is another hazard in the use of statistics to evaluate sexual problems. For the most part, sexual questionnaires are self-rating, that is, the subject evaluates himself. A study by Bell and Bell in *Medical Aspects of Human Sexuality*, for example, revealed that 82 percent of the women questioned rated their marriages "very good" or "good" and only 7 percent rated them "poor" or "very poor." We must ask ourselves whether the women in the sample were representative of the population as a whole or whether the women lied (our skyrocketing divorce rate indicates that a far greater percentage of the population is unhappily married). The questionnaire was anonymous and the researchers had no way of independently evaluating the accuracy of the women's responses. Many people are reluctant to admit that they have marital or sexual problems because they feel that such an admission would mark them as failures.

As an example of this feeling, let me tell you a true

story. I once stated that out of a group of ten doctors with coronary disease, eight had sexual problems (I had a single group in mind). When another doctor said that figure was much too high, I explained the "accusation method" to him. A professor at my university in Hungary told us that we should never ask a patient, "Do you have gonorrhea or syphilis?" He told us, since even Hungarians are reluctant to make such admissions (Hungary attaches no stigma to sexual problems), we should always ask a patient, "When did you last have VD?" Originally only two of the ten doctors volunteered that they had sexual problems, but when I used the accusation method (I already knew they were under tension and frustration), four admitted their sexual problems. This brought the total to six. Then, on the principle of *audiatur et altera pars* (let the other side be heard), I talked with their wives. The wives of two of the four who maintained that they had no problems contradicted their husbands. Indeed they did have problems, said these women, and one went so far as to say that she was contemplating either adultery or divorce.

For all of the above reasons, I do not produce my own statistics in this book—I frequently cite, however, the works of others. I personally prefer to use Freud's approach—the case history. Through the stories of average individuals and through the study of those groups with low rates of coronary heart disease, we can learn how to have healthy hearts.

THE ECTOMORPH

The ectomorph, the tall, thin, and bony man, seldom has sexual problems. When under stress he prefers solitude, and he is usually able to sublimate his sex drive and direct it toward spiritual or mental pursuits. The ectomorph is the type of man capable of becoming the most disciplined of monks, the ascetic, the hermit.

A classic example of the ectomorph is George Bernard Shaw. Although Shaw had a series of affairs, they were entirely mental. His famous romance with the actress Ellen Terry, for example, went on for years via correspondence. They were both afraid that an actual meeting, seeing each other in the flesh, might disrupt their relationship. Even though Shaw did marry, it is generally believed that the marriage was, by mutual consent, never consummated. Shaw devoted his life entirely to intellectual pursuits: he was one of the early Fabians (a highly philosophical group of socialists), lectured tirelessly on behalf of his favorite causes, and dedicated himself to the creation of a vast body of work intended to promote his theories. His letters alone constitute more prose than most authors turn out in a lifetime.

Bobby Fischer, the great chess master, is another example of the ectomorph. Chess not only requires a certain kind of mind but the passion of a lover. This most cerebral of all games demands the dedication and energy that most men would expend in sexual directions. The ectomorph is capable of devoting himself almost entirely to chess.

The Masai tribesmen of East Africa represent the typical ectomorph type. Although two-thirds of the diet of these herdsmen is derived from fat, the Masai have low cholesterol levels and rarely develop atherosclerosis, even in old age. A recent study showed that the Masai can burn up twice as much cholesterol as Americans do (50 percent of the cholesterol in the blood versus 25 percent). What accounts for this difference? We cannot accept as an answer that the Masai have a low rate of coronary heart disease because they "keep fit." No one has studied the sex life of the Masai or the influence of their body build on their susceptibility to coronary heart disease. No one ever may at this rate.

THE UNDERDEVELOPED NATIONS

In most of the underdeveloped nations of the world, heart disease is relatively rare. Almost every study of the health of people in these lands has revealed that their arteries do not become diseased, even in old age. Death from heart attacks is practically unknown in the rural parts of Asia, Africa, and Latin America.

There is some evidence, however, that men in these countries who move to urban centers develop higher blood cholesterol levels and a higher incidence of heart disease and its associated disorders. For example, Guatemalan Indians living an urban life have higher blood pressure than Guatemalan Indians living in rural areas. So do male Zulus who move into the city, as opposed to those remaining in small villages. Similar patterns exist in India, Korea, Malaya, New Guinea, Nigeria, Venezuela, Ceylon, Chile, Egypt, Haiti, Iraq, and other countries.

This difference has frequently been attributed to the stress of urban living that afflicts men in "civilized" areas. Dr. Ray H. Rosenman, say that "Western societies are now fraught with stresses that not only are restricted to industrialized societies but also are uniquely new and never before witnessed in any age of history. Epidemiologic surveys have shown that emotional interplay based on these new stresses has a dominant pathogenetic role in accelerating coronary atherosclerosis. . . ."

What are these uniquely new stresses? Certainly one of them is the breakdown of traditional family life and sex roles. An adult male has a very different role in an impersonal, fast-moving city (where his authority and status depend on the size of his paycheck) from what he has in a patriarchial village (where he is honored for his wisdom, strength, affection, and character). His reward and pleasures in the two settings are highly different, too.

Here is what one noted observer, Dr. Joannes J.

Groen, says of this difference: "Family conflicts such as we have met in the life-histories of our coronary patients were non-existent in traditional Eastern families. In contrast to the Western male the Eastern husband is sure to find at home at least one, sometimes even more, submissive wives, who always look upon him with admiration and affection, never compete with him or contradict him and who are always ready to be his humble servant especially in his sex life."

This is certainly in striking contrast to the position of the American husband and father, who may have to perform both economically and sexually in order to receive admiration and affection. As he reaches middle age and his performance in either one or both of these areas begins to decline, his frustration and insecurity mount. In traditional cultures, on the other hand, maturity is revered and honored, a man's value goes up with increased age, and sexual pleasure is considered his irrevocable right.

A perfect example of this kind of contrast exists in Israel, where Jews from various areas and cultural traditions have settled. Among them were around forty-eight thousand Yemenites, Arabian Jews with ancient, patriarchial traditions who migrated into Israel during the 1950s. Here they live among urbanized, westernized neighbors.

Ten years ago a group of scientists became curious as to why European Jews are prone to heart disease, cancer, and hypertension, while Yemeni (Oriental) Jews have little heart disease and retain health and virility into old age. An exhaustive research project headed by doctors from Tel Aviv and Jerusalem universities revealed significant differences in diet (the Yemeni Jews do not eat foods high in animal fat and refined carbohydrates) and in mental attitude (the Yemenites are deeply religious and fatalistic, worrying very little). The most interesting difference, however, is in their sex lives. Yemeni men are extremely active sexually (their women age faster and die younger than the men). In fact, until it was made a criminal offense, the

Yemeni Jews were polygamous, taking a new wife every eight or ten years. According to one research report, scientists concluded that "Yemenite men owe their longevity, virility, and health to the custom of marrying teenage brides at intervals, thus reinvigorating themselves."

THE HUNGARIANS AND OTHER EUROPEANS

But we can find healthy hearts even closer to home than Israel. We can find men living in industrialized nations, subject to many of the same pressures as we are, and eating similar foods, who have remarkably low rates of coronary heart disease. For example, among the heart-disease-ridden countries of Europe, there are exceptions: one is Hungary. Hungary has one of the highest longevity rates in the world and a relatively low incidence of heart attack. The Hungarian population over age sixty has become so large (17 percent as opposed to the world average of 4 percent), that economists feel that Hungary's "epidemic of longevity" may produce serious economic problems. This worry is refreshingly different and somehow more challenging than ours.

The Hungarian diet is high in animal fats such as lard and bacon, high in sugars and starches, and low in vitamin-rich fruits and vegetables. But Hungarian men are famous for their love of women, romance, and sex. The typical Hungarian views sex as a natural part of life that permeates all aspects of existence and that does not stop with advancing age.

Shortly after the Hungarian uprising of 1956, I visited Hungary and expected to see depressed, disturbed, sick people. To my surprise and delight, they were healthy, happy, and extremely friendly. I asked a Hungarian colleague of mine the reason. He answered, "The Russians took everything from us—fruit, vegetables, liberty, our homes—everything except love, sex, and sport. As long as we Hungarians can make love and have sport, we are happy and healthy."

Abkhazia, a region in the Caucasus Mountains of the Soviet Union, has more people over the age of 100 per 1,000 population than any other place in the world. Despite a relatively high caloric intake, they have low cholesterol levels and remain vigorous and healthy. And the aged play an important role in their communities and are honored and admired.

What is their secret? Professor G. E. Pitzkhelauri, the head of a study center in Tbilisi, has discovered that, with rare exceptions, all those who reach extreme old age are married. He feels that a regular, prolonged sex life is a vital factor. Many of the couples he studied had been married for ninety or a hundred years! They were grown men and women when France was ruled by Emperor Napoleon III, when Queen Victoria still had thirty years of her reign before her, and Albert Einstein was not yet born.

One one-hundred-year-old man confirmed that a happy marriage is essential. "My first six wives were all wonderful women, but this present wife is an angry woman, and I have aged at least ten years since marrying her. If a man has a good and kind wife, he can easily live a hundred years."

According to the World Health Organization, the Italians and the French have extremely low rates of coronary heart disease—despite high cholesterol and heavy sugar consumption via diets filled with pasta, pastry, and cheese.

But the French and Italians are known as great lovers, and they value their reputation and national image as such. They espouse *joie de vive* and *la dolce vita*. They openly admit to committing adultery and feel no anxiety about it. In fact they recommend it. In countries where marriages of convenience are relatively commonplace, one is free to seek love elsewhere—as long as the home and the family are not endangered. As one Frenchman said, "Never forget, give yourself body and soul to your wife and only lend yourself to your mistress."

"It is to that infantile, erotic oral peculiarity that the French owe their virtuosity in gastronomy, in love, and in poetry, which have made them justly famous" says Dr. Félix Mártí-Ibañez. A man with a mouth full of food, gazing at a young woman soulfully while leering at her, he says, is "simultaneously exhibiting the three passions— poetry, sex, and food—of the French people." When a man reaches forty in the United States, he is considered middle-aged, ripe for a coronary or a masculinity crisis. In France forty is regarded as the perfect age for a man. (The French regard a woman of thirty-five as the most highly desirable; in the United States she would be thought past her prime, even though that's the age when a woman's sexuality is supposed to be at its peak.) The French believe, with Molière, that "to live without loving is not really living."

Certain sections of Ireland have a remarkable distinction: they are the few areas of the world where men outlive women. What accounts for this extraordinary fact?

Despite the high levels of cholesterol in their diets, Irishmen have a low rate of coronary heart disease. One recent study, using sets of brothers, revealed that the brother who remained in Ireland ate a much greater amount of fatty foods than the brother who migrated to the United States, but lived longer and more healthfully. The large amounts of exercise common in Irish life may play a role (although the Finns get the most exercise of any nationality but also have the highest rate of coronary heart disease), but sex is undoubtedly important.

One Irish doctor attributes the low coronary rate to the fact that Irishmen suffer little from the current masculinity crisis. Ireland is still very much a man's country. Male companionship is valued and men, both married and single, have their own recreations. The single man, if he isn't satisfied, can sublimate his sex drive by drinking, singing, fishing, and working. The married man is the head of his household; any sexual problems in the marriage are far more likely to be his wife's. More American wives should recognize that "a night out with the boys" might make the next night a more exciting and erotic one for her. Husbands need the stimulus of male good fellowship. They'll come home feeling more manly.

THE AMERICAN MAN

Time magazine published an essay entitled "Americans Can—and Should—Live Longer." The article stated that compared with many other nations, such as most of the Western European and Asiatic countries, Americans do not live very long. The death rate for men from cardiovascular diseases is 50 percent higher in the United States than in Western Europe. As an American who lived and travels a great deal in Europe, I believe that the main reason for the relatively short life of the American male is that he is too busy making a living and has no time to learn the art of living. He doesn't know how to relax, how to play, and how to drink, how to eat, or how to make love.

In contrast, most Europeans take time to enjoy living even after middle age. They enjoy their food, their liquor, and their women without concerning themselves with cholesterol, calories, or age.

My observation was substantiated by Dr. Joan Gomez, a British psychiatrist who wrote *How Not to Die Young*, after she visited the United States. She stated that American men eat too much and that what they eat is rubbish. They don't get the proper exercise or enjoy the right relaxation, and she concluded that they don't know how to use the single best tranquilizer and the single best exercise—sexual intercourse.

But even in America, the country with the highest coronary heart disease rate in the world, there are exceptions. There are millions of men who live to a ripe old age without damaged heart muscles or arteries. It's difficult, if not impossible, to find out what all these men have in common besides their healthy hearts. No one, of course, has attempted to study their sex lives. However, two groups of such men have attracted the attention of medical researchers. One group is characterized by a specific racial background, and the other by a specific kind of community life. And both, it turns out, have a tradition of "natural," male-oriented sexuality.

The American Black. Coronary heart disease is rare among black men. Alexander R. P. Walker, writing in the *American Journal of Epidemiology,* postulates "an unknown environmental factor" that inhibits manifestations of the disease. Interestingly, the very few black patients with coronary heart disease I have encountered in my own practice did have sexual problems. Is it possible that a vigorous and active sex life is this "unknown factor"?

The Walker article reveals that the Bantu population of South Africa who composed this study group show little significant difference from American whites in terms of the traditional coronary risk factors. Overweight is common in middle age, their blood pressure is higher than the American whites', and their cholesterol level is virtually the same (212 vs. 220 for whites in the Evans County, Georgia, study mentioned earlier). At least half of the Bantu men he studied smoked, many quite heavily, and were becoming increasingly sedentary.

American blacks too have a very low incidence of coronary disease, but high rates for stroke. The tremendous environmental pressures facing the black man in our society might be expected to produce a great number of heart attacks.

Dr. Elijah Saunders, Chief Cardiologist at Provident

Hospital, Baltimore, states, "In spite of the fact that high blood pressure is common, we do not see an extremely high rate of hypertensive heart attacks causing deaths among blacks. What is it about black people which protects them from heart attacks yet makes them vulnerable to strokes? This is a paradox we do not understand."

Once again, Dr. Walker's unknown factor appears.

The Director of Harlem Hospital, Dr. Gerald Thompson, has pointed out that many patients dislike the medicines they are given for hypertension because of their side effects, which can include depression, physical sluggishness, and temporary impotency. At the same time, many hypertensive patients are reluctant to give up the rich, spicy foods to which they are accustomed.

One of my patients, a handsome black man in his early fifties, came to me because of impotence. He had been to another doctor who had restricted his diet because of high blood pressure. The patient complained that his sex life had deteriorated greatly since he had given up soul food. I felt that the worry and stress created by his impotency were more harmful than a spicy diet. The medication he was taking was responsible at least in part for his impotency, and I told him so. I advised him to eat the foods he liked in moderation but not to use salt or pepper. In addition, I gave him some tranquilizers and hormone tablets and urged him to keep taking his diuretic pills. He gave up the impotency-causing drug and three weeks later returned to my office. He reported a markedly increased sex urge, and he had a lower blood pressure than when I saw him last. He was so pleased at having his manhood restored and at being able to eat his favorite foods that his stress was enormously reduced.

Many physicians feel that the American black may soon have a much higher heart attack rate. The new upward mobility of the American black may, ironically, give him middle-class coronaries as well as middle-class possessions. As black men move into the mainstreams of American life, they become subject to the same stresses that cause disease in middle-class white men. The great pressures of business competition may lead to the neglect of home life (the "weekend husband and father" so familiar in suburbia); the once happy sex life suffers, wives become frigid, and the coronary-prone man is created.

If the American black is to escape the fate of his white brothers, he must not adopt in toto the life-style inherited from our Puritan forebears.

Roseto, Pennsylvania. The Italian community of Roseto, Pennsylvania, is an unusually stable one. Few people leave and few outsiders move into this town of 1,700. The inhabitants eat more animal fats than most Americans do, their diets are richer in calories, and they are somewhat overweight in comparison to most of us. They smoke at an average rate and their blood pressure levels tend to be high (although there is no evidence of any great amount of hypertensive disease). Despite these facts, the blood cholesterol levels of the citizens of Roseto are not high. During a recent twelve-year period, furthermore, the rate of deaths caused by heart attacks was less than half that of surrounding communities and of the United States as a whole. It would appear, in addition, that mental illness is less common in Roseto than might be expected. What accounts for all this?

According to a group of sociologists who spent three summers studying the community, the most striking feature about Roseto is its social structure. Unlike most American towns, Roseto is cohesive and mutually supportive, with strong family ties. The family was found to be the focus of life. Children relate primarily to parents, siblings, and cousins. Old people are not discarded when their usefulness ends, but continue to retain their influence over family affairs.

Most important, according to a World Health Organization Report and to a study by Dr. Stewart Wolf, "The men in Roseto are the unchallenged heads of their house-holds." W.H.O. observers concluded that the patriarchal family structure might "significantly reduce life stresses in males."

However, like the Yemenite Jews, when the Rosetans move away and change their way of life, their coronary heart disease rate begins to go up. Dr. Wolf reports that relatives of Roseto inhabitants who have moved to Phila-delphia, New York, or New Jersey, have the average American life-style, accompanied by its high coronary heart disease rate.

THE FULFILLED APOLLO AND THE FRUSTRATED MESOMORPH

There are many Americans with healthy hearts who have not been studied by researchers because they don't fall into an easily recognizable group. But the healthy in-dividuals I know have one thing in common: they have mastered the art of living.

Dr. A. C., an ectomorphic mesomorph (bony *and* muscular), the typical Apollo type, is one of them. He is a sixty-five-year-old internist who not only makes a good liv-ing, but who knows how to live well, drink well, eat well, and how good it is to make love. He enjoys golf and swimming. He can afford to play golf three times a week and he swims every other day in the pool of his apartment building. He has season tickets to the symphony and the opera. He is also an active member of his synagogue. He doesn't look his age and dresses in the latest fashions. He travels a great deal and likes to dance. He has a beautiful secretary and a charming nurse. He is admired by his patients, nurses, fellow doctors—by everyone. He is a hardworking, devoted doctor, more interested in humanity than disease.

He is one of the few doctors I know who outlived his

wife. He was happily married for thirty-six years. Before his wife died she told him to get married as soon as possible because "you need a woman."

A few months after her death he was besieged by many women and it didn't take him long to start his amorous adventures. After a year he decided to get married but the question was to whom. He had love affairs with two women, alternating between them. One was sexy and beautiful but not up to his artistic, upper-class social life; the other was an intelligent, rich widow, but cold and unaffectionate.

Just when the widow began to respond more warmly to his lovemaking and he was considering whether to marry her, along came a bombshell—an involvement with a young, gorgeous girl.

He still doesn't know how he is going to resolve his love problems, but one thing is likely: he will have a healthy heart until he is ninety.

But the "art" of living is not synonymous with money. Tom L. is an endomorphic mesomorph (muscular with a tendency to run to fat). In the end, as we shall see, he was less fortunate but less adventurous than Dr. A. C. He had worked as a pilot and in a real estate office; in his fifties he went through the male menopause, began to feel his loneliness, started eating heavily, and became fat. His doctor prescribed reducing pills because his chest pains indicated that he needed to lose weight. He came to me after his own doctor had moved. I refused to give him pills and suggested sex as a substitute. He had no girl friend so I suggested he find a reliable prostitute once a week. Another patient referred him to a manicurist who was a part-time prostitute. Tom soon stopped gaining weight, even lost a few pounds, and his chest pains disappeared.

Unfortunately, the girl was arrested for prostitution. However, she was freed because she was a first offender, but she disconnected her phone and my patient could no longer reach her. Then I received the following letter:

Dear Dr. Scheimann:

I think I've lost a few pounds since I saw you, but basically I feel I need an appetite depressant to keep my appetite under better control. This noon hour the choices of food for lunch where I work were not good (there wasn't a good meat dish available) and I finally chose chicken patties. They were small and I got hungry in midafternoon. At four o'clock I ate an item of food I usually am able to avoid (pie), as there wasn't much else available then. . . . I do not cook and I do not have a refrigerator, and therefore it's not easy to eat the foods one would prefer.

My last girl friend (sex) has moved away it appears. You once referred me to Mr. — in this connection. Hope you may be able to aid me again.

This letter reveals that the loss of Tom's girl had driven him back to food; even in this brief note his preoccupation with food is very evident.

I couldn't "aid" him again. I prescribed some reducing pills and hoped his chest pains would not return.

Had he been more imaginative and outgoing, he could have found a new girl friend. Instead, he had to rely on drugs to stop his compulsive eating. Fortunately for Europeans, they tolerate prostitution because they believe it is better for a man in need than the taking of drugs; they realize that sex often can be medicinal.

I hope that this chapter dealing with individuals, groups, races, and even nations in terms of low heart attack indices, gives us all ground for hope. Scientifically, we need to know more specifically about each of these incidents. There are seeming contradictions, true, but the fact that coronary heart disease can be rare or absent should of itself be great encouragement.

Now let us turn to sex as medicine and see if it isn't patently part of the answer.

10

SEX
IS
MEDICINE

PLATO STATED IN HIS REPUBLIC THAT WHEN A CITY NEEDS
many hospitals and doctors it is a bad city, that its citizens
would not require doctors if they had healthy minds in
healthy bodies.

Plato believed, as did the physicians, that a healthy
mind and a healthy body derived from living reasonably
(the classical goal of the "golden mean") and from har-
monizing life with the ways of nature. They were convinced that people who followed these principles had an
excellent chance of escaping disease.

The doctors of the ancient world did not specifically
discuss healthy sex; like healthy breathing, it was under-

stood as part of life, part of nature. If you stop breathing, you cease to live, and if you stop loving, many of them believed, you also cease to live. The ancients regarded a harmonious life as a happy one, which included the enjoyment of sex. They believed that a sexually happy person inevitably was a healthy individual.

Plato was an idealist who believed in a medicine even more powerful than sex—love. If they have love—whether for man, music, God, or some other ideal—many people, the ectomorph Bernard Shaw, for example, can live happily and healthfully without sex. On the other hand, it is possible to sicken, or even die, despite an abundant sex life, if one is without love. A few individuals, men and women, can be described as the "love-them-and-leave-them" type, but they are exceptions. For most people, both love and sex are necessary. Loving couples want a happy sex life together; they are unfulfilled and frustrated without it, because for them sex is a tangible, physical expression of their love for each other. The two cannot be separated.

Sex and love can be the cause of a broken heart or a disturbed mind, but they can also have a magical effect on health. Sex and love can be poison or potent medicine. They can, paradoxically, cause anxiety or cure it; they can disturb body chemistry and upset the body's hormone balance, but they can also restore them.

Love and sex if abused can be coronary risk factors, but they are more likely to be antidotes for them. Love and sex can destroy a marriage or save it. Love and sex can cause hostility and loneliness; they can create and promote tenderness and togetherness, the indispensable feeling of closeness. Love and sex can give you a downcast spirit or lift you up, exalt you until you have not only a healthy heart, but a joyful one.

SEX ANXIETY

Dr. John R. Graham, discussing what you can learn from a psychiatrist about heart disease, states: "We all recognize that anxiety leads to the secretion of catechols, and that they have a profound effect on the irritability of the heart." He went on to say that this irritability is greatly increased by too much drinking, both alcohol- and caffeine-containing beverages, and too much smoking, all of which may be caused by anxiety.

How can a psychiatrist or a modern physician stop the resulting overindulgence?

First he can simply tell the patient to stop drinking, to stop smoking, to stop eating a diet high in fats, and to start drinking caffeine-free coffee. These are, of course, wise and necessary suggestions, but let us suppose that the patient is the Apollo type, who resents restrictions. As Dr. Graham points out, the doctor must deal with "the aggressive self-made executive type patient, who will not follow any of the rules regarding coronary care. He is the fellow who smokes with oxygen in the room, walks to the bathroom when he wants to, and sneaks in some salt from the outside."

The psychiatrist can suggest that the restrictions be made, in Dr. Graham's words, "a challenge, not a requirement." Instead of ordering the patient to follow his instructions, the doctor must motivate him to do so. He should appeal to the patient's vanity and say these restrictions are an obstacle that he must overcome, just as he has overcome so many others in the past.

What happens, however, if the doctor is not a good psychiatrist and doesn't know how to challenge the patient?

What does the modern doctor do to relieve a patient's anxiety?

He prescribes a tranquilizer. This can be valuable

and very beneficial in some instances, but let us suppose the tranquilizer doesn't work (and very often it doesn't). Then the doctor can do one of two things—he can either increase the dosage of the tranquilizer or he can suggest psychotherapy. This sounds like an excellent idea. But, if the patient has no time, no money, or no desire to go into psychotherapy, or if he or she doesn't feel the need to (many patients react by saying, "I'm not crazy; I don't need a psychiatrist!"), what happens next?

The doctor has two choices: He can send the patient to a psychiatrist whether he or she wants treatment or not, or he can wait until the patient gets worse. If the patient is faced with a sudden heart attack, the doctor can act positively and convincingly and advise the patient as Drs. Robert S. Eliot and Daniel E. Mathers suggest: "To relieve your patient of stress risks, it's of great importance to remove him from daily stress patterns and life-style hazards, either by short hospitalization or a prescribed vacation." This, too, is an excellent idea. But you can only send a patient to a hospital or on a vacation once or twice; let us suppose that the patient's stress pattern and life-style don't change (and all too often they don't). What happens then?

Can we evaluate the methods used by the horse-and-buggy doctor, our medical predecessor, to stop the over-indulgence of patients?

The old-fashioned country doctor rarely advocated abstinence. There was a time in the United States when the national catchword seemed to be "What this country needs is a good five-cent cigar"; a good stein of beer and a hearty dinner were equally well regarded, and the country doctor agreed. He didn't tell his patients to stop smoking or to stop drinking high-cholesterol beer.

There was a time when he advised his patients to drink a cup of coffee down to the last drop because "it's good for you." There was a time when ham and eggs were a delight. The gigantic dinners greedily gorged by the

Victorians seem almost incredible today. Yet the country doctor seldom advocated avoiding caffeine-filled coffee, or told his patients to stop eating ham and eggs, or recommended low-calorie dinners. Instead he advised his patients to slow down and to have more fun. The doctor of that period believed in the power of pleasure. He knew that patients with more recreation, more play, will eat less, drink less, and smoke less also. He knew his patients personally, and could prescribe with conviction.

SEPARATION

The feeling of separation arouses the deepest fears of mankind. Man is a social creature; he needs the society of his fellows. If he is cut off from them for an extended period—as is a lone castaway, for example—it is difficult for any except the strongest to feel fully human. The same thing holds true for emotional castaways—male or female—who feel isolated from their companions even when surrounded by them in a physical sense. Babies playing peek-a-boo are experimenting with this fear; they risk being lost and alone because of the intense pleasure and relief of being found. They crow with delight when they peek out and see that they are not really alone after all, that it was "only pretend."

Today we deplore the communication gap, the credibility gap, the generation gap. The word "gap" is significant; a gap divides, it separates, it leaves one alone. Our fast-moving society cuts us away from our roots: we are no longer given a sense of security by union with nature (nature has become the enemy whom we must master); we have the small nuclear (mother, father, and children) family instead of the larger, almost clanlike family of the past; we change our cities, our homes, and our jobs with greater frequency; there seems to be little continuity in our lives. This ever-accelerating rate of change is what author Alvin

Toffler calls "future shock." All this creates a deep feeling of separateness (we no longer *belong* anywhere) and anxiety.

Sex and love provide a means of overcoming this separation and, therefore, of relieving this anxiety. Just as a wailing infant, feeling isolated and frightened, is soothed and comforted by the knowledge of its mother's physical presence—being held and cuddled and talked to—so the adult is soothed and comforted by the knowledge of another's presence, by holding and being held, by touching and communicating. Sex and love can bridge the gap between two individuals; they can unite two alone people and make them one for a time.

In many primitive cultures the bridge is built not between two individuals but among an entire group of individuals. The orgiastic states attained through drugs and/or group sex also relieve the individual of separation anxiety and make him part of a group. We are enhanced through communication with others. As long as these rites are approved by the group there is no guilt or anxiety about participation. It is only the nonparticipant who feels guilt.

SEX AND STRESSORS

A sexually frustrated or lonely man is apt to sublimate his sexual demands and substitute food, drink, and smoking for sex. Oral gratifications are necessary when sex and love are missing. In our infancy, sex and love and food are closely linked. A baby is cuddled while being fed; whether the milk comes from the mother's breast or from a bottle, the feeling of touching and warmth is associated with food. Just being fed is proof of being loved, proof that someone is caring for our needs. The adult who feels unloved (and untouched) turns to eating, drinking, and smoking because these activities are associated with love. Doesn't it follow then that the satisfied man is subject to fewer coronary risk factors because of less need of these substitutes? Case histories that prove this assumption are plentiful, but one story will serve as an example.

Lydia's romantic problem seemed simple: she couldn't keep a boyfriend. Perhaps, as one of her former boyfriends had told her, she was too much of a clinging vine, too anxious to get a boy for one to stay interested in her. Others had told her she was too nervous and too restless. There was good reason for her nervousness—daily she smoked three packs of cigarettes, drank more than fifteen cups of coffee, and imbibed at least five martinis and four bottles of beer. She was skinny, unattractive, and had halitosis.

One day she decided to take up yoga; this began to change her. She became totally dedicated to her study and attended the sessions of her yoga group faithfully. She stopped drinking alcohol completely and cut down to eight cups of coffee and two packs of cigarettes a day. She started to eat natural foods and took vitamins. Her mouth odor did not vanish (she still smoked too much), but it did improve. She was far less nervous.

At this stage she met Tom, an old acquaintance, who asked her why she no longer frequented the tavern where she had done her drinking. She told him of her metamorphosis and enthusiastically urged him to join her group. She felt that yoga could help Tom (who had also started drinking heavily) as much as it had helped her.

Tom, too, became a yoga disciple and in the course of his studies gave up not only drinking but smoking as well. He asked Lydia to quit smoking but she could not.

Then, a month later, something wonderful happened to her. Lydia found the strength to give up smoking and to limit her coffee drinking to four cups a day. Where did she find this new strength? She and Tom had begun a love affair. The love and sex she found in this relationship diminished her loneliness and anxiety and enabled her to give up the oral substitutes upon which she had been so dependent.

I asked her whether she thought that she would relapse and go back to her old habits of drinking and smoking if her affair ended. "No, Dr. Scheimann," she said, "I no longer feel unwanted. I am a new woman now—love or no love."

HORMONES AND BODY CHEMISTRY

Studies have shown that strong emotions and stress can produce marked changes in body chemistry. We have discussed the "fight or flight" syndrome—when we are frightened, adrenalin pours into our bloodstream, our hearts beat faster, and our breathing becomes more rapid. Our body is automatically preparing us for combat or for fast, efficient flight. Stress can disturb the balance of still other hormones in the body, and tension can produce abnormal amounts of heart-stimulating hormones. Recent studies have shown that tension increases the level of cholesterol in the blood.

Unfortunately, there are no experiments that attempt to discover the beneficial effects of sex and love on cholesterol levels. Why should this be so? Many doctors regard pleasure, specifically sexual enjoyment, as negatively as they regard too much eating or too much drinking. Many people—far too many physicians are among them—seem to feel that "anything that feels that good must be bad for you." This, of course, is the old bromide, not totally unbelieved, that medicine has to taste terrible to be effective.

There is hope, however, that this attitude is changing. An experiment reported in *Today's Health* (December 1972) indicates that pleasure can dilate the pupils of the eyes; perhaps the day will come when an experiment will prove, scientifically and conclusively, that coronary arteries and blood vessels are contracted by stress and expanded by pleasure. On that day, we will know that sex restores disturbed body chemistry, repairs hormonal imbalances, and, most of all, reduces the cholesterol levels in the blood.

SEX AND HYPERTENSION

One of the most crucial coronary risk factors is hypertension atherosclerosis; hypertension atherosclerosis causes narrowing of the coronary arteries. The disease is commonly called "hardening of the arteries." The most prevalent form of hypertension, however, is essential hypertension which is caused by emotional stress or tension, by anger or distress. For a doctor to take a blood pressure reading while the patient is under stress makes no more sense, therefore, than to take a patient's temperature while holding a match beneath the thermometer.

While the physician readily concedes that stress can elevate blood pressure, he is not so ready to admit that pleasure and relaxation can reduce blood pressure. As one doctor put it, "The blood pressure settles down when we settle down." Since sex is one of our greatest pleasures, we should not dismiss the sexual factor so lightly.

Drs. Wilbur W. Oaks and John H. Moyer, exploring the subject, recognized that "Hypertension, one of the most common diseases encountered by the practicing physician, is intertwined with sexual activity." They state that "many physiologic problems have a sexual basis, and certainly the hypertensive patient is not exempt from such life situations." This is rather an advanced position. Many doctors feel uncomfortable with sex and have no inclination or disposition to discuss it with their patients. The routine use of sexual history for diagnostic and therapeutic purposes is disturbing to them.

There is no doubt that psychological factors play a vital role in hypertension. Sexual problems may cause, or be caused by, the physical effects of hypertension; in either case, they cannot be ignored. Helping a patient with sexual frustrations may cure his hypertension (if the symptoms are a mask for underlying sexual problems) or at least help relieve it (removing an additional source of stress can't help but be beneficial).

I have had many patients who suffered from high blood pressure but whose subsequent happy sex lives brought those high levels down. The best example of this encouraging fact is T. A., who wrote a letter in response to an article of mine in *Forum* magazine.

T. A. was told that he had high blood pressure when he was forty-eight and was advised to cut down on his work, golf (which should have been recommended as relaxation!), and sex. This last was no hardship because he and his wife had a minimum amount of sex. She did not enjoy it and used the menopause as an excuse to avoid sex, saying, "We are too old for that sort of thing." T. A. and his wife found they had little in common, and each lived a separate life. Nonetheless, after his wife's death in a car crash, T. A. was filled with tension and guilt. When he had an examination, his blood pressure was dangerously high.

Shortly thereafter he met an attractive woman in her late thirties. He told her his troubles and her responsiveness and warmth led to their becoming lovers. A year later they were married. T. A. was worried about making a sexual adjustment because of his high blood pressure, but gentle lovemaking made him feel so much better that he began to experiment. He now describes his sex life as more exciting than the one he had in his youth. This story has a happy ending. T. A. ends his letter by saying his blood pressure is way down and that he feels "more energetic and relaxed than I have for many years . . . My new sex life, which in theory should have finished me off altogether, has done more for me than diet, drugs, and doctors ever could."

LONELINESS AND BOREDOM

During my lifelong study of unhappy couples I came to the conclusion that loneliness and boredom are the most crucial factors in broken homes and broken hearts.

The most widespread and most damaging illness in the United States today, many psychiatrists feel, is loneliness. Loneliness is the major cause of obesity, alcoholism, drug addiction, and compulsive sexuality in this country. Dr. Natalie Shainess has said: "Loneliness is dangerous because it destroys a person's will to live. He feels unwanted and wishes to die as an escape from the most fearsome experience a human being can have—the sense of isolation from his fellow humans." Loneliness leads to sickness because despondency can cause or aggravate physical diseases. "Anyone who is happy, who enjoys life," says Dr. Shainess, "has an infinitely greater resistance to physical disease than one who is lonely." We have discussed how married men and women live longer than those who are single, divorced, or widowed. According to the United States Public Health Service, divorced men over sixty-five, for example, have a death rate of 75 percent higher than married men in the same age group.

These are the "sins of commission" that we can ascribe to loneliness, but there is no way to measure its "sins of omission." How many great books were never written, how many beautiul songs never composed, how many pictures never painted because their potential creators were too lonely and depressed to work? We shall never know.

There are two types of loneliness. One is as old as man himself and is associated with mental depression; our medical forebears named it melancholia. The second is an outgrowth of our modern society and is associated with feelings of emptiness, boredom, or hopelessness. We have physical remedies and, drugs for mental depression, but no medicine that can cure the anxiety of loneliness in our troubled times.

The loneliness of modern man is both universal, relating to our society as a whole, and specific, relating to the individual. Much has been said about the universal aspect of loneliness, so we will confine our discussion to the more specific causes. There are many reasons for this specific loneliness—the adolescent identity crisis, the crisis of middle age, a basic inability to communicate—but the most important is the inability to make love. Sex can be a way of transcending these crises, a way of communicating; the person who cannot make love happily and successfully is not only deprived of a method of relieving anxiety, but suffers from great additional anxiety because he feels inadequate sexually.

We Americans talk a great deal about the sexual revolution; we tell ourselves that we are emancipated, that the old Puritan American ethic is dead. We are deluded. Far too many Americans still have an imbedded deep fear of sex; many have sexual hang-ups; one sexual act or another "isn't nice" or "is unnatural"; such people never find the real joy inherent in truly, totally making love.

This fear is especially common in women who are taught from childhood to deny their sexuality. The old idea that "nice women don't enjoy sex" but only submit to their husbands' baser desires lingers on. Many women who consider themselves emancipated suffer from this underlying fear of sex and, above all, a fear of loving and being loved. Mate-swappers, for example, claim to love sexual freedom and to derive great enjoyment from a constant switch of partners. Perhaps some do, but many others suffer from guilt; many swap because they are afraid of becoming emotionally involved with a partner; when sex becomes a purely physical act, with no desire to know the partner, one's sex life becomes mechanized, depersonalized, and, ultimately, unsatisfying.

For all too many Americans sex has become meaning-
less and artificial. Charles Reich, in his book *The Green-
ing of America,* states that we live in a world where the
genuine has been systematically replaced by the artificial.
A world that is artificial is also a world without life, and
a society that deliberately manufactures an artificial world
ends as a manufacturer of death. Sex and love can be a
way of breaking through this artificiality and reaching out
for meaning and authenticity. Alas, in the United States
today, this wonderful opportunity is being ignored and
wasted.

I am inclined to believe that in this country Venus is
dead.

One of the most important causes of loneliness today
is our inability to live alone *or* to live together with someone else. As Dr. Erich Fromm put it: "We speak of all
sorts of terrible things that happen to people, but we
rarely speak about one of the most terrible things of all.
This is being bored alone, and worse than that, being
bored together."

Life is a pendulum that swings between solitude and
companionship. Both states are necessary and unavoid-
able. There are times when we need to and are forced to
be alone and other times when we have to live together.
In order to be happy we must know how to cope with
both conditions. In order to prevent loneliness and boredom we must learn to achieve a balance between single-
ness and togetherness.

In order to achieve this balance I recommend two
old and reliable medicines—*normal love* and *normal sex.*
Coupling assures a couple a happier married life because,
for the man, it prevents the male menopausal syndrome,
masculinity crisis, and impotency (a sexually active man
seldom becomes impotent); and for the woman, it fulfills
the fundamental need of being wanted and feeling desirable, physically adored, and intimately caressed, while
slowing down the aging process in some inexplicable way

(not yet medically proven but a totally acceptable idea
to me). For both husband and wife, it promotes harmony,
togetherness, and tenderness, and thereby decreases hostility, self-destruction, and loneliness.

Father D'Agostino, a priest and physician, at the
Twelfth International Congress of Catholic Physicians
stated that "a lot of aggression is really a denial of sex. If
sex were liberalized—in a good sense—we would have
fewer wars and lynchings." Healthy sex is sex liberated
from guilt and anxiety. Liberalized sex can prevent the
sense of isolation and the sense of being unwanted and
lead to healthier, happier lives.

SEX AND EXERCISE

Obesity is a dangerous coronary risk factor in that it
aggravates many other risk factors, and other serious diseases as well; and sex is the best medicine for obesity. Sex
not only assists you in ending compulsive eating patterns,
but actually helps you to lose weight.

Dr. Neil Solomon, an authority in the field of weight
control, has commented that "sex meets all the requirements of a good exercise and it can be played year around."

Enthusiastic participation in intercourse involves virtually every muscle in the body, and each act of intercourse burns up approximately two hundred calories.

Drs. George Clark and Philip Bard believe that the
sexual response center of the brain is located in the hy-
pothalamus, the same area that controls appetite. It's even
possible that an increased sexual response could have a
dampening effect on the appetite center. For example, the
slight shortage of oxygen in the brain during intercourse
could depress appetite.

Perhaps most importantly, an active sex life prevents
one from turning to food as a substitute for love. Compulsive overeaters are often love-starved; a happy sex life

gives them the feeling of being loved, which is so necessary before an ingrained eating pattern can be changed.

TOTAL GRATIFICATION

At a symposium on "Society, Stress and Disease" held in Stockholm in 1970, a world-famous physician came to a very significant conclusion in regard to preventing heart disease.

Before examining this conclusion we must learn a little about the discussion that preceded it. Dr. Wilhelm Raab of the University of Vermont represented the viewpoint of most American doctors. The cure for heart disease, he felt, was in abstinence. He went so far as to suggest governmental regulation of the public's diet (control of the intake of saturated fats in dairy products and other foods), an organized exercise program (exercise breaks during working hours), complete elimination of all cigarette advertising, and the establishment of "retraining centers" to help people break faulty habits.

In response to this, Dr. Richard Lazarus of the University of California, Berkeley, reminded the audience that a life governed by fear of disease, dominated by preventive measures, and poisoned by anxiety induced by such measures might well be worse than life with disease.

Dr. Lazarus then raised his significant point, and here is a real contribution to heart attack prevention. "Absence of stress is," he stated, "a negative virtue; lack of anxiety does not automatically provide satisfaction, identity and meaningfulness. Accordingly, we must face the problem of not only how to eliminate the stressors, or to improve the coping, but also *how to provide positive states* of body and mind for individuals" (italics added).

Dr. Joannes Groen agreed and added "that it is the total gratification with respect to all possible activities which finally determines whether you will be more or less happy and satisfied with yourself. One very important element in this total gratification is sex."

The Bedouins, Dr. Groen pointed out, endure a highly monotonous, bleak existence, but they obtain great gratification from their sex lives. Work is relatively unimportant in their scale of activity, so boring work does not mean for them the dissatisfaction it would for a more highly work-oriented people. Since sex is the focal point of Bedouin life, a happy sex life provides sufficient gratification to make them content and healthy despite the other difficulties of their existence. They have a great amount of this all-important "total gratification."

We must provide these positive states of mind and body in our own country if we wish to enjoy good health, and sex will become a natural source of gratification for us just as it is for the Bedouins.

It is most encouraging that Drs. Lazarus and Groen can express such a viewpoint. Perhaps the medical world as a whole may come to accept the fact that abstinence is not only impractical in many instances, but can cause actual harm, while sex not only can enrich our lives but be good therapy as well.

SEX AND THE JOYFUL HEART

Dr. Alexander Lowen ended his excellent book *Love and Orgasm* by stating that "sexual difficulties are intimately bound to physical disturbances in the form of muscular tension, pelvic rigidities, spasticities of the leg musculature, and restricted respiration."

To prove his assumption he introduced the concept of the "open heart" and the "closed heart." He stressed that a sexually mature person has an "open heart" because he gives himself fully to those he loves. The individual with a "closed heart" is afraid to love. He knows the meaning of love, and he is aware of his need to love, but he cannot open his heart to the feeling of love. The fear of love produces a defense that takes the form of an "armoring" expressed physically in a chronic rigidity of the chest musculature. The heart becomes "closed" by being imprisoned in a rigid thoracic cage, which in turn limits respiration and inhibits feeling.

Dr. Lowen concluded that he can offer "no simple prescription for a satisfactory and healthy sex life. The sexual crisis that confronts this age will require for its resolution some major changes in thinking and attitude."

In this book I am not offering a simple prescription for a satisfactory sex life, but I am offering an approach that could save your heart.

First I shall expand Dr. Lowen's theory by reemphasizing that sexual difficulties or a "closed heart" can cause more severe problems than disturbed respiration, pelvic rigidities, or muscle spasms. A closed heart can cause coronary heart disease.

In the third part of my book I shall offer a rethinking or new attitude toward sex; also a prescription as to how we can expand the "open heart" to the "joyful heart" because a joyful heart is the best medicine for preventing heart attacks.

Once there was a man whose very name is synonymous with wisdom—King Solomon. He believed in the positive power of sex, because he had several hundred wives and concubines. Perhaps he didn't have the medical wisdom of the modern cardiologist but he knew something about a joyful heart, and he said:

"A joyful heart is a good medicine, but a downcast spirit dries up the bones" (Proverbs 17:22).

His message can be amended: if you satisfy your wife or husband sexually after many years of marriage, you have a joyful heart, and good medicine; if you do not, you will have a downcast spirit which will not only dry up your bones but harden your coronary arteries.

THE JOYFUL HEART

I am known as a skid-row doctor or,
as one of the columnists expressed it,
"the doctor for broken hearts and broken homes."
The majority of my case histories,
therefore, reflect unhappiness.
I do, however, have some case histories with
happy endings. I have selected a few of them
for this section to prove to my readers
that there is a way to change the broken heart
into the joyful heart.

11

THE
SCIENCE
OF
HEALING
SEX

FOR FIFTY YEARS I HAVE TOLD MY PATIENTS THAT SEX
properly used has the power to heal and rejuvenate. I
know—I've witnessed it in scores of cases. Yet for most of
these years my ideas were thought shocking, unscientific,
and, even to some of my closest colleagues, somehow un-
dignified, unworthy of my esteemed profession. Sex was
simply not acceptable as a doctor's prescription in my day.
Today the puritan ethic is dying and my ideas on the
power of sex to heal may at long last receive credibility, if
not ready acceptance.

The sexual revolution is upon us, and now society
knows that sexual problems can make people mentally

miserable and physically ill and should be cured in any and every way possible. These problems are no longer treated as shameful secrets, nor is it to my professional discredit that I do all I can to help people overcome them, or, at least, live with them. (Can you imagine my elation when a man who has become impotent confesses his innermost feelings and frustrations to me and I counter with my prescription for sex, and later he returns to my office following a second honeymoon with manly tears of gratitude in his eyes? Is there a greater reward for a doctor?)

Today it is common practice for couples to go to marriage counselors, sex clinics, encounter groups, marathons, and other forms of therapy to learn together how to cure their sexual hang-ups. In my day this would have been unheard of and, for that matter, unavailable. But although the idea of sex as a healing force is no longer as shocking as it once seemed, just accepting this idea isn't enough. To benefit from healing sex we must know how to use sex properly. Sex is not just a matter of doing what comes naturally; human beings, unlike animals, have to learn how to make love. Falling in love and getting married in themselves aren't adequate teachers. Neither is reading sex manuals: you can learn to cook from a cookbook, but you can't learn how to make love satisfactorily from a sex book. On the contrary, sex manuals can mislead and misinform you by exhorting step-by-step preordained procedures that repel and restrain you—and deny your unique individuality and the exquisite ecstasy in self-expression. Would your partner have it otherwise—how else can it be perfect if it isn't truly personal?

Sexual sophistication can be acquired only by experimentation and practice. If two partners really want to learn the art of lovemaking, they will put aside other considerations, and put their intimate relationship first; if they will concentrate on the art of lovemaking, they can, and they will, discover also, on the way, the mystery and the magic of healing sex. Supposedly any medicine is most effective when "taken as directed," and sex is no exception in this context. If sex is to heal, to strengthen, to rejuvenate body and soul, then the doctor who prescribes it must first instruct his patient on how to use it positively.

KINDS OF SEX—INTIMATE, THERAPEUTIC, AND RITUAL

What is healing sex? Some sexologists, including Dr. David Reuben, author of *Everything You Always Wanted to Know About Sex,* do not acknowledge that it even exists. Reuben propounds, a bit platitudinously, that there are three kinds of sex: sex for reproduction, sex for recreation, and sex for love. But, believe me, sex is more complicated than that. You may think of sex as a multifaceted gem, or a hydra-headed monster, but if you think about sex seriously, you know that it can involve much more than producing babies, having fun, or expressing love. For example: *Duty sex* is not sex for love or fun or procreation. Duty sex is an act either performed or submitted to in order to meet or satisfy an obligation.

Revenge sex and its sibling, *rebellious sex,* cannot be classified as sex for love, procreation, or fun (unless you consider revenge a sadistic form of pleasure). Yet they exist. The woman who, when she discovers her man has been cheating, goes out, searches for and finds a sex partner may or may not have fun. She may or may not fall in love, she may or may not get pregnant. She does, however, satisfy her momentary desire to avenge an insult. Those such as the fifteen-year-old girl I talked to who do what society deems immoral or illegal to thwart the establishment, use sex to defy and deride—not to love, not to have fun, or to make babies. Many prostitutes fit this category.

Promotional sex, commercial sex, compulsive sex, and *escapist sex* exist despite the fact that sexologists, sociologists, and theologians choose to ignore them. There are the wives who sleep with their husbands' bosses in order to abet a promotion. The "on-couch-audition" is no novelty either for aspiring actresses or ambitious career girls. Prostitutes give themselves for money. (Many wives are prostitutes in that they give out only after their mates give in.) Nymphomaniacs copulate without achieving satisfaction. Their compulsion is like that of the escapist, who fornicates out of boredom. Both are considered by most physicians to be symptomatic of a disease, but they engage in sexual acts that cannot be classified as sex for procreation, fun, or love.

We have already added six kinds of sex to Dr. Reuben's simplistic, circumscribed list of three. There are many more (this chapter will discuss another three not mentioned as yet) but my object is not to enumerate types or kinds of sexual encounters, but to discuss the practice of sex as a medicine.

There is an old Hungarian saying, "One cannot explain love, one can only practice it." In some ways, I must admit, one cannot explain healing sex, one can only describe it. Healing sex is based on a physical relationship that is free of guilt or anxiety. Fear does not heal. Submission, revenge, or rebellion does not heal. To heal means to make whole or sound. Lots of people fall in love and have sex. Lots of people have sex just for the fun of it but they, both lovers and "live-it-uppers," also have guilt and anxiety. That kind of sex does not heal—it may give temporary, physical relief to sexual frustration but it does not heal. I use the word love as it is usually applied in twentieth-century America to refer to a romantic, tender, and meaningful relationship between a man and a woman. When there is love, and when there is sex free from fear, guilt, or anxiety, only then is sex for love a healing sex. I call it *intimate sex* but I hasten to point out that the practice of healing sex is not limited only to those relationships based on intimate sex. *Ritual sex* and *therapeutic sex* are equally powerful healers if there is no guilt and no anxiety.

Let us suppose that a man is impotent, and let us say that one night this man meets a woman and, for one reason or another, that woman wants him and wants to give herself to him. Without fear or guilt, let us suppose that this man accepts her gift and her gift restores his vitality. That's instant intimate sex. It's also magic. In the opera *Faust*, such magic is attributed to the devil himself. But the impotent man whose body is restored to health by such magic is more inclined to attribute his miraculous recovery to a higher power.

Intimate sex, unlike ritual or therapeutic sex, is always associated with love and affection. This love and affection may be of short or long duration; it may be a light love or an intense love; one's partner may be an old acquaintance, a stranger, or even a friendly prostitute, it makes no difference. When partners respond affectionately to their erotic encounter, there is love—it may last for only an hour, a night, a year, or decades, but nevertheless, it is love.

Therapeutic sex does not depend on love to light the way. It does not require that both partners be sexually satisfied in the sense of experiencing pleasure or having fun. And it most certainly does not include the desire to procreate. Its only "must," its only requirement, is that the relationship be free of guilt or anxiety. Only with this concept in mind, can a wife understand how important it is to satisfy her husband to safeguard his health. She may not enjoy her husband as a sex partner, but if he is a good father, or even just a good provider, and she likes him enough to want to prevent him from having a heart attack, she must learn to practice therapeutic sex to prolong his life.

This is what Demosthenes, the great Attic orator and statesman, meant when he wrote around 350 B.C.: "We have courtesans for the sake of pleasure . . . wives to bear us children and be faithful guardians of our homes . . .

concubines for the daily health of our bodies." Thus concubines were therapists. In today's sex clinics they are
called "surrogate wives"—women who are employed, not
as courtesans to bring pleasure, or as wives to care for the
children and the home, but as concubines for the health of
body. A young San Francisco woman recently attracted
attention because she is supporting herself by free-lance
sex therapy. She has four or five male clients who for fifty
dollars a session learn how to make love effectively. The
surrogate wife—whether employed in a sex clinic, a massage
parlor, or a house of prostitution—has one major purpose:
to help and heal a man, to administer sex therapeutically.
Such a woman may be a humanitarian, or she may merely
be in it for the money. The point is, she's a professional
therapist, not a love-mate.

Ritual sex can also be healing. The ancient sex orgies
and rituals were founded on the belief that sex is magic
and holy. The very earth itself was made more fertile when
man and maiden offered themselves as a living sexual
sacrifice to the gods. Their "gift" had little to do with the
desire to procreate, to have fun, or to love. Like the young
women who, in order to worship Venus, went to the temple
and surrendered themselves to a stranger, sex was an act
performed without affection; it was a religious rite, necessary for the well-being of the tribe. Today, though few
women wish to worship Venus, there are many who idolize
film stars, folk singers, and sports heroes. An erotic encounter between idol and idolizer can benefit both. The man or
woman who has, even for one brief moment, satisfied his
or her idol, is not likely to doubt his or her sexual prowess
or physical desirability for life. And the man or woman
who has been so idolized is less likely to doubt or decry
his or her worth. Do the words ritual, religious, and holy
discomfort you? If you trace the derivation of the word
"holy," you will discover that holy in Old English has the
same meaning as "whole," "wholesome," and "heal" or
"healed!"

Today much of the methodology used in ancient sex rites applies to encounter groups and other communal experiments to help revitalize marriages, frigid females, impotent males; also to help people face up to discomfiting perversions such as compulsive exhibitionism, voyeurism, narcissism, and an inordinate interest in nudism.

The San Francisco chapter of the Sexual Freedom League, for example, offers various workshops for people interested in improving their lovemaking ability. Some of their rituals include the following:

> *Gestalt Encounter and Sensual Massage.* During this day and a half MassagEncounter session, we will be getting in touch with our bodies and, with encounter leader ———, will be dealing with the feelings that come up from the massage. Minimum twelve participants.
>
> *Touch/Feel Encounter.* New experiences in touching and feeling. Learning to turn people on, not off. Sharing sensual awareness. Exploring pleasure zones.
>
> *Sensual Movement for Couples.* Making love can, but often does not, involve sensation and feeling throughout the body. In order to make our entire body more sensitive to the flow and rhythm of our partner, we will learn body movement and breathing techniques. These are designed to make lovemaking more intuitive, flowing, sensitive and spontaneous.

Another unusual group located in Chicago, "Sexy Senior Citizens," consists of older people who use ritual sex in order to stay youthful in spirit and body. And, according to the members I have interviewed, it works. One couple forthrightly stated: "After twenty-five years of so-so marriage, we finally admitted, and then conquered, our sexual hang-ups." A sixty-four-year-old man said triumphantly, "My wife and I feel young again. We're newfound lovers."

To benefit from ritual sex you have to be willing to break a few rules you were brought up on. You may be bored with sex, or inhibited about whether to try it, but

if you are willing to do things that outwardly seem out-
rageous—because you believe the results will be worth it—
ritual sex can become "healing sex." But you must believe
in it. Ritual sex has always required a measure of faith:
faith in a god or goddess; faith in a concubine's power to
heal, or just faith in one's right to love and be loved in
return. Best of all, faith in the ritual itself. Such faith is
powerful medicine. It is like a drug or medicine that when
prescribed by one doctor can be totally worthless, and yet,
when prescribed by another doctor, can heal.

As James Russell Lowell said: "Science was Faith
once." So, I, too, say the science of healing sex was faith
once. I am not talking about blind faith. Blind faith is
quite a different thing: namely, hope. I am talking about
an understanding faith, a faith free of encumbrances, a
faith so strong it becomes "the substance of things hoped
for, the evidence of things not seen (Hebrews 11:1-2)."
Or, as the Indian poet, Tagore, wrote: "Faith is the bird
who feels the light and sings while the dawn is still dark."

The magic of ritual sex is not unlike the magic of a
witch doctor. It activates those intangible, invisible forces
within us that are essential to healing. But before these
healing forces can be activated, men and women must rid
themselves once and for all of fear, guilt, and anxiety.
Only then will these forces work for their benefit.

The most powerful, the most healing sex of all is intimate sex. Unlike therapeutic sex, it is not directly aimed at
healing. Yet it can have the healing qualities of the most
powerful medicine. Unlike ritual sex, intimate sex does not
require sexual emancipation, nor does it require exposing
our sexual feelings and actions to a group. All it requires
is affection and personal commitment. It thrives on love.

How does true intimate sex differ from what goes on
in millions of American homes? One difference is in the
length of time involved; another is in the importance of
the preliminaries as opposed to the goal. The average
American couple have a sex relationship (and I'm only

speaking of those lucky enough to still have one) that goes
something like this: At bedtime, after watching TV, the
husband snuggles up and kisses his wife on the neck, which
is followed by a kiss on the lips, after which the husband
begins to fondle his wife's breasts, stroke her clitoris, and
finally proceed to the sex act. From the beginning to end
their erotic encounter is completed in something less than
fifteen minutes. As one needlessly frustrated wife (so we
found out later) confided to me: "I felt like I was about as
unique as a urinal!" Her equally and just as needlessly
frustrated husband retorted, "I thought her attitude was
for-godsake-Harry-hurry-up-and-get-it-over-with!"

TOUCH, KISS, AND EMBRACE

Some people cannot love. Some people cannot make
love. But all people can learn to be intimate, if they learn
to touch. Touch can express more than words can convey.
Holding hands, cuddling, and hugging are forms of touch
that say "I like you." A pat on the back says "You're all
right!"

The first thing an infant does to explore the external
world is to reach out and touch objects. You don't teach a
baby how to touch; it's a spontaneous gesture. When you
touch your sexual partner, you, too, must explore. Unlike
an infant, you are not touching out of a desire to learn
about the external world, you touch to learn about the
mysterious, mystical inner world of your partner. Your touch
says, "I like you. I want to know all about you."

The child deprived of touch grows up angry. He is a
child deprived of a pleasure to which he is entitled. As Dr.
Alexander Lowen, stated in his book *Pleasure*, "Bodily
pleasure is the source from which all our good feelings and
good thinking stems. If the bodily pleasure of an individual
is destroyed, he becomes an angry, frustrated and hateful
person. His thinking becomes distorted and his creative

potential is lost. Pleasure is the creative force in life. Many
people believe that this role belongs to love but, if love is
to be more than a word, it must rest on the experience of
pleasure."

THE SEXUAL REVOLUTION

Had not the sexual revolution hopscotched the Atlantic,
had not America's puritan ethic been engulfed by a tidal
wave, this book would never have been published.

Many doctors, sociologists, and psychologists attribute
the beginning of the sexual revolution to Sigmund Freud.
As an admitted and practicing Freudian, I happily attribute
it to an Austrian musician, Johann Strauss, and his "lewd
and lawless waltz." A hundred years ago, a man and woman
never touched or embraced in public. Dancers were grouped
and occasionally they tapped hands and shoulders. Then
along came Strauss and the waltz. Suddenly men and
women were divided into couples, moving to the sensuous
strains of music, smiling at each other—and openly embrac-
ing. The effects were explosive. With music and dancing, a
new, intimate, exciting, and enchanting encounter came into
being. The waltz evoked desire, and as a wise man wrote:
"Desire for anything is the thing itself in incipiency."

There were protesters. Priests and clergymen objected.
They were quick to sense that here was the beginning of
a new concept of sex: sex as pleasure instead of reproduction. A book addressed "Most Urgently to the Sons and
Daughters of Germany" presented "Proof that the Waltz is
a Main Source of the Weakness of the Body and Mind in
Our Generation." But pontifications could not stop the
waltz. The sons and daughters of Germany were too dizzy
whirling to heed the warning.

First, they waltzed to a melody that boasted of the
beauty of the blue Danube, then they waltzed to a tune
that paid tribute to the emperor, and last they waltzed

to the love songs of operettas which decried the chaste life as the best life. The sexual revolution was in full swing. The whole of Vienna was spinning. The waltz and its enchanting embrace in public precipitated thousands of new love affairs—especially during carnival days when couples danced "under mask." The mask permitted one to lose his or her identity. The mask freed self from self; there was no fear, no sense of guilt, and no anxiety. Nobody gave thought to "what will the neighbors think?" Their neighbors would never know.

Fear, guilt and anxiety, as we have seen, are powerfully hard to surpress, to contain. Yet once removed, like a cork from a bottle of champagne, the wine of life rushes forth to express itself. This is a law of physics and a law of nature. It is interesting to note that a judge in Munich has recently recognized this higher law of nature. He ruled that adultery, when committed during carnival (that is, under mask), is no longer acceptable as grounds for divorce!

ONE NIGHT OF LOVE

The art of lovemaking can only be acquired by teaching, experimentation, and practice. No two human beings are physically or emotionally the same—similar, yes, but not identical. If a couple is willing to put one night or three hours out of the week aside for learning the art of amour, they can discover the mystery and the magic of intimate sex. This "one night of love" is potent enough to heal a broken heart; it is also potent enough to *prevent* a heart from being broken.

On this one night, you must clear your mind of all outside preoccupations. Forget the children, forget the dinner dishes, forget your office worries, forget your finances. Devote yourself, your entire being, to what is known as a wholehearted all-out sexual encounter. In

other words, "live for love." This night is a night to experiment. Do not seek so much to enjoy as to explore. You
must remember that when you marry someone you don't
necessarily know that person. When you fall in love you
have romantic, and often false, impressions. You are blind
and, when you are blind, the only way you can see is by
touching. So use the method of the blind—touch!

As you touch, as you explore, you stroke and fondle
and caress. Begin to note your own sensations and impressions. By doing so, you enlarge the meaning of touch, you
learn to know your partner. To have sex is to get to know
someone and touching is the first step to knowing. Talking
to each other is important, too. As if you were alone in an
unknown abyss, talk to each other. Cry out both your
pleasure and your pain.

On this one night of love, a woman should think of
herself as a mistress, a hoyden, a goddess of love—she
should surrender herself to herself and to her lover. The
act of sex is a giving of self, a surrender of self to the
oneness of the sexual embrace. Erich Fromm said: "Not
until the heart is joined to the genitals in the act of sex,
is it possible to attain orgiastic fulfillment in sexual love."

Do not kiss each other when you first touch, remember the waltz—touch, embrace, and then kiss. I am not
going to recommend any special place to touch or any
specified kind of kiss. What's appealing to one is not necessarily appealing to another. For example: one person likes
to have his or her ear touched or kissed or nibbled, another
dislikes it intensely. You must explore and experiment and
discover what your partner responds to the most. Sex
manuals when they insist on certain approaches and circumscribed techniques wreak havoc and consternation.
However, when you first start to kiss, your kiss should be
gentle, very tentative but affectionate. It should say "I like
you. You know you have the power to excite me." More
passionate and erotic kissing naturally follows, such as in
the erogenous zones. Not until your kisses have gone from

affectionate to passionate do I advise you kiss the breast, or touch the genitals. Pacing and timing do play an important part. Take your time. Enjoy each instant for itself.

Many women are multiorgasmic. A man who is unskilled in making love can become exhausted long before his partner is satisfied. But just by using his hands as well as his tongue, he can stimulate his partner to a series of orgasms before they climax together.

Far too many men, after satisfying their own passion, turn away and fall asleep. The good lover is delighted and determined to spend time cuddling and fondling his partner before and after intercourse. Foreplay and afterplay are important to a woman, and a man who enjoys both is likely to have the most responsive partner.

One of my patients, an attractive woman in her early thirties, told me a story that illustrates just how important the hand is during lovemaking.

Rita, a tall and dramatic brunette, had been married for several years. "Steve and I were happy together for the most part," she said, "but I was rather concerned over our sex life. In all the time we had been together, I had never once had an orgasm. At first I didn't care, but after a while I became upset. I knew that something was missing.

"I didn't think anything would come of my dissatisfaction. In most ways Steve was a good husband, and I certainly didn't want to leave him."

"Did you consider having an affair?" I asked.

"Not very seriously," she responded. "I was in love with my husband and he would have been too hurt. Then one day I met a man who changed my life. Steve and I had taken a cruise and the boat was returning home. One evening I wandered out to the deck with this other man with whom we'd become quite friendly. We sat on deck chairs and looked at the stars. Naturally, our conversation then turned to romance and love. Since this man, Bill, was a mature and an understanding person I found myself confiding my problem to him.

" 'That's easily solved,' Bill told me. 'Just lean back in your chair and relax.' There was nobody about and we were covered with blankets, so I did what he said. Gradually I felt his hand under my dress, moving across my thighs, caressing them, and then realized that he was going to use his hand to bring me to climax.

"I tensed up right away, and asked him to stop, but he continued while explaining that he had a great deal of experience with women. 'There's nothing wrong with you,' he said. 'You're not frigid; I can see you're beginning to enjoy it. It's just a matter of technique. Any woman can have a beautiful orgasm just from good hands.'

"You know," she said to me, shaking her hair, "he was right. I did have an orgasm. Right there under the stars, in fact. It was not only a great mental relief to me that at last I could achieve and experience an orgasm, but a great physical release as well I can tell you. Quite frankly, I felt marvelous.

"A few days later," she continued, "I summoned up the courage to suggest to Steve that he use his hands in this same way. I told him that I had read about it in a book as a simple, matter-of-fact way for a woman to achieve an orgasm. I was careful not to let him think I was one bit unhappy with him. I said I was merely looking for ways to make both of us even happier. He was willing to try it. It worked with him, too. Only much, much better. He was my lover, after all, not my confessor. Any qualms of conscience I had as a wife for sharing such an intimate confidence are long since forgotten. For now our sex life is infinitely more fulfilling and consequently our marriage is that much stronger."

Use your mind to communicate with your lover. Ask her what she likes and what turns her on. Don't be embarrassed to talk about sex. Verbalize your fantasies and be willing to explore hers. Anything goes as long as you both enjoy it! Use your imagination in devising new ways of making love.

A heart full of love brings understanding and good sex in its wake. A heart full of love makes up for many failings. Most women will forgive and forget lack of skill in lovemaking if they are sure that they are loved. Therefore always let your wife know that she is loved.

In his book, *The Marriage Art*, Dr. John Eichenlaub states, "Properly managed, the conditioning of sexual response can actually increase sexual arousal and enjoyment far beyond what either of you could expect through relationships with a variety of partners."

In order to so condition your sexual response, I suggest that this one night of love be the same night every week. If you think that is very unromantic, that sex should be "spontaneous," I would remind you that throughout the ages the most memorable, romantic nights of love have been planned ahead. Expectation leads to full enjoyment.

Seduction is defined as something that attracts or charms . . . an enticement . . . a lure. On this one night of love, seduction, not spontaneity, is your goal. I, therefore, recommend that on this special night, a wife douse herself with a particular favorite perfume, one she never uses at any other time. Like musk, this fragrance should be synonymous with sex for, in time, such a scent by its essence alone, will induce a conditioned response.

The one night of love ritual is a night for breaking rules. It is a night for forgetting phobias, prejudices, and all the no-nos you were taught by your parents or have absorbed from society. Forget all the things you were taught were not "nice." Put such concepts as "unnatural sex acts" out of your mind. Know that there is nothing dirty or obscene or unnatural about the human body—or any part of the human body. The human body can be no more obscene than a plant or a tree, or a bird, beast, or fish. A penis is a part of the body, as integral a part as a hand or foot; so too, are testicles, breasts, clitoris, and vagina. To kiss the lips is no more sacrosanct than to kiss the clitoris or the penis. *Try everything at least once.* Remember that beauty is in the eye of the beholder and "evil" or obscene sex acts are in the mind, and only the mind, of the man or woman who thinks, or accepts, them as evil.

Try practically every sex mode you can imagine. Seek out those sex acts which easily and naturally excite and satisfy you. Even if you don't think you'll enjoy a particular act, as long as it doesn't hurt you, try it. Most human beings have what society might deem "abnormal sexual fetishes," and most individuals satisfy these fetishes when there is an opportunity. Therefore, I would encourage you to make that opportunity—to try the unusual or "forbidden fruit" on this one night.

But forbidden fruit, I would remind you, is as taste-less as pap if you have no appetite. The most important aspect of lovemaking is to stimulate each other's sexual appetite, to touch, to embrace, to kiss, to arouse anticipa-tion and desire. To Europeans and bon vivants who enjoy sex fully, coitus without a kiss is a great sacrilege to Venus, much as the gulping of fine wine or aged brandy would be an offense against Bacchus.

The interest of most modern American lovemaking centers around petting and intercourse. More sophisticated people tend to think that if lovers acquire the art of oral-genital stimulation, they can ignore mouth kissing. Yet, mouth-to-mouth play is still the most expressive, romantic, and captivating sexual stimulation. This is especially true when one or both partners have highly sensitized oral erotic zones, which is not uncommon.

Probably no person is more aware of the importance of kissing than the call girl. After all, is not her profession the art of love? One such professional told me that a pros-titute very rarely kisses a client on the mouth: her kissing is a carefully guarded intimacy reserved for her own lover.

In her book, The Second Sex, Simone de Beauvoir confirmed this: "It has often been emphatically stated she [the prostitute] reserves for her lover the kiss on the mouth, as the expression of voluntary affection."

Dr. Frank Caprio, in his *Sex and Love,* notes that when a wife kisses perfunctorily or seldom at all, she is revealing the poor quality of her physical union.

A Hindu proverb says "a long kiss is better than a hasty coitus." Because of the vital importance of the kiss, partners should practice the art of kissing *continuously* during the one night of love.

THE RETURN-TO-LOVING RITUAL

Any kind of sexual experimentation and practice is relatively easy during the early romantic stages of marriage. But they become more difficult when the usual marital problems occur, especially if attraction and love have begun to subside. When this occurs, we need something akin to physical therapy and psychotherapy before we can hope to put the relationship back together again. Therefore, I recommend for estranged husbands and wives a Return-to-Loving Ritual.

The aim of this rewarding ritual or rebirth of sensitivity session is twofold:

a. To develop a sensitivity and an awareness of all the factors that would undoubtedly make the one night of love plan difficult if not impossible.

b. To tear down the wall of fear and distrust that exists between this husband and wife and to open up their hearts and minds to a marital rebirth.

This ritual uses meditation, yoga breathing exercises, and some controlled fighting or quarreling as well as open confession. These are important steps that help to release or reduce tension and hostility, which are not after all uncommon after many years of marriage. My aim is to restore a commitment to marriage. This approach does not criticize or take a person apart piece by piece. It tries to make the couple more aware of their specific and special problems *together* and more aware of each other's needs and desires.

The goal of this ritual is to help the couple change their hostile attitude to a friendly and, finally, erotic one.

No doctor can help a patient who has lost the will to be healed. So we must assume that a couple whose sexual relationship is nonexistent or sick wants to be helped. Remember, wanting is the only prerequisite for learning the art of lovemaking. If there is something—even if it is only some half-forgotten memory hidden dark and deep—that enables a couple to "give it one more try," then there is hope. There is even more than hope, there is the magic of a ritual that can restore them to health and to each other.

As stated before, and so important, is the fact that *you must believe in the ritual* if it is to have any power to help you. The ritual I am about to outline is designed to reawaken an awareness of each other's identity and individuality, to tear down the walls of fear and distrust, boredom, and frustration. As in one night of love, the couple must be willing to put one night of the week aside to concentrate totally on themselves. If you can afford it, I highly recommend that you seek the seclusion of a motel room. The change of scene helps to create a different and unfamiliar atmosphere and this in itself can contribute to the efficacy of the ritual.

There should be no predetermination to have sexual intercourse. Such an intention would be self-defeating. No hard liquor; no drugs; and if you must smoke, keep it to a minimum.

Most smokers are poor breathers and since we cannot overlook the importance of proper breathing for emotional and physical health, breathing exercises are an integral part of this ritual. Depression and fatigue are direct results of faulty respiration. Fear, anxiety, and frustration, and self-condemnation and hate are symptoms of stress-ridden depression.

Whether you are at home or in a motel, take off your clothes and, either nude or in nightwear, sit down facing each other. Put a single glass of wine between you and have a clock within sight. The lights in the room should be dimmed or completely extinguished and a candle (one of the votive-light types ensconced in a glass container is best) should be placed next to the wine.

At this point, you'll probably feel a little silly or, at least, a bit self-conscious, but grin and bear it or, better yet, laugh and admit it. Shared laughter is sweet indeed, and like the proverbial saying, "a spoonful of sugar helps the medicine go down."

Now, each of you must practice the special breathing exercises that follow. This will bring more oxygen into your body and it is oxygen that aids circulation and helps keep muscles and organs in prime condition. (For the impotent man, this is especially important since oxygen increases testosterone activity, as reported in the *Journal of the American Medical Association* in June 1972.)

Abdominal breathing is a technique that has been practiced by students of yoga for centuries. The instructions for abdominal breathing are simple: 1) Inhale slowly and deeply through your nose; at the same time, slowly expand your stomach as far as you can; 2) Exhale slowly and deeply through your nose; at the same time, slowly pull in your stomach as far as you can. Doing this routine, imagine your abdomen is a balloon you must fill with air, then empty. For a beginner, six or seven tries is enough. You can't expect to overcome years of incorrect breathing in a night.

You may be a bit wind-weary after the exercise, so relax, share the wine cup, and toast each other's efforts. Remember, *this is a ritual* and, like all rituals, it should begin with a prayer or a blessing, a wish and/or a positive thought. It need be nothing more than a "Here's to us!" but make it constructive. Look at each other, smile at each other for a moment or two. What's coming up next is the most demanding part of the ritual. It requires a great deal of self-discipline, concentration, and patience. But remember too, as Dr. Erich Fromm so aptly put it in his book,

The Art of Loving, "The practice of any art has certain general requirements, quite regardless of whether we deal with the art of carpentry, medicine or the art of love. . . . I shall never be good at anything if I do not do it in a disciplined way . . . concentration is also a necessary condition for the mastery of an art . . . and anyone who has ever tried to master an art knows that patience is necessary if you want to achieve anything."

When you have sipped your wine and put each other sufficiently at ease, you must begin to verbalize some of the hostile things you've been thinking about each other. But remember, your objective is *not* to wound nor to widen the breach between you but to heal and to bridge the gap. So that this "sensitivity encounter" cannot turn into a heated argument between the two of you, I suggest you limit it to no more than fifteen minutes *by the clock.* Discipline, concentration, and patience are absolutely essential if you wish to repair rather than rend, to heal rather than rupture. Reveal your pain, shame, disappointments, and frustrations to each other but *fix no blame.* When the clock chimes and your fifteen minutes have fled, stand up and hug each other. Choke if you must, but mutter some soft words of sorrow (if only for your mutual plight). If more people realized that to say I'm sorry is not to admit guilt or responsibility for the act which precipitated the sorrow, there would be far fewer bad memories in marriage.

Hug a little, cry a little, comfort each other as you would comfort a child. Then change pace! Slather your palms with a healing balm and give each other a back rub. Rub from neck to waist, vertebra by vertebra and rib by rib. Talk to each other, ask each other what feels good. Remember, touch relieves tension, it communicates, it heals. Remember, too, that you are taking part in a ritual: after the rub, comes the tub.

Taken by twos, a shower is sexy and a bath is balmy. Water washes away all sorts of grief as well as grime. Unless they are taught to be afraid of water, babies love their baths. Even the sound of a splash is a happy, carefree sound and the tickle or the sting of a brisk shower rejuvenates and restores and makes one happy just to be alive.

Once done, dry each other off and go to bed. Again I repeat, there must be no predetermined intention to have sexual intercourse but, if once abed the urge to merge comes over you both, then think about all that I have told you: touch . . . embrace . . . kiss . . . and kiss some more. Remember the mesmerizing magic of the waltz—you don't make magic happen, *you just let it happen!*

Everyone knows, or should know, that you can't master an art with one try. The return-to-loving ritual cannot teach you how to make love or heal marital boredom in a single session. Just as a child learns to walk by falling down, a couple learns to love by experiencing both the heady heights of walking upright and the knee scraping ache of falling down, getting up, and starting all over again. The important thing is that you have tried, and each time you try you will come closer to your goal.

In discussing the one night of love and the return-to-loving rituals, I have been talking about two facets of healing sex that relate to married couples. I therefore want to point out again that extramarital sex can also be healing sex. In the next chapter, we will examine the many facets of healing sex outside of marriage. But, before we do, however, I would like to tell you a story that illustrates both the benefits of one night of love *and* extramarital sex.

MARY, RICHARD, AND MADELINE

Richard and Mary, like perhaps half of all Anglo-Saxon married couples, I am sorry to say, were both bored and disenchanted with their marital sex life. Truth is, their sex life was nearly nonexistent. After their fourth child was born, Mary lost interest in sex. Richard spent more and more of his time at the office. A proud and ambitious man, Richard was determined to make it big in the business world. After all, he had a wife and four children to support and he was determined that they would live in the "right" house, attend the "right" schools, and belong to the "right" country club. In his drive to earn all those "rights," Richard committed a great wrong. He sublimated all of his sexual drives into his mania for making money. Stress and sexual frustration eventually caught up with him. The family doctor diagnosed "those terrible pains in the chest" as agina pectoris—the first signs of coronary insufficiency. The doctor warned Richard to slow down. He also reminded him that he was no longer a young man. "It's time you let one of the younger roosters do the crowing!" he remarked in a friendly man-to-man fashion just as Richard was leaving. Richard told Mary about the doctor's diagnosis and prescription. Mary promptly bought twin beds.

Then the inevitable happened. There is no such thing as a sexual stalemate or standstill. One fateful night Richard met Madeline. Their first brief encounter was by accident; not so the rest—they were by careful design.

At first, Madeline was content to be with Richard whenever he could conveniently arrange it. They literally thrived on newfound love. Richard's chest pains disappeared and Madeline's pretty face became radiantly beautiful with that inner glow that comes with loving and being loved in return. If Richard mentioned the difference in their ages, if he condemned himself because he was married and "taking advantage of her," Madeline merely quieted him with a kiss.

But one predictable Friday night when Richard was about to leave, Madeline burst into tears. "Richard," she wept, "you know I love you, but I can't go on this way. Weekends and holidays have become a living hell for me. You *have* to make a choice—your wife and family—*or me.*"

As the Bible says, "The spirit is willing, but the flesh is weak." Richard was caught in a battle between the two.

His lawyer warned him that he had no grounds for divorce and that, even if Mary agreed to one, Richard by rights (another sort) would be left penniless.

Ironically, it was Madeline who sent Richard to me. His chest pains had returned and she feared for his life. When I told Richard that I had known several men who gave up their wives, their children, and their fortunes for their Madelines and, in spite of what they lost, gained more, Richard wept. "You're the first person who has listened long enough to understand or to give me hope!" he exclaimed. "I can't give up Madeline! She brought me back to life. I'll die without her."

I suggested that Richard and Madeline not see each other for a period of six weeks. I told Richard I wasn't sure whether Madeline, half his age, was in love with him or with a father image. I also told him that I wasn't at all sure that he didn't still deep down love his wife. "Do you really want to replace Mary, or do you want Mary to be Madeline?" I asked him. "Mary could never be a Madeline," Richard scowled. "She doesn't enjoy sex, she just permits it."

"That may be so, Richard," I countered, "but I'll find that out for myself. Because of the seriousness of your condition, I want to see Mary for counseling at once. I also intend to see Madeline once a week for these six weeks."

When Mary came in, I told her bluntly that in my best medical opinion she would either be a divorcee or a widow within the next year. I asked her if she cared which, and she convinced me that she loved her husband too much to settle for either one without a fight. I then recommended that she and Richard try to practice my one night of love, starting with the return-to-loving ritual. "It can," I assured Mary, "save your marriage and your husband's life."

I said many things to Madeline in the next few weeks. I felt sure, even more so after a few sessions, that Madeline had transferred her love for her father to Richard. Later, I asked her, "Madeline, my dear, you are one of the most fascinating females I have ever met. Why do you want to settle for a secondhand Cadillac when you can easily with your charm have a brand-new Jaguar?"

Several visits after Mary had first come to see me, she was ten pounds slimmer and had changed both the color of her hair and her makeup. When she walked into the office for her weekly interview she did a quick pirouette, facilely, as fashion models do, and then she gleefully exclaimed, "It worked! Dear Dr. Scheimann, you are wonderful, and your one night of love works wonders, too." She blushed a bit, sat across from me, and smilingly said, "I'm now me— the true me, a sensuous woman, and I'm proud of it."

Both Mary and Richard were now deeply concerned about Madeline. They had no desire to hurt her, and Mary was most determined to help Madeline readjust to a life without Richard. I suggested that they treat Madeline to a few weeks' vacation abroad and they agreed. We handled it in a most delightful way. Richard told Madeline he had won a trip to Europe for two in a sweepstake. He explained that although he could not go with her, he wished her to enjoy the trip and had arranged to turn his half into cash she could use for shopping.

I will never be sure whether Madeline guessed that Richard had once again fallen in love with his wife or not. I know only this. A month after she left for Europe, I received a postcard from Switzerland. It read:

Dear, dear Dr. Scheimann:
Have found me a new Jaguar!
Many thanks—
Mad & Marv

12

WHAT
TO DO
IF YOUR
MATE WON'T

IDEALLY, A CORONARY CANDIDATE WHO REALIZES THAT HE can safeguard his health by changing his sex life should be able to do so within his own marriage. Ideally, if his wife loves him and wants to keep him alive and well, she will be proud of her sexual power and eager to use it to heal and strengthen him.

But life is rarely ideal. It is hard to convince some wives that their apparently strong strapping husbands are really vulnerable. Some will not or seemingly cannot practice the art of healing sex. Many wives fall short of fully satisfying the "fleshly needs" of their coronary-prone husbands.

If your wife fits one of these three categories, it must have occurred to you to look outside of marriage for sexual encounters. You can hardly avoid the temptation; reminders of it are all around you. Popular magazines tell single girls repeatedly that married men make the best lovers. A spate of best-selling books tell men precisely how to find, fascinate, and hold a mistress. Books, articles, statements from famous psychologists, moral and social leaders, lately even theologians, are all telling us that adultery isn't as bad as we used to think it was. Many, like me, even insist to the contrary that it is often a good and necessary thing for your health.

Moreover, there is increasing evidence today for both sexes that the old rumor is really true: everybody's doing it. Dr. and Mrs. John Cuber of Ohio State University announced after their five-year study of 437 professionals: "adultery is amazingly common among successful Americans. . . ."

And California marriage counselor Carolyn Symonds comments: "A new breed of husbands and wives is slowly arising . . . who allow each other openly acknowledged and guiltless extramarital adventures."

But you don't have to believe the experts; just ask your friends. Many of them will admit that they have strayed. Many of the rest will agree that there's nothing wrong with it. Our surface morality still says adultery is taboo, but it now takes only the slightest scratch to get beneath the surface to the reality. The reality is that these days societal pressures force people to be more embarrassed about being thought square and conventional than they are about being thought immoral or unconventional.

Not only is almost everybody doing it, but a surprising number of well-known people publicly approve of it. Dr. Albert Ellis, executive director of the Institute of Advanced Study in Rational Psychotherapy, for example, has said, "The man who resides in a large urban area and who never once . . . is sorely tempted to engage in adultery for purposes of sexual variety is to be suspected of being indeed biologically and/or psychologically abnormal; and he who frequently has such desires and who occasionally and unobtrusively carries them into practice is well within the normal range."

Of course Albert Ellis has long been known for his liberal views on sex. But today even our once conventional professors and doctors publicly state similar views. Anthropologist Margaret Mead has observed that the heavy demands of sexual fidelity are so onerous that a more honest and realistic relationship between the sexes is called for. The president of the Sex Education Council of the United States, Dr. Mary Calderone, maintains that extramarital sex can help, as well as hurt, a marriage. Dr. O. Spurgeon English, professor at Temple University Medical School, says: "We like the company of different people at different times and for different reasons. The same could apply to sexual activity. . . . An extra-marital affair carried out graciously and without condemnation is capable of bringing high benefits in a sense of well-being and vivacity." Virginia Satir, a therapist at California's Esalen Institute, regards affairs as "inevitable and necessary for many contemporary marriages if they are to avoid becoming stale and destructive."

Even the church—for centuries the most conservative, antisex of institutions—is getting into the act. The Reverend Hunter Leggit, a Unitarian minister, puts it this way: "Extramarital sex can be positive. It can be related to maturity, personal growth, better marriage and joy." And the British Council of Churches, in its report on sex and morality, refused to condemn adultery as necessarily immoral or as automatic grounds for divorce. It commented that casual sex can be "trivially pleasurable or mildly therapeutic." In a recent article in the journal *Forum*, the Reverend John Andrews, a Catholic priest, stated that he has frequently recommended adultery. "High on my list of priorities is the achievement and perpetuation of human happiness. If adultery will contribute towards this—for all concerned—then I strongly support it. Similarly, if a marrige will benefit from it—then again I support it. . . . Surely extramarital sex is infinitely preferable to broken marriages."

IF YOUR WIFE WON'T

The solution is obvious—so obvious that it's practically being pushed down your throat. But before you proposition your neighbor's wife or pinch your boss's secretary, hold on. If you are a coronary candidate—and most American men over thirty-five are—you must handle extramarital sex with extreme caution. Like smoking, it may be comforting, but it can be hazardous to your health. Like nitroglycerine, it can cause a fatal explosion if used incorrectly; but if used as directed, in small and pure doses, it can save your heart.

Now, I don't agree with the scare tactics of those doctors who announce that most men who die during intercourse do so while engaging in adulterous liaisons, implying that adultery is always dangerous and unhealthy. Adultery can be fatal if combined with fear and guilt or the excessive use of drugs and alcohol to loosen inhibitions. We have already seen how harmful anxiety and guilt can be. A sordid, guilt-ridden encounter with a prostitute is certainly not "healing sex" for a terrified husband suffering under a male climacteric; indeed, it can be harmful. On the other hand hostility, frustration, and boredom also can do harm, and the right kind of release with the right kind of partner can be rejuvenating and life enhancing. It can, literally, be a lifesaver.

Long before it was considered acceptable to do so, I stated publicly that adultery can save and revitalize marriages, as well as rejuvenate the partners themselves. It takes a very unusual couple not to get into a sexual rut after making love to each other for fifteen or twenty or thirty years. Bored couples could add a little spice by practicing my suggestions in chapter 11; but that takes discipline and planning—and a willing, devoted wife. They could also go to a sex clinic and learn all sorts of exciting new techniques, but that takes a thousand dollars or more, as well as mutual cooperation. For many couples, a simpler, far less expensive way, is to experiment with a new partner and then return to one's spouse with what one has learned.

It simply is not true that people are "naturally mono-gamous." And since so many people are practicing it suc-cessfully, adultery must be considered an important aspect of healing sex. But not without some guidelines for han-dling it. It's awfully tempting to believe all the adultery propaganda—its frequency and joys—that is flying around, especially for a middle-aged man with a wife who's not particularly sensual. But it should be taken, like much else, with a grain of salt. Like all forms of love and sex, extra-marital sex must be used properly in order to bring bene-fits. For the man who has not had a heart attack but has some of the characteristics of a potential coronary victim, there are special pitfalls as well as unique benefits to be gained from extramarital sex. We will first have a look at the other side of the marital picture.

IF YOUR HUSBAND WON'T

What shall a sexually frustrated wife do if her husband fails to satisfy her and doesn't believe in open marriage or give his consent to her committing adultery?

Before answering this key question, we could raise a few other questions of medical relevance. Is sexual frustra-tion as crucial a factor in women's coronary heart disease as it is in men's? Is it a factor at all? And if so, to what degree? These questions are difficult to answer because the plain fact of the matter is that there is no single reference work to date in medical literature that mentions that sex-

220 · THE JOYOUS HEART

ual frustration in females is a coronary heart disease risk factor. On the other hand there are a number of problems that women complain of that sexual frustration could cause: hysteria, neurosis, hypertension, nervousness, insomnia, and gastrointestinal disorders to name just some of the most common. Is it possible that a women's sex hormone, estrogen, neutralizes the dangers of sexual frustration?

Those doctors who are interested in emotional stress and heart disease believe, of course, that fear of impotence is the most damaging stressor for men with coronary heart disease. Women, however, have no fear of impotence; they can always satisfy their love object physically. An impotent man can't. That is most likely the reason why the few doctors who associate sexual anxiety and coronary heart disease refer only to men. The following quotation by Dr. Edward Weiss attests to this fact: "The coronary age is also the age of diminishing potency. Sexual problems creating tension occur, especially among men. Since men are much more likely to have coronary heart disease than women, these tensions are of particular significance. In almost 50 per cent of our coronary cases there were important sexual problems that antedated the attack, and most of these occurred in men. They were twice as frequent in the coronary group as in the control group. Loss of desire, quick ejaculation, a feeling of 'growing old,' preoccupation with the idea of 'loss of manhood' or the onset of the 'change in life,' and compensatory efforts to prove oneself still a vigorous man (a frequent source of stress and strain)—these are some of the problems that afflict men of this age." Not very informative about women, as you can see.

Some women relieve their sexual frustration themselves (as of course do a surprising number of American males, according to Kinsey, throughout life). But a woman's danger is more apt to be anxiety over losing a love object. This potentially could be very damaging to her coronary problems if the research I propose (see chapter 1) on sex and stress includes a goodly number of women and proves that their pattern is indeed similar to men's. I strongly suspect it is so.

Times are changing. There are more of the Atalanta type of women today who act like men, take on the same hectic business responsibilities as men, and chances are that for them sexual frustration is a highly possible coronary risk factor that must be dealt with. If you are an Atalanta type or a career woman you should have the same right as a man. This is true, too, if you know yourself to be sexually frustrated and have strong extramarital desires (and the capability of handling them). If you can't get your husband to grant you adultery privileges, despite strong and persistent insistence, then it is better to divorce him. But I don't recommend cheating on him. In women, as in men, this frequently creates more dire emotional problems than it solves.

SEVEN RULES FOR EXTRAMARITAL SEX

The first important rule for handling an extramarital affair is *don't do it unless you are emotionally, erotically, and physically prepared to cope with the consequences.* Sexual passion is not a toy for a coronary candidate; it involves powerful emotions that affect your physical health and mental judgment. If you already have a stressful occupation, if you already have problems with your wife, if you smoke, are overweight, or have high blood pressure, don't add extramarital stress to your problems until you have improved the other risk factors in your life.

For example, many middle-aged men blame their wifes for their symptoms of declining virility. They delude themselves into thinking that making love to a young girl will solve all their problems. A man like this often rushes into an affair with a luscious young adventuress. If she seems magically to restore his virility, he often ends up making a fool of himself and a martyr of his wife; it's usually hard on his children and his bank account and after it's too late he discovers that he has sacrificed a great deal and ended up with a selfish, dissatisfied, and restless young girl on his hands. He may then discover that his male climacteric symptoms return with a vengeance—and heart trouble is often on its way as well.

Many years ago I observed a middle-aged man who, unprepared, ventured into illicit sex with tragic consequences. One night I received a frantic call from one of my call girl patients. "I've got a sick client—hurry," she said. When I got to her room, the man was already imminently close to death. After I examined him, I called an ambulance—a private one so as not to involve the police. "He's married, Doctor," the girl told me, "and he's well known. Don't let them find him here."

When the ambulance arrived, the man was dead—but I refused to admit it, insisting that I still detected signs of life. "Put the oxygen mask on him and take him to the hospital—I'll check him there." At the hospital, in respectable surroundings, I declared him dead. There was no official record of the sordid circumstances that surrounded his death.

Later the girl told me, "I *knew* he was going to get a heart attack—I've learned to spot that type. He was frightened, he searched the apartment, looked under the bed and in the closets, kept asking me if the police ever came here. And when we finally did get into bed, he couldn't get it up—he was completely impotent. That's when he started clutching his chest."

That man would have been far better off seeking satisfaction from his wife. For him, illicit sex was poison.

My second guideline is a warning about professional discretion: *be particularly careful about extramarital sex if you are a doctor, clergyman, teacher, judge, or in political office.* Nobody gets too concerned about the private morals of most of society, but those who enjoy the community's trust are expected to set an example. If discovered, you'll be risking not only your marriage, but your career.

There's a half-serious bit of tongue-in-cheek advice popular among doctors that goes like this:

Don't have affairs . . .

But if you do, be sure you don't do it with a patient . . .

But if you do, be sure you don't do it your office . . .

But if you do, be sure to send her a bill.

Professional discretion is not an ironclad rule. Plenty of doctors, politicians, and judges do have extramarital affairs and benefit from it. Even ministers can, under the right circumstances. A lovely friend of mine, Julie, became intensely involved with her married minister, and is an example of this.

Julie had known Peter for years as her pastor and consulted him privately because of her own marriage problems. He counseled her and saw her through her separation and divorce. They developed a warm friendship, and he finally declared his own feelings for her. Peter was in his late forties and a typical Apollo. He was a mesomorph in build, and a natural, charismatic leader with a zest for life and people. He was slightly overweight and smoked moderately. His twelve-year-old marriage was virtually sexless; his wife, Joyce, preferred to dedicate herself to church work and other good causes. Peter had successfully sublimated his sexual emotions through his community work, his friendships, and his three adopted children. But now he was entranced by Julie, the first truly sensuous woman he had ever known. She was absolutely uninterested in remarrying, but found a passionate affair with a man like Peter, who was totally different from her husband, to be a satisfying transition for the first year after her divorce.

Peter blossomed during the relationship. His work suffered in no way; his sermons became even more inspiring. His wife was contented, naïvely assuming that her husband's late hours meant that he was more devoted than ever to God's work. Joyce, who hardly recognized that sexual passion exists at all, would never have been able to face the truth, and she never had to. For Peter and Julie the affair was a beautiful interlude that enriched both their lives and hurt no one.

One reason that they all benefited is that Peter was fortunate in his choice of a partner; another Julie might have demanded more and caused a scandal. This brings up rule number three: *choose the right partner.* This is probably the most important rule of all, because if you ignore it, following the other rules won't help at all.

Avoid unhappily married women, single women looking for husbands, or obvious sexpots who might lure you into forsaking home and family. Your best bet is a sexually liberated older woman who is sophisticated enough to revitalize you without jeopardizing your marriage. Whomever you choose, be sure you can meet her needs as well as your own.

If you are relatively young, I'd advise an affair with an older woman. Most young American husbands are sexually immature; sex with an experienced woman can improve your marriage—and you.

A mature man who wants healing and rejuvenating extramarital sex would do best with a middle-aged woman who also needs sexual variety and excitement. She can satisfy you and appreciate you. If she is independent enough to see you without jeopardizing her own marriage, she is an ideal partner.

A liberated, independent, and sophisticated single girl might also be a good choice. If she doesn't believe in the double standard, enjoys sex, and is in no hurry to get married, you can teach her a great deal about men, and she can give you a new lease on life.

If you are rich, an expert call girl or a reliable mistress can be the Aladdin's lamp that safeguards your virility and revitalizes you. She will make few demands on you other than economic ones, and she will do everything to please you sexually. If this kind of situation appeals to you, such a girl may be your best medicine.

Number four: *Be honest with your partner.* You can avoid all sorts of traps and entanglements if you remain scrupulously honest with your partner right from the beginning. This usually means making it clear that you don't intend to break up your marriage, that your wife and family will always come first. It might also mean telling her that you have sexual and health problems. Anything that you gain by lying to her or misleading her is usually in the long run not worth gaining.

This brings to mind the story of David. An attractive married lawyer, he began to show signs of impotence when he reached his late forties. He consulted his family doctor, who examined him and could find nothing wrong physically, suggesting that he consult a psychiatrist. David agreed. After four months of therapy, during which he discussed his childhood and his parents in detail, there was no improvement. However David had noticed the doctor's attractive secretary, Sonia. One day he left the doctor's office at the same time Sonia left for lunch. He invited her to lunch, she agreed to go, and they began to have regular luncheon dates. He became more and more attracted to her and wondered if she knew about his problem. Finally he asked her. "No, I hardly ever see the files on the current patients. The doctor is very careful about professional secrecy." That gave David courage to ask her for a date. She accepted. Now he couldn't decide how much to tell her; finally he decided to confess all. He admitted that he was married, that he intended to stay married, and that he had recently become impotent. She was sympathetic and warm and said she admired him for his honesty. One thing led to another, and they began to make love. A miracle occurred. His impotence disappeared—with his wife as well as with Sonia. David has always believed that Sonia cured him—and perhaps he is right. He later told me, "Sonia had more sense between her legs than that psychiatrist had between his ears."

If you're going to have an affair, you must decide how honest you are going to be with your wife about it. Ideally, you and your wife should both be free to enjoy extramarital sex without risking jealously and divorce. To my more sexually sophisticated, emancipated patients I recommend, instead of the old-fashioned contract of exclusive marital fidelity, a new covenant based on their needs and desires: "I will remain faithful to you as long as you satisfy my sexual needs. If you do not, I have the right to have sex outside of marriage, but I will remain your loving mate as long as you are a good wife and good mother (or a good husband and good father)."

I know many couples who have rewarding marriages and who love each other despite the fact that they know that their mates have extramarital relations. Open marriage is popular today among emancipated young American couples. They promise to love, honor, and cherish each other, but they withhold promising eternal sexual fidelity. They believe that it is almost impossible for all of one's sexual and emotional needs to be fulfilled forever by one person. Open marriage or adultery with consent changes the old, restrictive concept of marriage. It gives husband and wife the freedom to live as independent personalities. I'm not talking about swapping or swinging, or even telling your mate about your affairs. I'm talking simply about a general agreement to permit sexual freedom within the framework of a stable, affectionate marriage. Adultery with consent is an ideal partnership—a monogamy with sexual freedom. If both marriage partners agree that they may commit adultery if the need and occasion arise, there is no breach of trust, no dishonesty, no infidelity, and no guilt. Consented-to adultery is the best antidote to divorce. Then, too, if the husband and wife marry in their early twenties, they may have had no opportunity to relate to others, until adultery gives them such scope. Consented-to adultery gives them the freedom and independence to fulfill their physical, emotional, and intellectual needs. It allows them to live as personalities, rather than just wife and mother or husband and father.

However, in today's era of sexual permissiveness, many men and women need both the security of marriage and a sense of freedom. A coronary-prone male needs a secure home, a haven from the stresses of the outside world. A man with Apollo personality characteristics also needs variety, adventure, and freedom. Is it possible to have both? In some cases, yes.

This was true of George W., a forty-eight-year-old Chicago businessman who came to me complaining of chest pains diagnosed as angina pectoris, often a warning of possible heart attack. When I questioned him he revealed the typical life-style of a coronary personality. "I work too hard," he admitted, "but I have to, to get ahead. Sometimes I eat and drink too much and I know I'm a little overweight—but I do exercise. I play golf twice a week. Sex? Well it's not much anymore. I look at other women, but I'm scared to cheat on my wife. Now with this heart I guess I'm getting over the hill—it's probably too late for me."

I recommended medication, certain changes in diet, advised George to have sex once a week with his wife, and said, "Stop playing golf—it's no good as exercise. I want you to jog every day or swim at least one hour three times a week."

Five weeks later he returned—eight pounds lighter, free of chest pain, and glowing with happiness. "The swimming did wonders for you," I said. "Congratulations." George grinned sheepishly and said, "Doctor, I know the swimming was good for me, but it's sex that really changed me. At the health club I met a girl, and now we get together three times a week instead of swimming. I'm a new man."

I wrote about George (not using his real name of

course) in a *Forum* magazine article later, and one day I received a phone call from his wife. "I read your article, doctor," she said, "and I know that story was about George." I waited for a tirade. "That's all right, though," she went on. "I know all about George's girl friend. But could you please convince him to see her only once a week? He really needs the swimming too."

Relieved, I complimented her for her understanding and tolerance. She said, "I'd rather have him alive and cheating than faithful and dead."

Another wife once came to me wearing a stunning new mink coat. I complimented her, saying, "Your husband must have made a killing on the stock exchange." "No," she said, "he has a new mistress. He always gives me an expensive present when he gets involved with a new girl." "Do you mind?" I asked. "I think he really needs the girls," she said. "I don't mind as long as he's a good husband and a good father and makes me feel secure."

Which brings me to rule number five: *put first things first.* An understanding and tolerant wife can turn into a raging bitch if she thinks she is going to be badly neglected or discarded. Your wife and family must come first. You owe them this. As Simone de Beauvoir once put it, "Marriage is an obligation, a lover is a luxury." Always take care of your obligations before enjoying your luxuries. Spend weekends and holidays with your family; a wife has a right to become jealous and possessive if she's stuck alone with the kids every Sunday. That's why a married woman is quite possibly your best bet as an extramarital partner; she will have similar family obligations.

Adultery with consent is an ideal partnership—monogamy with sexual freedom. But it won't work if a man has hang-ups about the double standard—if he thinks it's all right for him but not for his wife. It won't work if either partner is the puritanical or jealous type. Unfortunately, many people today are either jealous, puritanical, or still believe in the double standard. For that reason, few couples are able to handle a totally sexually open marriage with success. That's why most extramarital sex is still conducted secretly.

So, rule six is: *Be discreet.* Even the ancients honored this. According to Jewish law, adultery was punishable by death; however there were never any executions for this offense because the conviction could be upheld only if the guilty parties were seen by three or more witnesses. Evidently, no one was ever foolish enough to fulfill these conditions.

So if you are going to be discreet, don't go with your mistress to places where you might be seen by those known to you and your family. Stay away from home territory; don't take unnecessary chances. And, no matter how tempting it might be to talk about it, keep your mouth shut.

The private nature of adultery was best expressed, strangely, by Alessandro Piccolomini, an Italian Renaissance bishop, in 1540 in his book *Good Form for Women:* "Secrecy is the nerve of love."

Dr. James McCartney, a New York psychoanalyst, ignored this rule when he published a paper, "Overt Transference," in the *Journal of Sex Relations* in 1966. He told of many cases in which, as part of this therapy, he became involved sexually with his patients. In 10 percent of his cases, he wrote, he found it necessary to perform such acts as "mutual undressing, genital manipulation, or coitus." This may sound very detached and clinical, but it got Dr. McCartney into a great deal of trouble. Although his credentials as a scientist and therapist were impeccable, and although none of his patients ever complained, the article caused a scandal and McCartney was dropped from the American Psychiatric Association. Before he could clear his reputation, he died from a heart attack.

If you can be discreet, if you are honest with yourself and your partner, if you put your family first, your romance can run its course, with no one hurt and everyone benefiting. But there's one more thing you have to know.

Rule number seven: *Know when to stop*. If your affair interferes with the welfare of your family, your job, or your health, then it must end. If the trouble it causes outweighs the happiness it brings, it must stop. An affair is like a vacation; eventually the vacation is over and it is time to return to the obligations of life.

Speaking of which, in many resorts temporary romances are taken for granted as part of a happy holiday. Temporary alliances form and drift apart, all in a spirit of fun and with no sense of future obligation. One young woman, Tanya, a civil engineer from Leningrad, told George Feifer, an American reporter her plans for her month's holiday. "I'll explore the beach for a day or two. When someone appeals to me, I'll get together with him. I may take a trip with him, camp out with him, rent a room with him. A vacation is dull unless you spend it with somebody new."

When asked if this would interfere with her marriage, she answered, "Nonsense. This is the twentieth century. I've a good marriage and I love my husband—but should I stop living when he's not with me? I hope he has fun on his holidays, too."

YOUNG SWINGERS AND MATE-SWAPPING

I believe it's possible to love more than one person at the same time: your lover or mistress as well as your wife or your husband. The only difference is that extramarital love rarely lasts, but marital love can last forever. Unfortunately, only a few people can enjoy consented-to adultery. You have to be rich to afford a mistress and at the same time satisfy your wife's material needs.

So if you are not an affluent American, you must

learn the art of lovemaking and seduction. But remember, the modern liberated woman is economically independent and can love you and leave you when she finds a better partner.

For husbands who are not wealthy or great lovers, I recommend the third type of adultery, which I've called "cooperative adultery." Perhaps you know of it as the mate-swapping game. It's great to play if you have a fairly attractive wife and are not too old and still physically attractive yourself. But you must know the rules otherwise you could come out a loser. They are as follows:

1. Don't get into it unless you are emotionally and erotically equipped to deal with the consequences.

2. Know your own motivation. Why are you anxious to swap mates?

3. Know your partner. His or her likes and dislikes, what is wanted from you as much as what you want from your partner.

4. Marriage and the family must come first.

5. Never on Sunday. Commit adultery every day of the week if you like, but one day at least should be spent with your family. For the Christian, Sunday should be the Lord's day; for the non-Christian, the agnostic, and the atheist, it should be a day for developing the superego, or the spiritual self. Leave one day to develop your spiritual and intellectual nature, to engage in wholesome recreations not involving sex. So I suggest that the swinger or mate-swapper, instead of staying up all Saturday night, quit his roistering by early morning.

6. Don't kill romance. If your spouse is in the grip of an infatuation, let it run its course. In time, he or she will have had enough and will be glad to get back to the home milieu. As one swinger put it: "This is a risk of the game—and it can't be stopped."

7. Be discreet. A gentleman or a lady *never* talks about his or her love affairs.

8. Avoid the use of stimulants, such as alcohol, marijuana, or LSD, to rouse you to sexual activity.

9. Enjoy sex for sex's sake. Don't use it as a means of escape or for expressing hostility. Nor is it healthy to use a partner to assert your own attractiveness or boost your own ego.

10. Be a good sport. Try to regard swinging as a card game; sometimes you lose, sometimes you break even, occasionally you win. Don't expect to succeed with your partner every time.

11. Know when to stop. If swinging, mate-swapping, or adultery interferes with your family's welfare, call a halt.

12. Home cooking is still the best, though a meal in a restaurant may be different and tasty. It's the same with lovemaking: an affair may have its joys, but the best sex is at home with one's spouse. Make it so. Keep it so.

I have observed that the happiest swingers are those who finish their escapades by achieving sexual satisfaction with their mates at home. Again, I have to emphasize that mate-swapping is feasible only for the young and attractive. You must have strong sex appeal.

Unfortunately swingers could become addicted to swapping. After the initial euphoria wears off, many become obsessed with sex, compelled to try more and more, to do anything and everything. This attitude dehumanizes and depersonalizes sex, and the oversatiated are often left with a boredom and emptiness that drives them to further experimentation. Eventually, this may bring swingers up against the masculinity crisis.

A male's ego may be shattered if his wife finds the other swapper more considerate, more human, and a better lover. The masculinity crisis and other emotional and psychological factors could cause a mental block and precipitate impotence. Usually, these blocks are temporary, but they can be of long duration or even become permanent.

A simple example of how a mental block can develop

is the man who leaves a hotel after having had just two cocktails. A friend sees him on the street and tells him he's drunk. This makes him think: "I've never gotten high on two drinks before. Maybe after so many years of drinking, there are some changes taking place in me I haven't become aware of." But he shrugs it off—after all, one swallow doesn't make a spring and one opinion isn't necessarily a valid diagnosis. But, a block farther on, another friend also tells him that he's drunk. So he immediately decides he'd better go home and lie down.

It's the same with sexual performance. Usually. adulterers get together because they are attracted to each other, whereas at a sex party people form pairs even though one party may not be attracted to the other. Quite often, a man will be a poor lover or fail completely, especially if his partner does not cooperate; she may then tell everyone that he is a failure in the bedroom. If this happens too often, the man's performance may be so affected that he becomes temporarily impotent. Another cause of impotence can be the expectation and criticism of a sexually sophisticated female swinger. What man wants to be judged or criticized in bed? He wants encouragement or praise and that's all.

ALOHA, I LOVE YOU, GOOD-BYE

One of the most important aspects of a love affair, whether it is brief or prolonged, is its ending. The final parting can make so much difference—if bitter, the happy memories are destroyed. If you wish to preserve and maintain all the benefits of happy memories that such an affair can bring, you must know how to say good-bye.

Parting should be gentle, without recriminations, and most important, properly timed. There is a natural ending to every affair—a day when parting becomes necessary because both lovers have received everything they can from the relationship and because holding on will spoil what has gone before. Prolonging an affair beyond this point serves no purpose and usually leads to disillusionment and disappointment.

It is not easy, I admit, to be sure when this point has been reached, and it is often not easy to act even when you know the time has come. The stories of Kenneth and Mei-Ling and Barbara and Peter are beautiful examples of such a parting.

Kenneth and Mei-Ling. Kenneth, a fifty-one-year-old professor of psychology, had shortness of breath, high blood pressure, and chest pains after exertion. He was going through the male menopause and developed sexual problems. He was advised to take a three-week vacation in Hawaii in order to get away from his normal routine and worries.

The very word *Hawaii* bespeaks romance. The profusion of perfumed flowers, the exotic fruits and swaying palm trees, the long sandy beaches, the constant warmth of the tropical sky, the endless pulse of the mighty Pacific, the throbbing rhythm of the hula and Hawaiian music, and the casual intermingling of ages, nationalities, and cultures—all these combine to give the islands an aura of mystery and magic. Hawaii is a land of enchantment and Ken found a miracle there.

Shortly after his arrival he met a lovely tour guide named Mei-Ling, who was a college student majoring in psychology.

He and Mei-Ling met late one moonlit night by the hotel swimming pool. They intended only to talk, but the spell of the evening carried them away. With the music from the hotel drifting by, they swam alone in the abandoned pool and then began to kiss and touch each other. For the first time in many months Ken had an erection. Almost afraid to believe his good fortune, he began to remove Mei-Ling's bikini. She responded passionately and they made love in the pool. The combination of the unusual setting and their need for each other produced a heavenly sexual experience.

After that enchanted evening they met every night. Their relationship was not only sexual but intellectual and spiritual as well. Mei-Ling was torn between the Oriental traditions of her family and her own desire to be independent. Ken was able to give her insight into herself and her needs. They discussed politics, philosophy, religion, every topic that interested them. They exchanged minds and hearts. And every other night they made love. Each time their lovemaking was joy for them both. Ken felt happy, healthy, rejuvenated.

At last the day of his departure approached. The night before he was to leave, Ken declared his love to Mei-Ling. He asked her to come to his college to study. He offered to pay her expenses and promised that if they were still in love after six months he would divorce his wife and marry her.

She kissed him gently and affectionately and whispered "Aloha." She explained to him, "Aloha means not only 'welcome' and 'good-bye' but also 'I love you.' We Hawaiians believe that love never lasts forever, so when we are in love we need to know how to say good-bye. I shall remember you for the rest of my life. You have helped me to find myself and made me a woman. You are a wonderful man and your wife and your children must miss you very much." She kissed him again and once more whispered "Aloha."

Although he knew this precious episode was over, Ken suddenly felt elated. He was loved by a beautiful and intelligent girl; they had shared their souls and been blessed by Venus. His masculine crisis was cured forever. Ken kissed Mei-Ling's hand and told her how much he admired her in every way.

"Now I believe your theory, Dr. Scheimann," Ken told me after his return. "Sex can save your heart—I feel young again—my chest pains and constriction are gone. Mei-Ling was wise enough to know that permanent love belongs to a good wife and mother even if a man turns to someone else because of needs she can't fill. Mei-Ling will always be one of my happiest memories."

Only when you possess Mei-Ling's wisdom, only when you know how to say good-bye, can your love affair have a happy ending.

Barbara and Peter found this out. When a woman falls in love with a married man or even a single man who is unwilling to commit himself, she must learn to say aloha. When Barbara realized that Peter was saying his good-bye by seeing other women, she wrote him the following letter:

Dearest Darling Peter,

Love, we have had the most beautiful year together. I never thought in my wildest dreams how happy and full of affection I could be. I used to think of myself as a cold person but you saw through that and gave me so many hugs and kisses and lots of love that I was able to give my all, my body and soul, and everything which comes with loving another.

The second time we went out I went to bed with you. I have never done that before and I guess I was very lonely and starving for affection. But you know, I'm not sorry I gave in so easily that night. You needed it so very badly and so did I.

Darling Peter, I don't know what has happened to us. It seems like my world has come crashing down around me. Honey, I think you know how I feel about your going to bed with other girls. I tried to accept it and I tried real hard, but I have too much respect for my own person and body to share them with you after you have been with someone else the night before.

Darling, I think you love me too, but you must find that out by yourself. Remember me by all the good times we had and not by the arguments we have had the past month.

Honey, I love you very much, but I cannot and will not take second place to anyone and that is where you have put me. If you ever decide that I am the one you love, my arms will be open and waiting. Until then,

All my love,
Barbara

Barbara was able to express her love and to remember all the good she had derived from the relationship. She was hurt but not bitter, and she was willing to welcome Peter back, but without destroying herself and her love.

Women in love, especially with coronary-prone men, should take the examples of Mei-Ling and Barbara to heart. Knowing when and how to say good-bye can prevent not only broken hearts but heart attacks as well.

13

SEX
AFTER
A
HEART
ATTACK

VOLTAIRE SAID THAT "PLEASURE IS THE OBJECT, THE DUTY, and the goal of all rational creatures." If he is correct, if pleasure really is our object, our duty, and our goal, we must ask ourselves a searching question: can, or should, a man experience the same sexual pleasures after a heart attack as he did before it?

Very few doctors today recommend complete abstinence, except for the period immediately after a heart attack. Many in fact believe, as I do, that complete sexual abstinence can be deleterious to health. Drs. Herman K. Hellerstein and Ernest H. Friedman are emphatic; they say that "deprivation of sexual function due to heart disease may be catastrophic."

A return to normal sexual functioning presents few problems if the patient is happily married and enjoys a healthy sex life with his wife. But what if the heart patient's wife refuses—whatever her reasons—to have intercourse with him? Especially to the Apollo, coronary-prone personality, the excitement and stimulation of healthy extramarital sex can be beneficial. But what if he is deprived of this stimulation because of mild heart disease, or because his wife fails to satisfy him, or because he is suffering from "middle-aged anxiety" and turns against her? Then the patient is in a potentially dangerous position.

What are the effects of the male climacteric? A man in his middle or late forties is undergoing biological and psychological changes. He knows that he no longer possesses the same sexual power and energy he once did; he knows that he is now "middle-aged" and that his youth is gone forever. In a desperate attempt to stop the clock, even to turn it back, he searches for romance and the illusion of being young again. Ironically, often the new woman in his life is not as attractive or as desirable as his wife. Many a woman who could understand her husband having a fling with a beautiful young blonde is astonished to find "the other woman" is middle-aged herself and far from stunning. The new woman's irresistible charm lies in the very fact that she is "new"; she provides proof of his prowess— he is sexually attractive; he is still exciting to women. She is a means of reaffirming his masculinity and is not an individual in her own right; she is valued more for what she does for his ego than for herself.

Just because a man has had a heart attack, he is not immune to these feelings. Indeed, a coronary may intensify them. A man accustomed to extramarital sex may seek to prove that he is still the same man he was. Even a hitherto faithful husband may suddenly feel that he missed something and be driven to find out exactly what that something is.

John L. is an excellent example of this. Like many other men, he experienced his moment of truth after a heart attack. A typical hard-driving mesomorph, he had given up the pleasures of sex in order to achieve power, status, and wealth. His determination to achieve this worldly success had left him little time or energy to devote to his family.

In the beginning this presented no problem. While the children were small and took up most of her attention, his wife did not object to his goals; she, too, desperately wanted him to succeed. But when the children began growing up and causing her the usual problems, she resented his absence. She insisted that he spend more time with the children but unfortunately he was too exhausted to do so. Because she felt neglected by her husband, she began nagging him for more time and more attention. He in turn responded by devoting renewed time and energy to his career. Their sexual life was deteriorating, but John didn't care; he wanted power more than sex, status more than family.

He started to eat more, drink more, smoke more; he had less recreation, less relaxation, less pleasure. Then he suffered his heart attack. While in the hospital he was forced to give up all the pleasures he had substituted for love—he could not drink or smoke or indulge in food. He was able to tolerate this strict regimen because his determination to get well was as forceful as his determination to succeed.

While in the hospital John was attended by a charming and attractive nurse who liked him because, like Apollo, he was a likable fellow. She was especially attentive to him. She was always reassuring and told him often that she had had patients far more ill than he was who had fully recovered. John experienced new feelings, new sensations, and an erotic awakening because of a young woman

who cared about him and who was interested in his welfare. He felt erotically stimulated if she only took his
pulse. The daily alcohol rub she gave him was pure delight.
He began to realize that he had been missing a part of
life he had last known and relished when he was young,
and now he wanted to feel young again. He wanted and
craved sex again.

One day he grabbed the nurse and kissed her.
"Johnny," she said, "be a good boy. When you recover you
can have all the kisses you want." "Even from you?" he
asked. To reassure him she answered yes and kissed him
very lightly. Two weeks later he confessed that he was in
love with her. When he learned that she was a divorcee
with two children and no boyfriend, he asked her to become his mistress. He told her, "I can't marry you, but I
can make you and your children happy. I will buy you a
home and give you everything you need." She didn't take
him seriously, but told him she would consider his offer
if he felt the same after he was well. She confessed that
she was attracted to him. John was willing and able to give
up drinking, smoking, and overeating, but he didn't want
to give up his newfound interest in sex and, more particularly, Margaret, his nurse.

Now, once again, I raise the question: Should this
man have played the hermit and closed his mind to the
possibilities of such an affair? I have discussed this question
with several of my colleagues and almost all of them,
despite the deeply ingrained puritanism of medical men
in general, replied that John could have benefited greatly
—provided, they agreed, that he kept his promise not to
break up his home and give up his family, that he was
completely recovered, and, most important, that he didn't
become too emotionally involved with Margaret. A sudden
heart-rending ending to a passionate romance, they felt,
might well be hazardous for him.

"What," I asked these doctors, "would you advise John
to do if he were your patient?" The overwhelming majority

replied that they would advise against such an affair. As one doctor put it, "I couldn't advise him to commit adultery —the vast majority of men who die during intercourse are committing adultery—it's too dangerous and I don't want to be responsible."

Is this attitude justified? Is this doctor correct, or is this another example of medical puritanism in action— willing to allow something in theory but forbidding it in practice?

Recently Dr. Lenore Zohman, the director of cardio- pulmonary (heart-lung) rehabilitation at New York's Mon- tefiore Hospital, stated that "eight out of ten men who die during intercourse do so while engaging with partners other than their wives." Such dire a warning, which is likely to produce untold anxiety, is especially unfortunate when it is not strictly validated. If I, a male sexologist with a liberal attitude toward adultery, have difficulty in getting complete sexual confessions from my male patients, can a female doctor with a negative predilection get trustworthy answers? Since the men upon whom she bases her statistics are, moreover, dead, they cannot speak for themselves.

In addition, Dr. Zohman's messenger-of-doom warn- ing overlooks the following questions:

(1) How many of these men had hearts so badly damaged that any kind of exertion (a two-mile walk, for example) might have killed them?

(2) How many of them experienced pain at the slightest exertion?

(3) How many of them suffered guilt and anxiety about committing adultery? (Indeed, what was their pre- vious extramarital affair pattern?)

(4) How many of them were impotent when they tried to engage in extramarital sex (impotency, of course, can produce an enormous amount of stress)?

Although Dr. Zohman is not alone in her views, many doctors have made different observations and have come to different conclusions. Dr. B. J. Allenstein of the City of Hope National Medical Center in Duarte, California, for example, says: "I seriously doubt that intercourse with anyone (wife or mistress) would really make any difference. . . . I don't see any problem here in relation to cheating."

Dr. Herman K. Hellerstein, a noted cardiologist, stated: "The commonly accepted opinion that sudden death often occurs during sexual intercourse is not supported by the available facts. Sexual activity was associated with sudden death in only 3 of 500 subjects with arteriosclerotic heart disease, and in 2 of these 3, extramaritally."

As you can see, the experts are far from agreeing with each other about the hazards of sex, and particularly extramarital sex, after a heart attack. Physicians who share Dr. Zohman's viewpoint should have been taken aback by the account in *Sexual Behavior* of a coronary patient who was helped by adultery. Dr. William S. Kroger described the case of a patient who was married to a woman who was both frigid and selfish and who could not be won over despite the patient's fervent attempts. After being advised to change his own attitudes (since it was evident that his wife could not or would not change hers), the patient found partial relief by acquiring a mistress.

In the face of these conflicting statistics and opinions, I must stress again and again my own conviction that adultery is an explosive; it can be as dangerous as dynamite but, taken in small doses and with the proper precautions observed, it can be as helpful and as needed as the nitroglycerine that often is prescribed for heart patients.

What did become of John and Margaret? In the end there was no love affair. Margaret knew from experience that men tend to make promises in order to obtain sexual gratification and often break them after they are satisfied. She was reluctant to have an affair with a married man. John, too, was afraid of having a real affair, especially one which he knew had little chance of ending happily. Once he had recovered and his passion had settled down somewhat, he decided that he "preferred life instead of love." He became health conscious; he didn't take up smoking again, cut down on the fat in his diet, and curtailed his drinking. He did not, however, give up sex. After receiving his doctor's permission, John resumed sexual relations with his wife. Because she could not give him satisfactory fulfillment, he began visiting a reliable and friendly call girl twice a month. In this way he received the benefits of healing sex from both his wife and the call girl.

What made these experiences "healing sex"? John felt no fear, no guilt, no anxiety, and no emotional involvement. This kind of sex is like sport and exercise—body and mind are rested and refreshed. John recovered completely and was able to resume all his normal activities without any difficulties. He lived a healthy and safe life because he had significantly reduced all his coronary risk factors.

For John, adultery was not dynamite but nitroglycerine.

After studying many patients like John and drawing upon the experiences of other physicians, I offer the following guidelines for sex after a heart attack, based on questions most often asked by coronary patients. But I must emphasize that *your own physician must be consulted before you engage in sexual activity.*

Each patient is different and, while I can offer general information and guidelines, only a doctor familiar with your coronary condition and your medical history can give you specific instructions tailored to your needs.

> QUESTION: When can I resume my sexual activities?
> ANSWER: Resumption of sexual activity depends on your general health and on the extent of your recovery. It depends on your mental attitude toward sex and sometimes on the attitude of your doctor.

A recent issue of *Sexology* discussed the five classifications used by doctors to describe damaged hearts.

Class A: No restrictions on physical activity.

Class B: No restrictions on ordinary physical activity but unusually competitive efforts are prohibited.

Class C: Strenuous work or play must be avoided and ordinary activity moderately restricted.

Class D: Marked restriction on ordinary physical activity.

Class E: Complete rest required; all exertion to be avoided.

Only your own doctor can tell which classification fits your condition and how much sexual activity you can indulge in.

If you are completely recovered, have no symptoms (such as chest pain, palpitations, and shortness of breath), if your blood pressure is normal, if your electrocardiogram remains stable, and if you can perform other physical exercises, you can probably resume sexual activities.

It should be stressed that all cardiologists are not in agreement as to what constitutes recovery. Dr. Perry Blumberg, for example, says that sex may be attempted if the patient can walk three blocks briskly without any symptoms. Dr. Nanette Wenger feels that sex is no more demanding than many routine activities such as climbing up a flight of stairs. Dr. John Naughton says that intercourse requires about the same energy as "walking briskly at a rate of 2 to 2½ miles per hour, or perhaps walking up a flight of steps." Your doctor may have his own definition. Most doctors agree that the energy expenditure of sexual intercourse falls into the mild to moderate category.

If you can pass whatever exercise test your physician prefers and if you can handle your usual activities, then you can most likely resume sex after nine to twelve weeks. Some doctors recommend a longer period of abstinence of course, but in general three months is considered sufficient.

Some medical men, like myself, believe that you

shouldn't wait three months if sex is vitally important to you. If you happen to be an ectomorph you can probably wait three months, or even a year, with little difficulty, but if you are the Apollo type, such a long wait may cause its own (and more serious) problem. For one person, abstention from intercourse may seem a small sacrifice, while for another individual such abstinence may seem the equivalent of impotency and may produce dangerous anxiety and depression. As Dr. Robert A. Bruce says, "Sometimes abstinence because of fear generates anxiety and tension that may be more stressful than carefully paced intercourse with an understanding spouse."

A comparison may be drawn between sex and work. Dr. Ray H. Rosenman says that, if sex becomes work, "perhaps the patient should wait a little more than nine to twelve weeks." It seems very likely, however, that the opposite is also true. For some individuals sex, like work, is an obligation. These are the people who should be careful about resuming their activities. For others, sex, like work, is necessary for self-fulfillment. These are the ones who doubtless should resume their activities as soon as possible.

Drs. Risteard Mulcahy and Noel Hickey reported on a series of Irish coronary patients who returned to work earlier than is customary. This quick return "was not associated with an increased long-term morbidity or mortality in these patients. In fact, the mean annual mortality of the group . . . compared favourably with mortality reports of similar subjects from other centres."

Drs. Mulcahy and Hickey felt that many doctors and patients are too cautious and attribute this to the "notion that exercise, physical work or employment responsibilities are harmful to patients with a history of coronary heart disease, a notion which has no scientific or epidemiological basis of support."

At St. Vincent's Hospital in Dublin, where this study was carried out, rehabilitation begins at the moment of admission. Early recovery and fast return to a normal life are assumed to be routine. The coronary patient is encouraged to begin walking four or five days after admission and a program of gradually increased exercise is started.

Another study, done at the Chelmsford group of hospitals in England, indicates that prolonged rest is not only no more safe than earlier ambulation, but may in fact be more hazardous. Early recovery and fast return to normal life lessens the risk of respiratory problems and thrombo-embolic complications and benefits the patient psychologically, economically, and socially.

Another factor to be considered is the attitude of the patient's wife. If prolonged abstinence depresses her, says Dr. Henry N. Massie, the "hostility and lovelessness in the relationship could be far more threatening than the excitement of love-making."

If sex is very important to you or your wife, or to both of you, and if your physical symptoms have subsided, ask your doctor if you can resume sexual activities early in the post-attack period.

QUESTION: I read somewhere that there are special positions that can prevent danger during intercourse. Is that true?

ANSWER: Sexual positions undoubtedly can make a difference in the amount of energy used. One position that involves minimum strain for either partner is the side-by-side position. Neither partner has to bear the weight of the other and there is a good deal of variety possible. The amount of movement is more important, however, than the position itself. Each couple must decide which positions they like best; they may choose to avoid the most strenuous of them (sitting and standing positions). These precautions apply only to those with moderate to severe heart impairment. If the impairment is slight, sexual intercourse is no more dangerous (often less so, in fact) than hundreds of other daily activities.

QUESTION: Before my heart attack I occasionally cheated on my wife. My doctor tells me not to fool around anymore. What is your opinion?

ANSWER: I always emphasize that adultery is dangerous if one has guilt or anxiety about it. Dr. John Naughton, quoted earlier, agrees that the fear and guilt often caused by adultery may make intercourse far more stressful than the simple act of sex itself. The fact that you asked this question reveals to me that you do have doubt or fear. If you are going to engage in extramarital sex, you must have a positive attitude toward it. I would recommend, therefore, that you follow your doctor's advice and remain faithful to your wife.

QUESTION: Is group sex dangerous after a heart attack?

ANSWER: This depends on how much your heart was damaged and on the extent of your recovery. If your case was a mild one and if you found group sex relaxing and pleasurable, you are free to continue—at your own risk. You must bear in mind that, despite your previous experience with group sex, your wife may become anxious and this can affect you. Others, finding out about your heart attack, may warn members of the group not to have sex with you. This rejection may cause new stress. My advice would be to forget swinging and to concentrate on having a satisfactory sex life with your wife. Perhaps swinging won't cause another heart attack, but it didn't prevent the first one either.

QUESTION: A friend of mine, also a coronary patient, uses poppers. He says that poppers are the best defense against a second heart attack. Would you advise using them?

ANSWER: Many doctors advocate the use of nitroglycerine tablets placed under the tongue for prevention of chest pains during intercourse. Very
little, however, has been written about amyl nitrite
(poppers). According to Dr. Donald B. Lauria,
amyl nitrite can delay ejaculation and thus prolong
orgasm, but he also stresses that it has dangerous,
and even life-threatening, side effects.

Even if these side effects were not present, I do not
believe that prolonged orgasm or a long sex act is advis-
able for former heart patients. We know too little about
what the drug can do and the coronary patient cannot risk
the "adverse cardiovascular effects" cited by Dr. Lauria.

Amyl nitrite is often used during intercourse by members of the drug subculture (and often in combination
with other drugs). While mixing amyl nitrite with marijuana or lysergic acid diethylamide (LSD) may produce
fascinating reactions, it is more likely to prove extremely
dangerous.

It is interesting to note that poppers are particularly
popular among homosexuals. Why should this be? We simply do not know. Doctors interested in the correlation between sex and heart attacks would have to conduct a
study of the rate of heart attack among sexually active
homosexuals who use poppers versus the rate among sexually active heterosexuals who don't use them.

QUESTION: Dr. Scheimann, you seem to be contra-
dicting yourself. You've said in the past that sex
is like dynamite, but that when used in small doses
sex can be as helpful as nitroglycerine. Why don't
you prescribe adultery for men who have had
heart attacks?

ANSWER: This is a very pertinent question. I don't
prescribe adultery for heart patients because I
don't have enough data to do so. I know many

hundreds of coronary-prone men who are enjoying extramarital sex who have not had heart attacks, but until I know of many hundreds of men who have had heart attacks who are enjoying adultery and showing no adverse effects, I am reluctant to prescribe it.

QUESTION: I am completely recovered from my heart attack and I have a positive mental attitude toward adultery. My doctor has given me permission to have extramarital sex. Nevertheless, I would like to know the best way to prevent another heart attack.

ANSWER: Although I have emphasized repeatedly that sex can save your heart, we doctors know that *there is no medicine absolutely guaranteed to prevent heart attacks.* We can only offer suggestions and precautions.

These are some individuals who should never commit adultery:

(1) Men who have not fully recovered from their heart attacks and who have not received permission from their doctors to resume normal activities.

(2) Men who have guilt and anxiety.

(3) Men who develop chest pains or other symptoms during sex.

(4) Men who weigh 20 percent over their correct weight (as determined by an insurance table or doctor's chart).

(5) Men with significant hypertension.

(6) Men who smoke ten or more cigarettes a day or who use comparable amounts of cigar or pipe tobacco.

(7) Men with elevated cholesterol or serum lipid levels.

(8) Men who don't exercise.

(9) Men in psychic stress situations.

(10) Men with a low tolerance for frustration.

Men who are not included in the above list should pay careful attention to the following precautions. These four "rights" may save you from a second heart attack.

The Right Time. Select a time when you are not likely to be tired; make a date for morning rather than evening, or select a time when your work load is light. Do not choose a time when you have overeaten or when you have a cold or upset stomach. Remember that while extramarital sex is a tranquilizer before a heart attack, it isn't one afterward, so be sure you are relaxed and not tense. If you feel tense when you have a date, take a nitroglycerine tablet or have a mild drink (excess alcohol, however, can make it difficult to achieve an erection, so drink sparingly!).

The Right Place. For your rendezvous, don't choose the backseat of your car, or a romantic haystack, or a place where your office can reach you. Select a spot where you can have sex in comfort and privacy. An air-conditioned motel away from your neighborhood is an excellent choice (heat and humidity add to stress and air conditioning helps you to relax).

The Right Way. Before your heart attack you were free to be adventurous and daring; you could perform any sexual act that struck your fancy, try any new position, and so on. After a heart attack you must be more careful and choose techniques that cause the least strain and exertion. Avoid extensive foreplay and select nonfatiguing positions that offer satisfaction in a relatively brief period of time.

The most important part of your new lovemaking technique is proper breathing. Proper breathing is not only healthful, it enhances pleasure. As Dr. Alexander Lowen says in his book *Pleasure*, "The better one breathes, the more alive one is. . . . We do not realize that inadequate breathing reduces the vitality. . . . The inability to breathe fully and deeply is also responsible for the failure to

achieve full satisfaction in sex." Breathing also helps reduce tension. If you begin to feel anxious or strained during lovemaking, hold still for a moment and breathe deeply.
Almost immediately you will begin to relax. You can then
return to lovemaking with renewed vigor and enthusiasm.

The Right Attitude. Before your heart attack presumably
you could enjoy the challenge of an extramarital encounter
or an exciting affair. You were free to be a magnificent
lover and win any woman you wanted. You could take
special pleasure in winning that "hard-to-get" woman. Now
you must change your attitude. You must think in terms of
gratifying yourself first; your partner must be, to some degree, a sex object, who is willing to satisfy you. For this
reason it is important to choose the right partner.

The *Ananga Ranga,* or Hindu book of love, written
over a thousand years ago, still offers good advice in regard to adultery. The translation made by Sir Richard Bur-
ton lists seven reasons for refraining from adultery, but
then goes on to say, "despite all the ignominy, disgrace,
and contumely, it is absolutely necessary to have connection with the wife of another under certain circumstances."
The Hindus believed that adultery was preferable to obsession. If you can think of nothing but the woman you
desire, if you feel that you are going mad, if your health
suffers, if you cannot carry out the regular business of
life—then, says the *Ananga Ranga,* you should commit
adultery.

My advice for the choosing of a proper partner for
extramarital sex:

Don't choose another man's wife unless she has an
open marriage. Don't choose the wife of a close friend, or
the wife of your worst enemy. You'd be asking for trouble.
Don't have sex with a woman who has difficulty in being
aroused. Choose a woman who is a "sexpot" or who does
not place much importance on orgasm. Many women are
altruistic enough to find sufficient gratification in pleasing

a man. Find a woman who cares not only for you but for your heart. There are many lonely single girls, divorcees, and widows who will be happy with your companionship as long as you give them affection and a little love. Many women are happy to have a sex partner, or to be subsidized, even when the sexual relationship is not exactly what they would choose.

A business executive who was my patient told me that his secretary had become his nurse after he had a heart attack. She saw to it that he took his pills, watched his weight, made him get enough rest, and limited his appointments. She arranged his travels, made his reservations, and saw that he was properly entertained. I told him that I had read of an escort service which provides pretty girls for tired and lonely businessmen and asked him whether his secretary could make such arrangements for him. He laughed and said that he had made the same suggestion to her. She replied that he should remember his coronaries—he didn't need to fool around with an escort service when he had his wife and her to take care of him!

As you can see, sex need not be less pleasurable after a heart attack. Your techniques and approaches will be different but they can be just as much fun. Sometimes they can be even better than they were. A heart attack is not the end of your sex life, but a new beginning.

14

IF
YOU ARE
A WOMAN

In the fifth century the Greek playwright Euripides wrote: "Man's best possession is a sympathetic wife." This is still true today (substitute "greatest asset" for "possession" though). And I venture it will be so tomorrow and for all time. How often I have met extraordinary men of great promise only to find later that they had even more, or just as, extraordinary wives. Each time I would say to myself—yes, it figures.

Womankind has long been the symbol and the guardian of the home. Because the modern-day housewife of necessity is a cook, bottle washer, nurse, chauffeur, housekeeper, accountant, interior decorator, and so on, in short a Jacqueline-of-all-trades, much is expected of her. On a popular TV show, "To Tell the Truth," one truth-telling panelist was a young man who had just finished a study at Cornell University. He concluded that the average modern housewife would earn better than $9,000 were she paid for such services at today's going rates. This figure seems too modest but in fact she's priceless, because you can't buy her loyalty, determination, and tolerance and the positive example she sets for others in the household.

Too often this was taken for granted. Thus her role was maligned and her chores seemed demeaning. Now that women have asserted their rights and many have a family and a career, will the female role—the mother image as we once knew it—drastically change? Yes and no. Yes, it will change, just by her independent salary which automatically makes us recognize her value. And, in most cases, we must add the $9,000 to this figure. No, it won't change —it's contrary to Mother Nature, at least for mothers. Life holds just a few rare diadems and one of them is, and always will be, the love, the friendship, the understanding, and compassion of a good mother. With the passing of a mother, she takes something from the earth reserved for her alone.

Too many husbands, too business-minded, cannot appreciate a sympathetic or helpful wife. In their offices, in pursuit of greater assets toward wealth and status, they lose sight of their most valuable asset—back home. Inevitably this leads to unhappiness for all.

In terms of the investor, a good wife is far more valuable than a blue-chip stock because money cannot buy health or prevent heart attacks, but a loving wife can. She is good currency. We have seen that the lowest heart fatality figures by far are for happily married men and women. But the highest by far are unhappily marrieds— even higher than the widowed or divorced, who are less healthy than singles. So if you wish to live, *marital happiness is the single best prescription for health.*

Just as a man needs a woman, a woman needs a man in her life. Naturally, she wants to keep him healthy.

What can she do to make sure that he stays well, especially in their later years of long life together? Let's see if we can fully establish the power of a woman to prolong her husband's life.

The most important thing, of course, is to find the right partner. I know this from my own experience. My first marriage was unhappy because my wife and I were not right for each other and consequently I was not a good husband. If you have a good husband, you are fortunate; your happiness is that much more assured. But if your husband is average, you can teach him to be better. To achieve this, you must modify the traditional "love, honor, and obey," to "satisfy, understand, and compromise."

THE MALE MYTH

We know that men are not the strong, tough fellows they like to appear. Society has taught them what a man ought to be, and they are trying to live up to that unrealistic image. In fact, from birth to death the male is weaker than the female. Perhaps nature has arranged for more males than females being conceived because fewer males are carried to full term and fewer still survive the hazards of birth, infancy, and early childhood. All through childhood, girls are taller, stronger, and healthier than boys. During adolescence, boys seem to catch up but, despite the fact that they become taller and heavier, they are still physiologically weaker. This difference is intensified in the years after menopause. Estrogen relieves many menopausal symptoms for women; however, the male hormone does not ease the aging process for men. Women who worry about losing their looks can more artfully use cosmetics and even resort to plastic surgery; such aids may seem permissible for actors and other male entertainers, but there remains an uneasy suspicion that "real men" don't go in for such things.

Men die at earlier ages than women. Business reversals or a serious illness may convince a man that he is old. The resulting depression may lead to further illness, to alcoholism, or to the feeling that his life is over—that there is nothing left for him but death. Today the number of widows is steadily increasing and, because of the shortage of men in the older age groups, the possibilities of remarriage for widows are steadily dwindling. Today's lonely widow (or those divorcees who would have had it otherwise) could have kept her man—healthy and happy.

I know of at least one psychiatrist who considers the American male an easy candidate for homosexuality, impotency, and alcoholism. Can this frightening picture be verified? At least part can. Today men are affected by impotency at ever younger ages. The new aggressive attitude toward sex and the mounting masculine crisis combine to produce this ego-threatening ailment—one that strikes men at the very heart of their self-image. It is difficult for a woman to understand the psychic importance of potency. A woman can engage in sex when she's not in the mood, even against her will. She will enjoy sex to varying degrees depending on circumstances, but she is always *biologically* ready for it.

It is not that simple for men. The mechanisms of erection are a complicated blend of physiologic and psychologic factors and it is relatively easy to disturb them. Since a man feels that sex constitutes the very essence of manhood (a real man makes many conquests), loss of sexual potency can destroy his sense of identity. Women must try to understand how damaging impotency can be, and they must avoid contributing to it by undermining the male ego. The man who cannot relax and enjoy sex because he does not measure up to his wife's demands, because she does not reach orgasm every time, or because he is a failure in bed, is a strong candidate for impotency.

Men suffer from loneliness just as much as women do.
You may wonder how this can be true. After all, men go
out into the world, they meet new and stimulating people,
they make friends. It is women who stay home with no one
but the children for company. It is true that most men have
more acquaintances than their wives, but acquaintances do
not solve the problem of loneliness. Only friends can do
this, and the average man has business companions and
fellow workers rather than friends. The business world is
often cutthroat, and it is difficult to trust the man who is
after your contract, your promotion, or even your job.

The working man rarely has time to make friends—he
is too busy earning a living, commuting, trying to succeed.
All too often he has little time to spare for his family;
friends cannot be fitted in at all.

Common interests of a noncompetitive type promote
friendship, but the ambitious man has no time to develop
such interests. One sad example familiar to everyone is the
elderly man whose work has been his whole life. Once he
retires, or even slows down, he finds that he has no other
interests.

In the United States culture is generally cultivated
more by women than men. When women attend lectures,
visit art museums, and go to concerts, their men look on
indulgently; maleness discourages men from doing so even
if they have the time, energy, and interest. Watching a
baseball or football game is the more acceptable recreation
for men. A man may enjoy sports events but he cannot
structure his life around them. As he grows older, he gives
up participation in the more active sports. He then needs
activities that will enrich his life and add meaning and
dimension to it. A love of art or music, or a dedication to
any hobby that he finds fascinating, will keep him enthusiastic and young at heart. Too few men turn in this direc-
tion.

The new consciousness of women and the sexual
revolution (the relaxation of the double standard, the

"new morality," and, of course, the pill) have remade American life almost overnight. No one expected these rapid changes, and most of us don't know quite what to feel, or do, or say about them. Usually, the American man was stunned and rather shocked by this new attitude on the part of the American woman, and quite unprepared to fulfill his wife's liberated emotional and sexual demands. Even the male swinger who professes to delight in the new freedom for women—since he now expects an abundance of sex partners—is threatened. He no longer "makes" girls, seducing them through his own cleverness and irresistible charm; he is now required to "satisfy" *them,* and if he fails they will not hesitate to tell him so in no uncertain terms. As Phyllis and Eberhard Kronhausen remark in their *Sex Histories of American College Men,* "It seems as if the male sex has not had sufficient time to assimilate the changes in the sexual behavior of women."

Until quite recently a man's wife was not only his inferior, she was often his property. Sex was a man's right and a women's duty. Now this is changing. A woman can refuse to make love, she can control her pregnancies, she can have affairs without fear. In the past she was a slave; now she controls not only her own sexual destiny, but her husband's as well—and all men need her affection, tenderness, and warm, loving sex, the coronary-prone man most of all.

TODAY'S LIBERATED WOMAN

In this revolutionary new world, we must undergo a metamorphosis. Sex must become free without being mechanistic or dehumanized. The marriage contract must become more liberal without losing its sanctity. The modern woman must become liberated without hurting her partner. Liberated sex and marriage are the best antidotes for the troubled man—and woman—of today.

If you pride yourself on being an old-fashioned wife, one who believes that the husband is the head of the house, and if you are married to a forceful, dominant man, you can satisfy his need for admiration and respect with few reservations. If, however, you are, or want to be, an equal partner, you may find your path more difficult.

The most important thing to remember is that there is no inherent conflict between being liberated and being feminine. Indeed, only the truly liberated woman can be fully feminine, and the old-fashioned wife can be just as liberated as her more vocal sisters.

A truly liberated woman can be known not by what she does but by what she is. A woman who finds happiness in being a housewife, who derives contentment from her role of wife and mother, and who does not desire a career, or even a job, finds liberation in her own home. A woman who takes a job because she feels that a liberated image requires it, that she is a failure because she is happy to be at home, is no more liberated than a woman forced to remain home when she really wants to work.

If you are content to stay home and are not compelled to work for financial reasons, you are a lucky woman. You have the time to pursue your own interests, the time to watch your children grow, and the time to make your home a real haven from the rigors of the world.

But what, you ask, if you are not happy staying home —should you give up your dreams and sacrifice your own goals to domesticity? No, you should not (a miserable wife makes a miserable home), but you must be careful how you go about running your career.

There are hundreds of thousands of women who resent being "office widows"; if you find your husband's dedication to business hard to accept, it will be much harder for your husband to be an "office widower." Our society has taught him to believe that he should be your main concern, and outside interests are difficult for him to tolerate. For both partners' happiness, therefore, it is extremely important for the career woman to retain her femininity and to avoid being the aggressive, castrating woman. A man can understand and even be proud of his wife's success as long as he knows that he is necessary to her. A woman can be an executive or a brain surgeon and remain completely feminine, just as a man can be an artist, a poet, or a ballet dancer while remaining completely masculine.

Telling a man you love him because he is your life, because he is all you have, places a great burden on him (how can he ever measure up to that?); you must tell him instead, "I am not entirely dependent on you. I have other interests and other satisfactions, but they make me appreciate you more. I am *me* whether you are here or not, but I am *more me* when I am with you."

This is the greatest compliment you can give your husband. What man would not be thrilled and gratified to find that he enriches his wife's life, that he helps bring out the best in her, and that his presence is felt in everything she does? To make each other "more me" is the essence of love and liberation. People in love ought to enhance each other; only men and women who are liberated can give to each other fully and freely, without reservation and resentment.

As a woman, one way for you to reach this happy state is to become sexually responsive. You must learn the art of making love. "One night of love" can help you as much as it helped Mary (see chapter 11). Of the many books that have been written about the sexually emancipated woman, they can inspire but they cannot teach. You can learn to be sensuous only by participating in sex in a new way. You must, like Mary, shed your inhibitions and fears and learn to truly enjoy sex. Even if you don't love your husband, you probably want to protect his health for the sake of the family. If your husband is stubbornly unwilling to experiment with you, you can do what many other women do—learn with another man. Mme de Pom-

padour achieved fame, wealth, and power because she was
sensuous enough to capture a king—using methods she
learned from other lovers.

SIX SEXUAL TABOOS

To be a sexually exciting woman you must observe
the following taboos.

Don't be a sex critic. If you are sexually ignorant, you cannot judge your partner. Remember that the man you consider a lousy lover may be terrific with someone else. Remember that if you are expert you can help him to become
a better, more understanding lover (as Mei-Ling did for
Kenneth). Criticizing and complaining will make him so
anxious and tense that his lovemaking is bound to get
worse, not better.

Don't be an Olympia. Olympia was a doll in *The Tales of
Hoffmann* who had to be wound up with a key before she
could function. Many wives respond to their husbands'
sexual needs as porcelain dolls would—they comply, but
they participate without passion, without life. Such mechanical sex is bad for both partners.

Don't be a Sleeping Beauty. The Sleeping Beauty wife remains much like Olympia, but entirely passive during lovemaking. Often she is literally asleep or half-asleep during
intercourse and contributes nothing to it but her body.
This kind of sex can destroy a marriage. When your
prince kisses you, wake up, and *come alive.*

Don't be a blackmailing wife. One woman whose husband
had taken her to fine restaurants and given her extravagant
presents before they were married deeply resented the loss
of these special attentions. As a wife, she was not courted

and wooed so constantly. "If he doesn't show me he loves me," she decided, "he only wants me for sex." From then on, she rebuffed him—unless he entertained her, or bribed her with presents.

This form of sexual blackmail demeans both husband and wife. She becomes a married prostitute, providing intercourse in exchange for rewards, and sex is no longer the spontaneous expression of love and admiration it should be.

Don't be a touch-me-not wife. This woman protects herself from her husband's sexual advances. She is as afraid of being seduced as the most inexperienced fifteen-year-old, and she can always find some excuse for avoiding sex: "The children might hear." "Don't mess up my hair—I just had it done." Or she may start an argument late in the evening ("You can't expect me to feel loving after you insult me"). She may stay up night after night watching television (though this is a wife's most frequent complaint about a husband), retiring only after she's sure her husband is asleep. She finds sex threatening or repellent but doesn't want to admit such feelings; she simply finds excuses to avoid sex as often as possible.

Don't be an apathetic wife. One doctor complained that his wife of twenty-one years never seemed interested in sex. "I rate my sexual performance well above average," he wrote. "On the other hand, my wife has always had a low libido. She seems to regard me as a sex maniac. Once a month a sexual interlude, timed to her own choosing, is presented to me like a sacrificial gift. This emasculation has been going on for years."

Men frequently demand sex from their wives caring little or nothing for women's wants and needs. And many women present their husbands with sex as a gift, with as little concern for them. One is as bad as the other. *Each individual must regard mutual sex as a gift given and a gift received.* Only by learning to enjoy sex, only by becoming happily sensuous, can frigidity be overcome. Frigidity not only destroys a woman's pleasure (or dampens it considerably), it can cause her husband to suffer feelings of guilt and rejection and it can seriously damage their marriage.

A PRESCRIPTION FOR MARRIAGE

Encourage your husband to participate in some sport; join him in it. Exercise is necessary if you want him healthy. You can both find pleasure in some moderately vigorous activity, and it will be an added, shared interest.

Prepare nutritious, well-balanced meals. A low-fat diet is better for you both and may save him from a heart attack.

Plan interesting vacations; explore new places together. Play is very important after a man reaches thirty. Help him to enjoy life more.

Feel free to comfort him when he needs it. A truly liberated woman doesn't need a strong man all the time. Let him know that you love him, especially when he feels bewildered and unhappy. You go to him for comfort; let him come to you. If you can reassure him that admitting his feelings doesn't make him less masculine in your eyes, your husband will be relieved of great stress.

Guide him to the land of passion. Learn to be a free and uninhibited sex partner. This doesn't mean that you must swing or swap mates with your neighbor—just that you are willing to experiment with one man, the one you love.

Give him freedom. A man who feels trapped often seeks other women just to prove that his wife doesn't dominate him. Even if you are uncomfortable with your husband's extramarital flings, remember that outrage and nagging will only drive him away. Try to accept what you can't like. If you can do this, the odds are that he will come home to you and be a better husband for it. A man likes to feel free and to know that he is with a woman because he wants to be, not because someone says he should.

Two case histories illustrate this very well.

RON

Ron was a bachelor in his early fifties who had never married because he valued his freedom too much. One day his sexual freedom came to a sudden end. The swinging club he belonged to ruled that singles were no longer eligible. He had difficulty in finding a steady partner because after a while most swinging single couples break up —the girl wants a husband.

Then Ron met a lonely divorcee, Mona. She was happy to be his partner because she wanted a companion. Above all, she wanted sexual fulfillment and not a husband. She got her desire and was greatful to Ron. She became his steady partner, although they seldom had sex together.

One evening everything changed. It was in the winter and a snowstorm was predicted. Only three couples showed up for a party. Ron was paired with a very unfriendly partner and he was impotent.

This is a common complaint among aging swingers after a period of depersonalized sex. The older man needs more affection and stimulation.

Ron's partner was uncooperative and uninteresting, so he became impotent. Ron was concerned that she would "advertise" his failure. Mona sensed his anxiety and reassured him affectionately that he was still a great lover. She used the art of seduction that she had learned from swinging. It was a great success—beautiful sex in front of everyone. Then came the unpleasant part—the long drive to take Mona home—the part he always disliked. The snowstorm worsened and Ron was tired. Mona suggested that he sleep at her place because there was already seven inches of snow. They went to bed and the first time they cuddled they were aroused. Once again they had beautiful sex. The best part happened the next day, because of the snow. Mona insisted he spend Sunday with her. She prepared a fantastic dinner—and he proposed to her. Not because he needed a swinging partner but because he needed Mona, who was able to demonstrate what a wife can do.

After their marriage they swung very little because, as Mona expressed it, "We are very busy. When I was a divorcee my married friends ignored me, now we get so many invitations we just have no time for swinging."

What worked for Mona was that she never was anxious to get married and she believed in sexual freedom.

REX

On his way to New York for a meeting of television executives, Rex noticed a beautiful redhead waiting to board the plane. He was immediately attracted but lost sight of her in the crowd. After they landed, she was in front of him, and he speculated on how to meet her. Just then she turned around and said that she had heard him discussing television with the man seated next to him. She explained that she was a beauty contest winner and asked for his advice. Rex suggested that they share a cab downtown and offered to help her in any way he could.

When he asked her to dinner, she hesitated, but finally agreed when he assured her that he was married and that there were no strings attached. He took her to one of New York's finest restaurants and then to a glamorous nightclub. As they danced in the small hours of the morning, Rex told her that he loved her. Much to his delight and amazement, she replied that she loved him.

For the next four days they spent every moment together. They did all the traditional lovers' things—walking in Central Park, eating hot dogs, going to the top of the Empire State Building, and so on.

When the time for parting came, it seemed that the world had come to an end. Wild schemes ran through Rex's mind—changing his name and running away to Mexico, divorcing his wife, killing himself. In his heart, however, he knew that he could not leave his wife who had never done anything to hurt him. He just didn't know what to do.

When Rex reached home, he told his wife the whole story. He explained that he loved her very much, that he wouldn't think of leaving, but that he needed help. Although she was shaken, his wife did not react by accusing or blaming him; instead they sat and talked and eventually agreed that he should see the girl again to resolve his feelings.

As soon as he saw her, he realized he still loved her. But he knew they could not meet again. They spent several days talking, going for walks, just being together. Then they said good-bye forever.

"That was five years ago, Dr. Scheimann," Rex told me. "I still love her."

Rex may still love that girl, but he is still married to his wife and their love is as strong as ever. His wife told me that it wasn't always easy for her to understand and accept Rex's infidelity, but she tried her best because she loved him and didn't want to lose him. She knew that he would always come back to her.

15

THE
MATURE MIND
AND THE
YOUTHFUL
HEART

THERE IS LITTLE QUESTION THAT A NEW MODE OF LIVING
is the prescription for the coronary-prone, stress-ridden,
and postcardiac. In coming to this conclusion—via the immediate needs of my own patients—I did not until now
realize to what extent all American society—civilization itself—could benefit from my five-point program. The strains
of modern-day living, though mostly subconscious, are
real and must be met by each of us.

FOUR-POINT PLAN FOR LIVING

No household can be happy, faced with a heart problem or not, without relating to the first four points of my

plan: (1) love—men and women need love as much as they need bread and water. Sex, a facet of love, anticipates point (2) partner. But there is no love to give another without first loving yourself. If I were a full-time marriage counselor, I would be sure that the couples who came to me had something positive to bring to the marriage. Too many couples think their problems will be solved by gaining a loving mate. Personal problems should be confronted and solved before marriage. An engagement period is a good time to find out about each other, and to evaluate oneself. But the truth should not be blinded by love. In fact, the opposite should be true. It is precisely love that can enable us to open up to ourselves, as we have the strength and goodwill of another to uphold us. (3) Home is where love is, without physical limits, whether a mansion, trailer, or a room. (4) Faith (I humbly admit my good fortune in having religious faith). It would be difficult for me to counsel one who lacks it. But what joy there must be in finding faith. Many people say defensively, "I have faith. I mean, I believe in God in my own way, but I don't go to church." The first statement is the telling, all-important one. God doesn't work just on weekends at scheduled services. Lacking religious faith, formalized or not, you must have faith in yourself, faith in your partner, a faith in your mutual ability to create a home and family together. This is the absolute minimum for a happy, wholesome life together.

FIFTH POINT

We come to the fifth and final point of my plan for a new mode of living: 5) self-knowledge. In placing self-knowledge last it occurred to me that self-knowledge should perhaps come first, since it affects love, partner, home, and faith. Then the story of the wedding guest in the Bible came to mind: "and the last shall be first." You might consider its dual position as relevant to man-woman.

Self-knowledge is dynamic, changing throughout life. How much better to keep up with our changing selves than to discover one day we're changed and no longer recognizable. Life *is* change and to make a success of living is to mold that change into continued growth.

Inscribed over the entrance to Apollo's oracle at Delphi were the words "Know thyself." Man's desire to know himself and where he fits in the universe is the basis of all religion and philosophy. It was this longing for self-knowledge that led him to eat the forbidden fruit; it is this longing that distinguishes him from all other living creatures.

Self-knowledge demands strict honesty; we must become aware of our faults, confess them to ourselves, and resolve to overcome them. This admission and ventilation of our flaws is an important part of formalized religion and professional psychiatry—two ways of learning more about ourselves. I do not endorse either psychiatry or religion without reservation. Religion has been one of the forces in the world that is responsible for crippling ideas in the minds of many people regarding sex. Psychiatry, while holding great promise for the future, is really only in its infancy as a profession. But there is still much to be learned from both psychiatry and religion, and the step of confession I have learned from them is most important.

All too often this therapeutic confession and penitence is misused and made the basis for persuasion and reeducation when it should be regarded as an essential method of self-revelation. I do not speak here of the traditional confessional as such, but of the need to admit our weaknesses to ourselves so that we can resolve to improve. This is the technique used so successfully by Alcoholics Anonymous, for instance.

Penitence helps not only the problem drinker but also the coronary-prone, power-hungry, ego-centered modern Apollo—the doctor, the executive, or the high-level administrator who tends to think of himself as godlike (the same applies to Atalantas). "Why not?" asks his subconscious. "I control the fates of others; I am treated with deference; my pronouncements are eagerly awaited. I'm an important man." But this modern Apollo lost a great deal when he exchanged his toga and lyre for a suit and briefcase. He has forgotten the other half of his nature; he has suppressed the poet and the lover and lost the knowledge of true good and evil that only a whole man can possess.

If the modern-day Apollo can be brought to recognize his present predicament, he can begin to find himself and become once again a happy and healthy man. Penitence is the first step and it is, therefore, exceedingly valuable. A lovely story from rabbinical literature illustrates this very well.

An angel who had angered God begged for forgiveness. God replied, "I will forgive you if you go to earth and bring me back the greatest treasure it contains."

The angel happily left on her mission and traveled the face of the earth. She returned to heaven triumphant, crying, "I found it, God—the last breath of a soldier who died for his country." God said, "A soldier can be persuaded to die willingly for the sake of false ideals. That is not the treasure I seek."

The angel returned to earth a second time determined to try doubly hard. "I've found it this time, God," she said when she returned—"the last drop of blood shed by a mother who sacrificed her own life to save her child." God answered, "A better choice than before, but mother love is instinctive. A salmon too, must die for her offspring. That is not the treasure I seek."

In desperation the angel set off a third time. She searched and searched; she visited every nook and cranny of the earth, every mountaintop and every valley in her eagerness to overlook nothing.

Finally she returned to heaven. "I really do have it

this time, God. I've brought you the tear of a repentant sinner."

God smiled. "You are forgiven, little angel," He said. "That tear is the greatest treasure on earth and that sinner is the treasure I seek."

If you are resolved to be honest with yourself and to study your character and temperament objectively, there are many methods of gaining self-knowledge. You can try psychoanalysis, psychological personality tests, group therapy, "rap" sessions, or encounter groups. Once you have confessed to yourself, however, I believe the most effective method is to confess to your beloved or to a close friend. The meditation, discussion, and arguments described in "one night of love" (chapter 11) are apropos here.

After confession and penitence you will be more able to tolerate stress and frustration; you will be easier to live with; you may suddenly discover that you *like* yourself (which is very different from loving yourself—something all humans do without even thinking about it).

Your new insight can give you the most valuable human qualities you can possess—kindness, compassion, and communication. Just as a woman becomes more feminine through these qualities, a man becomes more masculine. Such a truly masculine man, who loves and is loved, can be unattractive (like Cyrano de Bergerac) or old and fat (like Pierre in *War and Peace*), but he will be sought after and esteemed as friend and lover.

LEARN HOW TO PLAY

I have emphasized that Americans are far too busy earning a living or bringing up a family to learn how to live. Now that you have stopped running long enough to begin your self-analysis, you must ask yourself if you know how to play. No matter how healthful your activities are, no matter how well rested you may be or how good your diet is, none of it will work if you don't play. Only through play can you mature and still remain young. You learned how to eat and drink; why not how to play and make love? Your stomach may alert you to food, and a joyful heart teach you something of the art of loving, but learning to play is extremely difficult for an adult.

If you feel guilty about playing (a surprising number of adults do), remember that play is more than simple fun. Play teaches us about life. Just as children practice being grown up when they play, an adult through play learns how to stay young. It is far more valuable than momentary enjoyment—it permeates our lives and even enhances our working hours by adding variety to our days.

Naturally, each individual differs as to what constitutes play and relaxation. If you are a mesomorph, for example, you are more apt to enjoy adventurous, competitive games—golf, tennis, swimming. If you are an Apollo or Atalanta mesomorph, try music and art as well as sports. Learn to dance or to play a musical instrument. This can have some bonuses: I once asked a seventy-eight-year-old bon vivant the secret of his amazing success with women. "It's easy, Doc," he said. "I play my guitar and sing Italian love songs—no woman can resist that."

One prominent businessman organized a family orchestra. He, his wife, and their three children provide the music for church dances and other local events. He is one man I'm sure will never have a heart attack.

Take up photography or collect rare books. Such hobbies not only pleasantly divert you and provide topics for conversation, but they lead to feelings of creativity and accomplishment. Take your spouse to art shows or to the theatre. A common interest often offers the promise of partnership in other activities (such as exciting sex).

If you are an endomorph, the sociable, convivial companion, you love group activities. Take up a sport your whole family can enjoy—boating, fishing, or baseball, for example. If you have musical inclinations, join a band or glee club. You are likely to make an excellent Scout leader, so, if you have children, think seriously of working with their troop.

If you are an intellectual ectomorph who prefers solitude, you are likely to have chosen your hobbies already. Your interests are probably well developed and hopefully you find them mentally and spiritually stimulating.

The mesomorph, the endomorph, and the ectomorph must all remember, however, that these hobbies are for the purposes of play. You must not let them become obsessions. We all know the kind of golfer who is miserable unless every game is played superbly. Winning is delightful to be sure, but if you cannot derive some enjoyment from the game itself, win or lose, it is not play.

No matter what your personality type, there is one game you and everyone else must learn: to play in bed. Sex is one game that will not interfere with your other hobbies—indeed, it will be enhanced by them. Make love to the *Zampa Overture* (known as "the masturbation overture") or to Ravel's *Bolero* (*Bolero* has been called the musical expression of orgasm). Whisper love poems during foreplay. Begin your love game by drinking wine or champagne. Use your new camera to take "lewd" photographs (learn to develop them yourself).

If you are devoted to athletics you will be happy to learn that recent studies indicate that good sex makes good athletes. Joe Namath, famous both as a football player and as a ladies' man, says forthrightly, "Personally, I think it helps."

Lovemaking should be an expression of your personality. Varied interests will undoubtedly provide you with fascinating ways of playing the game of sex, if only you will let yourself go. Inhibited sex can be pretty grim for either partner—relax and learn about the subterranean you. One physician I knew did precisely that and revolutionized his life.

Dr. L. at first glance bears no resemblance whatsoever to Apollo. He's overweight, short, not particularly good looking. Yet today he lives like Apollo because he acquired a mature mind and a young heart.

He married at an early age, but his dedication to his work destroyed his marriage. "You're not married to me," his wife charged. "You're in love with your laboratory!" Fortunately, he had a female laboratory assistant who greatly admired him and who taught him how to make love. He always managed to take enough time from his crowded schedule for her. Their affair was relaxing for him because he felt no real emotional involvement; fame was still his great desire.

But it ended abruptly when he had to move to a distant city where he became the head of the pathology department of one of the finest hospitals in the Midwest. This new post demanded his entire attention. He neglected sex and failed to exercise. As the years went by, he began to feel dissatisfied. He had achieved his ambitions; he published articles frequently, his colleagues admired him, and he had become a noted authority in his field. Other physicians asked his advice and no one dared to question his diagnoses. All this, he found, was not enough. Something was missing.

Dr. L. began to question the value of science. He found no answers, only endless problems. When he realized that he was doing autopsies on his friends—middle-aged men dead long before their time—he determined that he would not die without having experienced all that life could offer.

He had inherited some money and he set out to increase it. Wealth became as important to him as his laboratory. The money he made, however, was not used selfishly. He wanted it to make others happy too. He bought a luxurious mansion with an indoor swimming pool and installed a sauna. A large yacht was his next acquisition.

Twice a month he entertained lavishly. Sometimes

his guests were old friends and sometimes they were new friends—people who knew him not as a distinguished, rather stuffy physician but as a bon vivant. The yacht became an exotic pleasure barge with beautiful women and lots of sex. He lost weight, purchased contact lenses, and became known for his fabulous parties.

His square friends enjoyed his wine and music parties. As they watched him play his guitar while the yacht sailed through the moonlight, they marveled at the change in him.

Today Dr. L. has the best of two worlds. His work still excites him because it is no longer his whole life and his play is richly satisfying.

The last time I spoke to Dr. L., I learned that another great change had taken place in his life. He had fallen in love with a young, vivacious woman. She was more conservative, however, and agreed to marry him only if he promised never to see other women in his own home. At first, he was reluctant to accept even this minor restriction, but as his love kept growing he eventually consented. His wife is now pregnant and he is overjoyed at the happy prospect of fatherhood.

The elaborate parties and extensive experience he gained during his indulgent years have freed him from the hang-ups and pressures that destroyed his first marriage. He is now fully capable of devoting himself selflessly to his family. He is truly participating in and enjoying life. Love has turned his pleasure palace into an even more rewarding, far richer home.

LEARN TO BE SENSUOUS

In previous chapters I have discussed the benefits of healing and rejuvenating sex. Here we are considering another aspect of sex—sex that can keep your heart young by prolonging biological youth.

This is not ritual sex which relieves anxiety and the fear of separation; it is not therapeutic sex which cures sexual problems; it is not intimate sex which expresses love and brings joy.

What is this new experience? It is the erotic or sensuous sex glorified by the ancient poets (Ovid's *Amor*) and the Hindu writers of the *Kama Sutra* and the *Ananga Ranga*. Erotic sex begins when a baby is given suck and continues, as Sartre says, until death—if it is practiced. Sartre calls this sex "an intentionality that the body experiences." This form of sex does not depend upon being young. Indeed, the older you are, the more erotic your sex can become. *Erotic sex declines only when you lose interest in sex or in life itself.* These losses begin in the mind.

The majority of experts proclaim that the male sex urge is strongest in the late teens and early twenties, and then begins to decline. This unfortunate idea has been misinterpreted by the public.

One of my patients, a thirty-six-year-old man who was sexually inadequate, conveniently blamed his age. "I neglected sex during my good years," he explained. "I was too busy studying. By the time I was ready to resume sex, I was past my peak. It's too late now, I guess."

It may be true that purely physical sex declines early, but this animal sex (and I am not using "animal" in a pejorative way) is really the least satisfactory form of sex. When you are nineteen or twenty you may have more orgasms than when you are forty, but they will be less satisfying than the fewer, but more effective, orgasms of the mature man.

If a man believes his sexual appetite is, or should be, declining, it may in fact begin to do so. Your brain is your most important sex organ. If you *think* you are "over the hill," you will soon have an unhappy sex life. On the other hand, if you feel potent and sexy your sex life will be wonderful—even if you are eighty.

We must consider some of the mechanisms of aging in order to understand the correlation between erotic sex and continued youthfulness.

Dr. Irving S. Wright has stated that "we now have evidence that biological aging need not progress at a rate determined purely by the passage of time. The clocks by which individuals live and die operate at widely different rates."

What factors influence these rates? One extremely important factor seems to be the endocrine system. Our bodies manufacture a variety of hormones for a variety of purposes. We do not as yet fully understand the relationship between hormones and sexuality. Many researchers, including the eminent Hans Selye spoken of in chapter 1, feel that the hormones which regulate growth and sexual development play an important role in aging. It appears likely that the pituitary and thyroid glands and the gonads influence the aging process. Kinsey and his associates, in their classic *Sexual Behavior in the Human Female*, have concluded that there is a close relationship between pituitary and gonadal hormones and the development of sexual responsiveness. They found that a high level of thyroid secretion correlates with high levels of sexual response while low thyroid secretion correlates with lower sexual response.

Some experts believe that abundant sex produces a higher level of hormonal secretion which may in turn retard aging.

Erotic sex, furthermore, may help fight the dangers of cholesterol. Joan Arehart-Treichel revealed a significant correlation between cholesterol, heart attacks, and breast feeding in *Science Newsletter*. Breast-fed babies, she reports, have higher cholesterol levels than bottle-fed babies during the first year of life. Despite this, the underdeveloped nations, where breast feeding is most common, have very low heart attack rates. Researchers are wondering if elevated cholesterol levels activate some biological mechanism that depresses cholesterol levels in later years.

These experts would do well to consider the effect of erotic love (that is, breast feeding) on these infants. It is a well-documented fact that deprivation of love stunts growth. Perhaps the erotic gratification of being suckled helps produce a positive state of good health.

I strongly urge that we begin the fight against heart disease while our patients are children. This is a viable idea, because if the boy or girl of eighteen is taught about erotic love, he is far less likely to be a coronary patient at forty—she at fifty or sixty.

Young people should learn something about sensuous sex before they marry. The years of bachelorhood provide a golden opportunity to explore sexuality without guilt or inhibitions—or familial obligations. Singles can experience variety, and they can experiment at will; they can learn what the French call *l'art pour l'art,* the joy of doing something for its own sake. They can enjoy a number of partners and find sex that can be uninhibitedly erotic and totally satisfying.

What do I mean by erotic sex *and* satisfying sex? Modern sex books do not tell you. You must turn to the ancients for the answer. They understood the mysteries of lust, sensuality, and the libido because sex was part of their heritage and religion, a holy and natural part of life that had no connection with sin and sickness. The answer is really very simple: you must provide your own definitions. Each individual responds to a stimulus in a different way. Tom may find one stimulus intensely erotic, John may find it repugnant, while Mary is merely bored by it. Each makes his and her own distinction and each is correct.

One grave problem with many sex manuals is that they overlook this vital fact. They seem to assume that sexual response can be programmed as I stated in chapter 11. You must learn about your own sexuality. Remember the words of Apollo: "Know thyself."

Discovering sensuous sex, learning all its ramifications,

is a long process. Don't be in too much of a hurry to begin. A teen-ager does not yet have the mature mind needed to profit from sensuous sex. A young man takes ten to fifteen years to learn the art of sensuality. An old Mexican proverb says that a man should marry three times: When he is young he should marry an older woman in order *to learn* about sex; when he is middle-aged he should marry a middle-aged woman in order *to practice* what he has learned; and, finally, when he reaches old age he should marry a young girl in order *to teach* her what he knows.

We, like the Mexicans can divide our sex lives into three ages:

> the years from 20 to 40—the age of learning
> the years from 41 to 60—the age of maturity
> the years from 61 to 80—the age of teaching

During the age of learning you are busy struggling with life, making your way in the world. Play can ease the difficulties of the transition to adulthood. A child enjoys learning to ride a bicycle even if it means a few bad falls. You may fall and be hurt and disappointed, but don't give up. Keep these three rules in mind:

(1) *Be sex-oriented.* Make sex a normal regular part of your life. Let it be a hobby or gratification like eating, drinking, or sports. Sex is one habit-forming indulgence that is not dangerous.

(2) *Get the right teacher.* In Europe, an older husband usually instructs a much younger bride. In the United States boys and girls of the same age, equally ignorant and equally clumsy, are initiating each other. They grow up thinking of themselves as sexually sophisticated when they are, in fact, inexperienced children.

Follow the European custom and experiment with older companions, or, for males, an expert prostitute. Dr. Eleanor Rodgerson, says that older women are often much more relaxed and make better sex partners because they enjoy intercourse. In many primitive societies, reports Dr. Rodgerson, women anticipate reaching menopause with great pleasure; once they pass the child-bearing age, they can enjoy sex without fearing pregnancy and without following tribal taboos pertaining to menstruation.

If you're a man and don't like the idea of an older woman or a prostitute, find a plump or a plain girl. They tend to be excellent sex partners. Although a beautiful woman may seem more alluring, remember that she may be spoiled and used to being courted. She will expect you to gratify her. A less attractive girl often has had the opportunity to think more of others and thus will be more interested in pleasing you. She has learned to be sensuous because she does not compete for men solely on the basis of looks. She needs something else to offer, and has it.

(3) *You must believe in sexual freedom.* René Guyon, the noted French writer, believes that only complete sexual freedom produces sensuousness. Guyon feels that sex is the only means modern men and women have of communicating with nature, and he recommends sexual freedom as "the true remedy for psychopathic disorders caused by repression and censorship." You should, says Guyon, have relations with as many partners as possible. "A man who has known only one woman, or a woman who has known only one man, is like a person who has read only one book." Even if you don't wish to go as far as Guyon suggests, do experiment with a number of partners. Learn which types turn you on the most. Be patient and be a good sport. Sometimes you gain and sometimes you lose, but satisfaction comes more often as you mature.

Maturity should be valued. By the time you reach forty, you are generally settled in your career and making a fairly comfortable living. Many of the pressures that drive young men to drink and drugs (the age group from twenty-one to twenty-four contains more problem drinkers than any other according to a University of California survey) are alleviated.

But when you reach maturity, you must reflect on what you have learned about yourself. Remember the importance of honest self-confession. Dr. George A. Ulett, of the University of Missouri School of Medicine, reminds us that the inability of many executives and physicians to admit their emotional weaknesses is often dangerous.

Remember the value of penitence. Your mate deserves understanding as much as you deserve it. Be responsive to your partner, sympathize with your partner's needs and aspirations, offer tenderness and companionship, and you just may discover that this person you thought you knew is unbelievably sensuous. Now is the time for you to enjoy the rewards of your previous experimentation. You may find out that the best-selling book title is true—life does begin at forty. Orientals call the years after fifty "the rich years," and consider them the most rewarding of all.

If you want to have a happy, habitual sex life after the age of sixty, you must change your attitude toward old age. American doctors have done their best to perpetuate the myth that sexual desire and ability decrease markedly after forty or fifty. European and Oriental physicians, on the contrary, have long emphasized that age alone does not have this effect.

I know many men, and I am confessedly one of them, who have had more and better sex after middle age. Some time ago *The New York Times* interviewed a number of internationally known septuagenarian and octogenarian European men. Almost every one reported leading an active sex life in his seventies and eighties.

Another fallacy of our culture is that an old person is an undesirable and a poor lover. Only the Americans have the distorted image of the "old libertine." Only in the United States can you hear such expressions as "dirty old man" or "lecherous old man." In Europe there is a positive and reassuring attitude toward elderly lovers. The French express it by saying "The best stew is made in the oldest pot"; in Hungary it's "The old man is not an aged man." Old people—men and women—are just as sexy as young people. Study after study, including those of Masters and Johnson and Simone de Beauvoir, have patently disproved the myth that most men become impotent after middle age. We now know that a man's enthusiasm and ability as a lover are determined not by his age, but by his past sexual experience and his present attitude toward sex. Our complicated sexual reactions are triggered by emotions, not by hormones.

The old Hungarian proverb that says "the most important sexual organ is the brain" is true. As long as he can communicate—and has a woman he's interested in—a man of any age can be a superb lover. The same is true of a woman. It is personality, not biology, that determines sexuality in people.

Victor Hugo, Charles Chaplin, Picasso, Pablo Casals, and Marc Chagall in their seventies and older were loved by young women. And the world is full of less well-known ones. A remarkable man is Chief Njiri Karanja of Kenya. This 109-year-old has a five-year-old son and thirty-four wives! "Marriage," says the chief, "is good for man."

One of the most outstanding examples from the animal world died recently in California. Frazier was a lion who reached the age of twenty (equivalent to ninety in a human) while remaining virile. A team of fifteen doctors received special permission to perform an autopsy on his body to find out his secret. During the last years of his life he produced thirty-five offspring and had sexual relations with eleven young females who had rejected younger suitors for him.

A friend described him: "Frazier came from Mexico, but nobody knows exactly when or where he was born. His teeth were gone, his muscles were flabby, his hair ragged—but he sure was good at one thing. The females were crazy about him."

Frazier's memory will linger on—a few days after his death zookeepers announced that one of his lionesses was three weeks' pregnant.

16

EPILOGUE: THE JOY OF SEX AND THE POWER OF LOVE

IN EARLIER CHAPTERS I DISCUSSED THE DIFFICULTY MOST doctors have dealing with sex. They are often reluctant to listen to the intimate sexual troubles of their patients because they think of sex problems as embarrassing, or even frightening. A great many of them, in fact, know little about the subject and fall heir to much of the misinformation common to laymen.

The wives of doctors, however, know a great deal about sex and love and they, unlike their husbands, are not unwilling to talk about their knowledge. I discussed sex and love with many such wives and I realized that the more we learn about these topics the more we become aware of how little we actually know and how important it is to increase our knowledge. I have always appreciated women, and not surprisingly, from them I learned to appreciate a woman's point of view.

One doctor I know took a very typical attitude. "All this nonsense about sex!" he snorted. "You Freudians never think about anything else. Sex simply isn't that important." His wife, however, sided with me against him, and told her somewhat abashed husband that sex was indeed important, and that she wished he would think about it more. And seriously.

The most rewarding conversation I had about sex occurred on my way home from the AMA International Convention in Tel Aviv in 1973. During the long flight from London to New York, I was seated next to Linda L., the wife of a specialist in internal medicine. When I discovered that she had majored in psychology while in college, I began to tell her about this book. After asking many questions about my theories, she commented, "I just finished reading a book called *The Joy of Sex* that I think you would find fascinating. That book convinced me that joyful sex can prolong my marriage, just as your ideas have convinced me that joyful sex can prolong my husband's life."

She paused, looked meditatively at her sleeping husband as if ordering her thoughts, and then turned back to me with a smile. "I love my plants and I know that talking to them affectionately and taking loving care of them helps them grow. I love my little boy and in order for him to grow up with a healthy body and a healthy mind I have to communicate with him and let him know that I care about him. It isn't enough just to love somebody; you have to *express* that love and make the one you care about *feel* loved."

When I admiringly agreed, she went on. "That was my problem for a long time. I love my husband but he's always busy with his patients and I don't have enough opportunities to sit down with him and talk quietly and affectionately. Now I've overcome this dilemma. The best way for me to express my concern and love for my husband is through joyful sex. Instead of being mechanical and just physically satisfying, our sex is now *communication*. All the tenderness I don't have a chance to say, I put into sex."

She grew thoughtful, turned to look out the window at the Atlantic far below us while she searched for the right words, and finally continued. "I've read a lot of books on sex, but most of them are terribly disappointing. They simply didn't mean anything to me. But Dr. Comfort's book was like a personal letter written with me in mind. When my husband neglected me, I developed an inferiority complex. I decided that it was my own fault. I felt too demanding, too neurotic, too immature. I thought I was getting too old to be attractive. I don't feel that way anymore. I have a whole new attitude toward sex, an adult form of play and that healthy play is good for us. With his book I was able to convince my husband that joyful sex would be good for him, good for me, and good for our family life. Now sex is just as important to him as his career or making money."

I asked her why she thought such a transformation had been possible. She replied that her love for her husband was the main reason for her success.

"Many women," I cautioned, "stop loving their husbands for one reason or another. Will you still be able to enjoy sex with your husband if that happens?"

She shook her head no vigorously. "Sex to me is an expression of love. If I ever stop loving my husband, sex will seem lifeless because I believe that love is life."

During our lengthy discussion I stated that love means different things to different people, but obtaining joy from sex requires only one form of love—erotic love, a purely physical attraction at first which leads to an act of sexual gratification. The very act of sex, I argued, produces an emotional response because sex involves giving, taking, and sharing. The physical need to be close to the object of erotic love creates an affectionate and tender response to the partner who turns you on and who wants to make love to you.

Erotic love, I explained, forms a link between two people who are willing to give themselves to each other. This love as we saw in chapter 11 may be brief, lasting only a night or two, or more long-lived, continuing for a year, a decade, or even a lifetime; it may be a "light" love or an intense one, but nevertheless *it is love.*

I told Linda of some of my own amorous adventures which had given me and my partners joyful sex and a sense of sharing even though we were not what society calls "in love with each other."

"That's all right for you," she responded. "Perhaps in Hungary the women are more sexually sophisticated, more able to play erotic games without guilt or fear of being hurt. In France, I know, they believe in sex for its own sake, which is fine. American women, though, are more romantic. You may call it old-fashioned, and I suppose maybe it is, but we need and want love before we can truly enjoy sex."

I kissed her hand and replied, "You may be old-fashioned, but you are a fascinating, mature woman."

THE IMPORTANCE OF LOVE

Since my conversation with Linda, I have questioned many women about their attitudes toward love and sex. In the course of these interviews I learned something very interesting. Linda was right. Although American women are becoming more sexually sophisticated than ever before, and even though the women's liberation movement has started to free them of many inhibitions, women still want love. Now, however, they no longer demand that love take place in a conventional setting, within the confines of marriage.

　Some women find love with one man but others feel free to love more than one. They may marry, live with a man, form communal bonds, or enjoy group sex. Others have given up men altogether and find love with other women. Whatever form their search for love takes, they are not willing to do without it.

　Feminist author Phyllis Raphael, for example, believes that in the past a period of uninvolved sex was useful because most women until recently were inhibited about sex. Now, however, she says it is time for love to become important again. Many women think, she points out, "they can enjoy sex for the hell of it as easily as a man. But many of them have been finding out that the answer isn't as simple as they thought." She has decided that the best sex is a result of a relationship, an interaction between people that comes only with time: "I won't settle for second-rate sex. I want the best, and you don't get the best in one night, any more than Rome was built in a day."

　Chryssa Dobbson makes the same point in a *Cosmopolitan* column in a more picturesque way. "Really good sex comes only when you grow sensitive enough to another person to know what pleases him or her both in and out of bed . . . a skill hardly likely to develop overnight. You can't learn to play a musical instrument in a day; what horror to imagine trying to learn a *different* musical instrument each afternoon."

　Obviously, the problems of modern women affect men as well. The coronary-prone man, who desperately needs a rich and satisfying sex life, cannot obtain all the benefits of sex if his partner is unhappy or disinterested.

　It is not enough for him to keep himself young through exercise, hobbies, and sex; he must devote himself to keeping his woman young as well—and in love.

　How then can a man make a woman feel truly loved? One way to begin is by studying the techniques of great lovers. Their reputations may be somewhat exaggerated, but they must be doing something right.

Dr. Comfort added to the title of his book *The Joy of Sex* the subtitle *A Cordon Bleu Guide to Lovemaking.* This phrase calls to mind not only the French way with food, but the fame of the French in the romantic arts. For some reason a Frenchman is able to convey his appreciation of women in a subtle yet concrete fashion.

One young woman I interviewed had experienced this at a party one evening and the impression it made on her was indelible.

"Almost everyone there was European," she told me, "so there was something in the atmosphere from the very start. At the time I just sat back and enjoyed it, but since then I've tried to anaylze the feeling, to understand what made that evening so different.

"The men were very young, boys really, but they had already mastered the ability to make a woman feel unique. They concentrate on *you*, gazing into your eyes and making it obvious that you are the most fascinating female they have ever met. They know how to flirt beautifully, with tenderness and finesse. Instead of making a pass as though it's a social obligation, the way Americans do, they act as if they can think of nothing more wonderful than just looking at you or holding your hand.

"The pass comes later, but subtly, in a manner that says 'I long for you,' not 'I'll take you.' There's nothing crude or unpolished about it. Five minutes after you meet, he's wooing you."

She paused, trying to recall the fleeting sensations that had made the evening a vital one. "When you dance, for example, it's almost like making love. It becomes very sensuous, very intimate. One man told me I had the loveliest vertebrae in the world! No American could come up up with a compliment like that.

"Frenchmen are extremely masculine and make you feel ultrafeminine. And yet, there's none of the locker-room attitude that most Americans equate with masculinity. Frenchmen regard women as special—different to be sure, but definitely not inferior. You sense that they truly enjoy talking to a woman—that they would rather be with you than discussing football or the stock market.

"A lot of it is a game, of course. You're not expected to take their passion seriously. When they say they adore you, it's taken for granted that this is a convention, a rule of the game. Their attitude is simple: 'I am a man of the world, you are a sophisticated and desirable woman; what could be nicer than our being together?'

"Underneath you feel a real love for women, not just a woman, perhaps, but an appreciation for the whole sex. In the course of one evening, a Frenchman makes you feel more cherished and desired, more *special*, than you've ever felt before."

American men can learn a great deal from this story. Every woman needs to feel individual, to know that she has a special place in her man's thoughts. She wants to be loving and she wants to be told in return that she is loved and lovable.

Leonardo da Vinci's *Mona Lisa* expresses something of the eternal mystery of women. Critics have debated for centuries whether the haunting, enigmatic young woman was in love or pregnant, or to settle for "mystifying." Leonardo used his artist's hands, his ingenious mind, and his poet's heart to represent in paint the wonder that he saw. This should be every man's goal. The deep, subtle understanding Leonardo achieved can be yours, if you are willing to try. A happy, fulfilled wife is, in this sense, a true work of art. The husband who is willing to give of himself is an artist—and it will save his heart . . . and life.

NOTES

CHAPTER 2

Page

35 CARRYER, HADDON M., M.D., and Others, "Analysis of 2,812 Examinations on 569 Subjects at Mayo Clinic," *Industrial Medicine*, May 1972 (Reprinted from *Mayo Clinic Proceedings*, Vol. 46, Nov. 1971).

36 MAILER, NORMAN, *The Prisoner of Sex* (Boston: Little, Brown and Company, 1971).

36 Bell's speech reported in *Chicago Daily News*, June 21, 1967.

38 GINSBERG, GEORGE L.; KROSCH, WILLIAM A.; and SHAPIRO, THEODORE, "The New Impotence," in *Archives of General Psychiatry*, March 1972.

38 STEWART, B. LYMAN, M.D., "Viewpoints: Is Impotence Increasing?" *Medical Aspects of Human Sexuality*, Vol. V., No. 10, October 1971.

40 MANNES, MARYA, "Let's Face It," *McCall's*, February 1966.

45 BARNARD, CHRISTIAN, M.D., *Heart Attack* (New York: Delacorte Press, 1971).

CHAPTER 3

50 TOFFLER, ALVIN, *Future Shock* (New York: Random House, 1970), p. 165.

52 MACE, DAVID, Ph.D., and VERA, *Marriage: East and West* (New York: Doubleday & Company, 1966), p. 218.

55 MAY, ROLLO, Ph.D., *Love and Will* (New York: W. W. Norton & Company, 1969), pp. 40, 42, 43, 45.

59 COMFORT, ALEX, M.B., Ph.D., *The Joy of Sex* (New York: Crown Publishers, Inc., 1972), p. 19.

CHAPTER 4

66 ALLEGRO, JOHN, *The Sacred Mushroom and the Cross* (Garden City, New York: Doubleday & Company, Inc., 1970).

67 DURANT, WILL, Tiresias, quoted in *Our Oriental Heritage* (Vol. I of *The Story of Civilization*) (New York: Simon & Schuster, Inc., 1954).

Notes

Page

68 FRAZER, JAMES G., *The Golden Bough* (New York: The Macmillan Company, 1927; 1950).

69 FROMM, ERICH, Ph.D., *The Art of Loving* (New York: Harper & Row, Publishers, 1956).

70 YOUNG, WAYLAND, *Eros Denied* (New York: Grove Press, 1964).

73 DUBOS, RENÉ, and PIRES, MAYA, *Health and Disease* (New York: Time Inc., 1965).

74 MENARD, WILMON, Ph.D., "Love Marquesan Style," *Sexual Behavior*, Sept. 1972.

76 HARLOW, HARRY F., Ph.D., "The Development of Affectional Patterns in Infant Monkeys," *Determinants of Infant Behavior*, ed. B. M. Foss (New York: John Wiley & Sons, Inc., 1961).

77 JOURARD, SIDNEY M., *The Transparent Self* (New York: Van Nostrand Reinhold Company, 1964).

80 McGRADY, PATRICK M., JR., *The Youth Doctors* (New York: Coward, McCann & Geoghegan, Inc., 1968).

CHAPTER 5

83 LOWEN, ALEXANDER, M.D., *Love and Orgasm* (New York: The Macmillan Company, 1965).

83 MONTAGU, ASHLEY, Ph.D., *Sex, Man and Society* (New York: G. P. Putnam's Sons, 1969).

85 LEWINSOHN, RICHARD, *A History of Sexual Customs* (New York: Harper & Row, Publishers, 1971).

86 YOUNG, WAYLAND, *Eros Denied* (New York: Grove Press Inc., 1964).

87 WYLIE, PHILIP, *Generation of Vipers*, Annotated Edition (New York: Rinehart & Company, 1955).

88 COMFORT, ALEX, *The Anxiety Makers* (New York: Dell Publishing Co., Inc., 1967).

89 DUFFY, JOHN, "Masturbation and Clitoridectomy," *JAMA*, October 19, 1963.

89 MONTAGU, ASHLEY, *op. cit.*

89 YOUNG, WAYLAND, *op. cit.*

91 (DR. LESLIE H. FARBER) quoted in Peter and Barbara Wyden, *Inside the Sex Clinic* (New York: The World Publishing Co., 1971).

92 LIEF, HAROLD, "Sexual Attitudes and Behavior of Medical Students. Implication for Medical Practice, in Mar-

Page

riage Counseling in Medical Practice," edited by Ethel M. Nash, University of North Carolina Press, 1964.

93 SHATIN, LEO, Ph.D., "Sex Knowledge of the Freshman Medical Student" in *Diseases of the Nervous System*, July 1967.

93 WOODS, SHERWYN M., "Sexual Problems of Medical Students," in *Medical Aspects of Human Sexuality*, February 1972.

94 PAULEY, IRA B., M.D., "Influence of Training and Attitudes on Sexual Counseling in Medical Practice" in *Medical Aspects of Human Sexuality*, March 1972.

95 OAKS, WILBUR, M.D.; MOYER, JOHN H., M.D., "Sex and Hypertension" in *Medical Aspects of Human Sexuality*, November 1972.

97 WEISS, EDWARD, M.D., *Psychosomatic Aspect of Heart Disease* edited by Morris Fishbein (New York: Hanover House, 1960), p. 122.

CHAPTER 6

110 HURST, J. WILLIS, M.D., "Can You Predict a Coronary Incident?" *JAMA*, November 13, 1972.

CHAPTER 7

116 RUSSEK, HENRY I., M.D., *American Journal of. Medical Science*, June 1962.

116 "Role of Emotional Stress in the Etiology of Clinical Coronary Heart Disease," *Diseases of the Chest*, July 1967.

117 CASSEL, JOHN C., M.D., "Review of 1960 Through 1962 Cardiovascular Disease Prevalence Study," *Archives of Internal Medicine*, Vol. 128, Dec. 1971.

119 Silvia Sikes study mentioned in *Living with Your Heart* by Harley Williams, M.D. (Chicago: Henry Regnery Co., 1970).

120 LAPIN, BORIS A., and CHERKOVICH, GENJA M., "Environmental Change Causing the Development of Neurosis and Corticovisceral Pathology in Monkeys" in *Society, Stress and Disease*, Lennart Levi, editor (New York: Oxford University Press, 1971).

Page
120 WAHL, C. W., editor, *New Dimensions in Psychosomatic Medicine* (Boston: Little, Brown and Company, 1964).
120 CHAZOV, EUGENE I., "Daily Dozen a Day to Keep Cardiologists Away," in UNESCO *Courier*, April 1972.
121 VAN HEIJNINGEN, KITS H., M.D., and TREURNIET, N., M.D., "Psychodynamic Factors in Acute Myocardial Infarction." *Int. J. Psychoanal.* 1966, 47:370–74.
123 DUNBAR, FLANDERS, M.D., *Emotions and Bodily Changes* (New York: Columbia University Press, 1938).
124 SHELDON, WILLIAM H., *Varieties of Human Physique* (New York: Harper & Brothers, 1933).
125 DUPERTOIS, C. WESLEY, and FRANCHESINI, LELIO, "Body Build and Heart Attacks," in *Science Digest*, Jan. 1971.
126 FRIEDMAN, E., quoted by Kester, Edwin, Jr., "Your Personality Can Be a Matter of Life or Death," *Today's Health*, Feb. 1973.
127 RUSSEK, HENRY, M.D., "Role of Emotional Stress in the Etiology of Clinical Coronary Heart Disease," *Diseases of the Chest*, Vol. 52, pp. 1–9, July 1967.

CHAPTER 8

137 MILLER, RICHARD, M.D., "Humility and Compassion—Why Hast Thou Forsaken Us," *G. P.*, October 1964.
139 RUSSEK, HENRY, M.D., " 'Progress' in the Treatment and Prevention of Coronary Heart Disease," *The American Family Physician*, Sept. 1971.
140 FRIEDMAN, SAMUEL, M.D., "A Cheerful Look at Our Obituaries," *Medical Economics*, October 4, 1965.
140 KING, HAITUNG, Ph.D., "Health in the Medical and Other Learned Professions," *Journal of Chronic Diseases*, Vol. 23, 1970.
141 SCHNITZER, KURT, M.D., "To My Colleagues Who Are Still Alive: Slow Down," *Medical Economics*, Nov. 6, 1972.
144 HACKET, THOMAS, M.D., "Can You Handle the Medical Man's Menopause?" *Medical Economics*, June 19, 1972.

CHAPTER 9

Page
154 ELLERBROEK, WALLACE, M.D., quoted in *National Inquirer*, June 24, 1973.
156 BELL, ROBERT R., and BELL, PHYLLIS L., "Sexual Satisfaction Among Married Women." *Medical Aspects of Human Sexuality*, Dec. 1972.
158 MANN, G V., M.D.; SHAFFER, R. D., M.D.; and RICH, A., M.D., "Physical Fitness & Immunity to Heart Disease in Masai," *Lancet*, Vol. 2, pg. 1308, 1965.
159 ROSENMAN, RAY H., M.D., "Emotional Factors in Coronary Heart Disease." *Postgraduate Medicine*, Oct. 1, 1967.
160 GROEN, JOANNES J., "Social Change and Psychosomatic Disease." *Society, Stress and Disease*, Vol. 1 (London: Oxford University Press, 1971).
160 MILLER, BENJAMIN, M.D., and GALTON, LAWRENCE, *Freedom from Heart Attacks* (New York: Simon & Schuster, 1972).
162 IBERT, J. C., and CHARLES J., *Love—the French Way* (New York: Signet, 1963).
164 "Americans Can—and Should—Live Longer," *Time*, July 10, 1972.
164 GOMEZ, JOAN, M.D., *How to Die Young* (New York: Stein & Day, 1971).
165 WALKER, ALEXANDER R. P., M.D., "Coronary Heart Disease—Are There Differences in Racial Susceptibility?" *American Journal of Epidemiology* 90:359–64, 1969.
165 SAUNDERS, E., M.D., quoted by Jack Slater in "Hypertension: Biggest Killer of Blacks," *Ebony*, June 1973.
167 STAPLES, ROBERT E., "Sex and the Black Middle Class," *Ebony*, Aug. 1973.
167 WOLF, STEWART, M.D., "Psychosocial Influences in Myocardial Infarction and Sudden Death." *Society, Stress and Disease*, Vol. 1 (London, Oxford University Press, 1971).

CHAPTER 10

173 GRAHAM, JOHN R., M.D., "What You Can Learn From the Psychiatrist About Heart Disease," *Consultant*, Dec. 1972.

Page
174 ELIOT, ROBERT S., M.D., and MATHERS, DANIEL H., M.D., "Sudden Death," *Consultant,* Dec. 1972.
179 OAKS, WILBUR W., M.D., and MOYER, JOHN, M.D., "Sex and Hypertension," *Medical Aspects of Human Sexuality,* Nov. 1972.
180 T.A., "Sex and Blood Pressure," letter *Forum,* Aug. 1972.
181 SHAINESS, NATALIE, Interview in *National Enquirer.*
183 FROMM, ERICH, Ph.D., *The People in Your Life,* edited by M. M. Hughes (New York: Alfred A. Knopf, Inc., 1951).
184 SOLOMON, NEIL, M.D., and SHEPARD, SALLY, *Truth About Weight Control, How to Lose Excess Pounds Permanently* (New York: Stein and Day, 1972).
185 LEVI, LENNART, M.D. (editor), *Society, Stress and Disease,* Vol. 1, *The Psychosocial Environment and Psychosomatic Diseases* (London: Oxford University Press, 1971).
186 LOWEN, ALEXANDER, M.D., *Love and Orgasm* (New York: The Macmillan Company, 1965. Signet Book, pg. 319).

CHAPTER 11

197 Sexual Freedom League, National Newsletter, March 1971.
199 LOWEN, ALEXANDER, *Pleasure* (New York: Lancer Books, 1970) pg. 11.
205 EICHENLAUB, JOHN, M.D., *The Marriage Art* (New York: Dell Publishing Co., 1969).
206 DE BEAUVOIR, SIMONE, *The Second Sex* (New York: Bantam Books, 1961).
207 CAPRIO, FRANK S., M.D., *Sex and Love* (Englewood Cliffs, N.J.: Parker Publishing Co., 1959).
210 FROMM, ERICH, Ph.D., *The Art of Loving* (New York: Harper & Row, Publishers, 1956).

CHAPTER 12

216 CUBER, JOHN, DR. and MRS., quoted in *National Observer,* September 9, 1972.
216 SYMONDS, CAROLINE, Opinion: "How Does an Affair Affect A Marriage," *Sexual Behavior,* September 1972.

Page

216 ELLIS, ALBERT, quoted in *National Observer*, September 9, 1972.

217 ENGLISH, O. SPURGEON, M.D., *Pageant*, March 1969.

217 LEGGIT, HUNTER, REV., *Sexual Behavior*, February 1972.

217 ANDREWS, JOHN, REV., *Forum* magazine, December 1972.

220 WEISS, EDWARD, M.D., *Psychosomatic Aspect of Heart Disease* edited by Morris Fishbein (New York: Hanover House, 1960), p. 121.

229 YOUNG, WAYLAND, Reference to Alessandro Piccolomini's book *Good Form for Women* in *Eros Denied* (New York: Grove Press, Inc., 1964).

230 FEIFER, GEORGE, "Yalta, the Soviet Playground," *Holiday* magazine, October 1967.

CHAPTER 13

238 HELLERSTEIN, HERMAN K., M.D., and FRIEDMAN, ERNEST H., M.D., quoted in *Freedom from Heart Attacks*, by Miller, Benjamin, M.D., and Galton Lawrence.

243 HELLERSTEIN, HERMAN K., M.D., "Heart Disease and Sex," *Medical Aspects of Human Sexuality*, June 1971.

243 KROGER, WILLIAM S., "Sexual Frustration," *Sexual Behavior*, Dec. 1972.

245 BLUMBERG, PERRY, *Medical Aspects of Human Sexuality*, June 1971.

245 WENGER, NANETTE K., M.D., discussion. *Medical aspects of Human Sexuality*, June 1971.

245 NAUGHTON, JOHN, M.D., *Medical Aspects of Human Sexuality*, July 1972.

246 BRUCE, ROBERT A., M.D., "Exercise and the Postinfarct Patient," *Cardiovascular Review*, 1971.

246 MULCAHY, RISTEARD, M.D., and HICKEY, NOEL, M.D., "The Rehabilitation of Patients with Coronary Heart Disease," *Journal of the Irish Medical Association*, October 21, 1971.

247 MASSIE, HENRY N., M.D., *Medical Aspects of Human Sexuality*, May 1972.

249 LAURIA, DONALD B., M.D., Commenting on original article by Everett, Guy M., M.D., "Effects of Amyl Nitrite ("Poppers") on Sexual Experience." *Medical Aspects of Human Sexuality*, Dec. 1972.

Page
251 "Heat, Humidity, and the Heart," *Medical World News,* Nov. 19, 1971.
251 LOWEN, ALEXANDER, M.D., *Pleasure* (New York: Coward, McCann & Geoghegan, Inc., 1970).
252 MALLA, KALYANA, *The Ananga Ranga or The Hindu Art of Love* (New York: G. P. Putnam's Sons, 1964).

CHAPTER 14

259 KRONHAUSEN, DRS. PHYLLIS and EBERHARD, *Sex Histories of American College Men* (New York: Ballantine Books, Inc., 1960).

CHAPTER 15

278 WRIGHT, IRVING S., M.D., "Atherothrombosis: A Concept of Aging," *Medical World News Geriatrics,* 1972.
278 AREHART-REICHEL, JOAN, "Childhood Preventatives against Adult Heart Attacks." *Science Newsletter,* June 10, 1972.
280 ROGERSON, ELEANOR B., "Beyond the Menopause," *Medical World News Geriatrics,* 1972.
281 GUYON, RENÉ, *A Case for Sexual Freedom* (Hollywood, California: International Publications Inc., 1963).

CHAPTER 16

285 COMFORT, ALEX, M.B., Ph.D., editor, *The Joy of Sex* (New York: Crown Publishers, Inc., 1972).
288 RAPHAEL, PHYLLIS, "Sex for the Hell of It," *Forum,* May 1973.
288 DOBBSON, CHRYSSA, "Love Is the Best Aphrodisiac," *Cosmopolitan,* June 1973.

INDEX